Freedom in America

FREEDOM IN AMERICA

A 200-Year Perspective

Edited with an Introduction by

NORMAN A. GRAEBNER

The Pennsylvania State University Press

University Park & London

Library of Congress Cataloging in Publication Data
Main entry under title:

Freedom in America.

1. Civil rights—United States—History. I. Graeb-
ner, Norman A.
JC599.U5F74   323.4'0973   76-43022
ISBN 0-271-01234-X

Designed by Larry Krezo

Printed in the United States of America

Contents

Preface

In July 1975 Professor Norman A. Graebner, Edward R. Stettinius Professor of Modern American History at The University of Virginia, came to Penn State as a Distinguished Visiting Professor of History and Director of a special bicentennial project, Freedom: Then, Now, and Tomorrow. This book, *Freedom in America: A 200-Year Perspective,* is one result of that project.

After two hundred years of struggling for freedom in America, what are the conditions that will sustain freedom in the future? This question was central to Professor Graebner's intellectual inquiry and public education effort.

The project included a series of public forums by many prominent scholars whose thoughts are expressed in this book. It also included a series of one thousand town meetings for residents of the state. Based on democratic principles, the original "New England town meeting" was effectively educative. These meetings—as a continuing education program of Penn State's Department of History—had that intent.

Because of its broad scope the project required special funding. The University is indebted to the Public Commission for the Humanities in Pennsylvania, an affiliate of the National Endowment for the Humanities, and to the Bell Telephone Company of Pennsylvania for their financial support. We appreciate as well the enthusiastic participation of other colleges, universities, organizations, and agencies, especially The Pennsylvania Federation of Women's Clubs.

Professor Graebner's conclusions—and those of the other scholars— are diverse. They do tend, however, to focus on one theme: the future of Freedom in America rests with a reaffirmation of the principles of human dignity and the maintenance of an environment capable of sustaining them.

We are proud to have been a part of this project. We regard *Freedom in America: A 200-Year Perspective* as an enduring and appropriate observance of our nation's first two hundred years.

Kent Forster
Head
Department of History, Penn State

Floyd B. Fischer
Vice President
Continuing Education, Penn State

Introduction

Norman A. Graebner

Only the tyrant, living in a secure environment and operating above the law, is, at least in theory, free to do as he chooses. For the remainder of society freedom is an elusive condition, circumscribed by a wide spectrum of personal, social, economic, and governmental restraints. Freedom is bounded most fundamentally by the nature of man and the physical universe. Merely to remain alive human beings must accept a myriad of restrictions on individual appetites, actions, and desires. Only those who yearn for self-destruction can afford to ignore them. Even the restraints imposed on mind and body by the demands of meaningful employment can be severe. Personal choices are limited as well by levels of intelligence and the capacity to think. Effective advertising or propaganda can affect the freedom of those unable to analyze or resist it. Poor health and poverty can set serious limits to choice. No less significant are the intellectual and moral limitations which society imposes on those whom it intends to respect and honor. Social customs and mores, and the restraints they impose, set the limits of necessity and respectability and thus, for most, the limits of free choice. Freedom is boundless for none. Those are most free who accept personal and social restraints as the necessary price which they and society must pay for a minimum of order, decorum, security, and satisfaction.

Restraints, of necessity, must be public no less than private, for freedom, in practice, must be limited by regard for the freedom and welfare of others. Freedom can be defined as mastery of the human and physical environment in which one chooses to function. Thus freedom in its economic and political context is, in large measure, an exercise in power, for there is a strong relationship between wealth, position, and intelligence and the range of choices available for the individual citizen. It is the restraints on the stronger and more aggressive members of society that permits the remainder to be free. Freedom with restraint for none creates chaos; freedom with restraint for some creates injustice. Thus any state which claims a semblance of fairness and order must impose on its citizens a variety of public constraints. What matters in the quality of a country's freedom is not the presence of limitations on individual or group behavior, but the nature and necessity of the restraints. A free society concerned with excellence dare not apply restrictions capriciously or defy the essential rights of individuals to the full exertion of mind and body in the pursuit of legitimate purposes. Public responsibility for the many dare not eliminate the competitive. Inequality is unjust only when it denies a person that for which his nature is suited. As Russell Kirk has written:

> Ability is the factor which enables men to lift themselves from savagery to civilization, and which helps to distinguish the endeavors of men from the routine existence of insects. Ability is of various sorts: there are philosophical ability, mechanical ability, commercial ability, directive ability, and persuasive ability. But all these are various aspects of the special talents, produced by intelligence, which is independent of routine or of brute strength. . . . But these men commonly are few in number; and though it is impossible to create such Ability by state action, it is altogether too possible that state action may succeed in extirpating the Ability of a whole generation—or, of a whole people.

Freedom in America cannot be divorced from the colonial experience, for that experience fashioned the peculiar qualities of freedom as the Founding Fathers sought to define and practice it. It is the close association of the idea of freedom with the creation of the Republic which renders liberty a central theme in the nation's Bicentennial. To perfect their freedom the English colonists established not only their independence from Britain but also governments best designed to perpetuate the freedoms which they had won. Even then the implications of freedom, when defined in political terms, exposed a variety of purposes.

Fundamental to eighteenth-century American freedom was the concept of personal liberty: freedom from the impediments of class, tradition, or governmental favoritism which enforced servility and thereby limited the economic opportunity and social recognition for all but a privileged minority. European governments seemed oppressive simply because they supported the established class structure. Personal disabilities might render individuals unequal in any circumstance, but the imposition of legal restrictions on the inheritance or acquisition of property, the exclusion of most from political and governmental rights, the broad denial of access to the means of production, and the absence, for laborers, of any claim to the product of their labors resulted not from nature but from social and political traditions. It was not strange that Americans, living in a free environment, quickly removed all vestiges of the European class system.

In at least two important respects the English colonists in America escaped the restrictions which European society imposed on its masses. The colonists faced provincial regulations in the form of fixed wages and fixed prices for agricultural products. Shopkeepers and artisans required licenses, but they did not face the heavy restraints imposed by the European guild system. They could, moreover, escape local restrictions and improve their conditions by moving freely from one community or occupation to another. Mobility early became a central ingredient of the American dream. In addition, the colonists early acquired the right to own and accumulate landed property. Primogeniture had no chance against the abundance of land in America. The failure of primogeniture removed all restrictions on economic and social advancement based on class. In the colonies all citizens could escape the limitations of special privilege in the form of large estates or the exclusive ownership of tools and raw materials and become members of the proprietary class. Even indentured servants could move to newly opened regions, obtain title to land, and thereby better their condition. To blacks alone were the rights of possession and accumulation denied.

For Americans, living in a free environment with ample opportunity for movement and accumulation, the major restraints, then, lay not in nature but in government—whether hostile, arbitrary, or merely useless. To Americans political liberty had never been a mere abstraction.

For them it described a condition, long attained, where the individual enjoyed constitutional safeguards against compulsion or the threat of compulsion. As the Englishman Thomas Hobbes defined it, "Liberty, or freedom, signifieth, properly, the absence of opposition. . . . A FREEMAN is he, that in those things, which by his strength and wit he is able to do, is not hindered to do what he has a will to do." Thus the notion of liberty—that human beings have certain inalienable rights that transcend the power of governments—was neither new nor peculiarly American; nor was the notion that government, to secure these rights, could exist only by the consent of the governed.

Americans claimed no more than their rights as Englishmen, but in the eighteenth century, those rights were extensive. They had received affirmation and reaffirmation in documents and practices which spanned the centuries from the Magna Carta to the Glorious Revolution and the English Bill of Rights of the late seventeenth century. Indeed, the idea of the absolute moral worth of the individual had roots in Greek and Christian thought. Building on English precedent, the American colonies early established the principle that beyond certain procedural restraints there were absolute limits to state authority. Colonial Americans expected no less than fair treatment in their dealings with government and the observance of due process procedures in their courts. The rich and ample American environment merely emphasized the benefits of freedom and encouraged resistance to any infringements upon it. From its beginning the American Revolution was an effort to conserve that which already existed, the rights of liberty and property. Still it was not, by eighteenth-century standards, a conservative revolution, for it introduced massive changes in the outlook and institutions of society.

Eventually the American colonists rebelled against British rule simply because they regarded the London government an impediment to their evolution as a free people. Still such convictions came slowly and incompletely. As late as 1763 Americans agreed that the advantages of membership in the British Empire far outweighed the liabilities. British power, to their deep satisfaction, had in the great French and Indian War freed the northern and western frontiers from French encroachment. The Navigation Acts which confined colonial trade to the ports and ships of the Empire were not onerous; those that might have been troublesome the British did not enforce. For a century Americans had learned to accept imperial regulations, employing techniques of obstruction and delay when necessary to defend their interests. Meanwhile British mercantile policy assured Americans access to British markets.

Suddenly cords of empire which appeared indestructible began to unravel. Parliament's postwar regulation and taxing policies, backed by more efficient methods of enforcement, came with such speed and force that the older colonial strategies became almost totally obsolete. Moreover, the crucial acts of 1764 and 1765—the Sugar Act, the Currency Act, and the Stamp Act—touched American interests as had no previous actions of Parliament. What disturbed Americans especially was Parliament's determination to exercise freely both the taxing and the commerce power, the two powers of maximum imperial coercion. At issue was not the magnitude of the British exactions, but the fact that they were imposed by a government in which the Americans had no voice. Parliament, speaking for the Empire, gave the colonists the simple choice of submission or forceful resistance. To avoid either alternative, the colonists required some recourse, short of revolution, which would permit them to restrain the misuse of Parliamentary power. At the same time this restraining power demanded safeguards from public abuse. In their resistance some Americans turned to violence. But even as Parliament, under pressure, withdrew the most onerous laws, it claimed full authority in the Declaratory Act of 1766 to impose restrictions on the colonists.

During the critical decade that followed the Declaratory Act American radicals agreed generally that the British government had embarked on a systematic course of oppression. The Stamp Act, wrote Andrew Eliot in 1766, had been "calculated . . . to enslave the colonies." The *Newport Mercury* asserted that the act could "deprive us of all our invaluable charter rights and privileges . . . and involve us in the most abject slavery." In 1770 some residents of Boston passed resolutions which proclaimed that "a deep-laid and desperate plan of imperial despotism has been laid, and partly executed, for the extinction of all civil liberty. . . . The august and once revered fortress of English freedom—the admirable work of ages—the BRITISH CONSTITUTION seems fast tottering into fatal and inevitable ruin." What reinforced that conviction was Parliament's involvement in the East India Company monopoly of the American market and the events that followed the Boston Tea Party—the Coercive Acts which closed the port of Boston and severely limited the government of Massachusetts. Even George Washington, in 1774, accused the English government of "endeavoring by every piece of art and despotism to fix the shackles of slavery upon us." The measures of Parliament, he lamented, resulted from a deliberate process and included "a regular, systematic plan . . . to enforce them."

Only for a minority of colonists did liberty require independence from British rule. Still, the conflict came to that, largely because Parliament and the king in London refused to compromise the authority of empire. Faced in 1775 with open resistance in Massachusetts, King George III gave the colonists the choice between submission and triumph. The king expressed the British position clearly: "I do not wish to come to severe measures, but we must not retreat. . . . [T]here is no inclination for the present to lay further taxes on them, but I am clear there must always be one tax to keep up the *right*." Forced by British intransigence to choose between total submission and violent resistance, many Americans chose to fight. In the absence of compromise—and the British rejected all compromise—the American escape from submission required a victorious war. In part to acquire needed European assistance, the Second Continental Congress accepted the logic of fighting for independence. On July 4, 1776, the Congress announced that intention to the world in the form of the Declaration of Independence, brilliantly phrased by Thomas Jefferson. That decision divided the colonists and sent many Tories abroad, but it secured the needed French support which assured the success of the independence venture.

Not even the governments which the new American states created after 1776 eliminated the public fear and distaste for political authority, still associated with kings and governors. Reacting to the recent experience with Britain and the royal governors, the states no less than the Congress eliminated the executive almost entirely from their governmental structures. Congress, the only national governing body, lacked the power to tax, to regulate commerce, to enforce laws, and even to control foreign relations. What filled the power vacuum was the legislatures of the states.

For American radicals this was indeed a democratic triumph, for it seemed to place political power in the hands of the people. Still for conservative Americans the state legislatures comprised not a democratic triumph, but a disaster. Political philosophers of the century, both American and European, had long asserted that any unchecked power —king, parliament, or legislature—would ultimately become tyrannical. Their assumptions proved to be accurate. Legislatures as representative as any in history confiscated property, promoted paper money schemes, passed tender laws, placed burdens against the recovery of debts, and in other ways challenged the principle of justice, especially when applied to property rights. The unbridled rule of the majority, wrote John Adams, was leading to mass tyranny. The lack of wisdom and steadiness in government, James Madison agreed, was "the grievance complained of in all our republics." Any government that granted the majority whatever it preferred, became, for the minority, scarcely distinguishable from monarchy. Eventually the fears of legislative power, added to the general weakness of the national Congress to conduct foreign affairs and coerce the states, led to the movement for a new constitution.

For those who believed that liberty in America required some restructuring of government, the answer lay in a new separation of powers. As Jefferson explained, the best form of government was one "in which the powers of government should be so divided and balanced among several bodies of magistracy, as that no one could transcend their legal limits, without being effectually checked and restrained by the others." That Convention which met in Philadelphia in May 1787 to amend the Articles of Confederation managed instead to write the Constitution of the United States. Experience decreed against monarchy and legislative dominance. What would best protect the liberties and interests of the American people, the Founding Fathers concluded, would be a strong government imbued with the powers of taxation and commerce, but circumscribed by clearly defined limitations and a system of checks and balances based on the separation of powers among the executive, legislative, and judicial branches. The political theory of the Revolutionary era, with its emphasis on inalienable rights, constitutionalism, consent, separation of powers, limited government, and an ethical, ordered liberty, thus found its ultimate expression in the Constitution.

Those who opposed the Constitution—and some who favored it— hesitated to entrust their liberties to a document of such power. They looked to a bill of rights which might define those inherent liberties that lay outside the legitimate power of government. Jefferson, then in France, wrote to his fellow Virginian, Madison, to urge the adoption of such a bill of rights: "A bill of rights is what the people are entitled to against every government on earth, general or particular, and what no just government should refuse, or rest on inferences." Madison agreed to add the Bill of Rights to the Constitution when it became clear that ratification was doubtful without special guarantees of personal liberty. The Bill of Rights appeared as the first ten amendments to the Constitution, adopted by the first Congress under the new Constitution, and ratified in December 1791. Madison argued for the amendments and almost single-handedly carried them through the Congress, not because, he wrote, "they are necessary, but because they can produce no possible danger and may gratify some gentlemen's wishes."

Freedoms enumerated in the Bill of Rights generally restrained the government from interfering in the thoughts and actions of the individual: freedom of opinion, freedom of religion, freedom of occupation and economic enterprise, freedom from arbitrary arrest and judicial injustices. From government most Americans wanted no more than a few necessary and understandable rules, drawn by men whom they had elected. Alexander Hamilton had the vision of a powerful state, serving the interests of an expanding national economy based on wealth, banking, industry, and commerce. But the followers of Jefferson were concerned less with power than with the right to create a future which squared with their notions of simplicity, democracy, and freedom. They preferred a society of prosperous, property-owning merchants, artisans, and farmers, each free to progress in accordance with his own industry and free from the restraints which individuals of great power and wealth might impose.

For Jefferson, no less than for his contemporaries, the American Republic established a new order of competence in human affairs. Civic duty and moral virtue would combine to assure the new society its glorious destiny. Democracy—a government of self-rule—could flourish only if based on a foundation of morality. As Jefferson explained to Thomas Law: "I consider our relations with others as constituting the boundaries of morality. Nature hath implanted in our breasts a love of others, a sense of duty to them, a moral instinct. . . . The Creator would indeed have been a bungling artist had he intended man for a social animal without planting in him social dispositions. I sincerely believe in the general existence of a moral instinct. I think it is the brightest gem with which the human character is studded, and the want of it as more degrading than the most hideous of bodily deformities." Democracy would meet the requirements of society only as long as the people shared common perceptions of justice and necessity—and were willing to act upon them. Even a concerned, well-informed public would not restrain all passions, ambitions, and abuses, but it could limit the unfair and destructive exercise of power. Nothing would corrupt a democratic order more assuredly than coercion, obscurantism, and public addiction to personal ends. Moral self-discipline and a general concern for the whole were essential elements in the preservation of freedom in a democratic society.

Jefferson's vision of an ideal America was one simple enough to permit such unity of purpose. For that reason he favored a sparsely settled agricultural nation of self-reliant farmers and tradesmen. For him a high degree of economic equality was essential so that society could maintain the rights of all people to free choice of occupation. He feared manufacturing and trade because they magnified the opportunities for gain and thereby posed a greater threat than did agriculture to equality, to virtue, and to the institutions congenial to them. Jefferson understood that economic conditions determine the qualities of culture and politics. Human beings, conditioned by their culture, would hold some things dearer than others and struggle for what they prized, including wealth and power. Jefferson feared above all the rise of extremely rich and extremely poor, for gross inequality would endanger the country's democratic liberties and create a culture in which material acquisition would become the chief measure of success.

Long before the Civil War the expansion of commerce, industry, and urban life in America had shattered Jefferson's vision of a simple agricultural society. Even the notion that a free society required a moral foundation became the victim of prosperity, for wealth magnified the power of individuals to defy the dictates of virtue. Some Americans noted the dangers which prosperity posed to free institutions; they doubted that the nation could long sustain the expectations of the Founding Fathers. As early as 1829, Lyman Beecher warned his countrymen that the Republic's power and prosperity would be short-lived unless they observed its traditional moral restraints. Already under the surface the United States was becoming a land of competition and tension, of recklessness and indifference to suffering, of preventable disasters and environmental desolation. Rapid expansion—already the hallmark of American success—demanded no less a price of prosperous society. And in a country which measured success by its prosperity even such qualities could be virtuous.

This identification of happiness and success with material achievement encouraged Americans to ignore the unpleasant, the evidences of failure, the existence of the considerable unhappiness around them. Despite the growing inequality, liberty served the interests of most, maximizing the opportunities for gain without necessarily multiplying the occasions for rancor. But for the multitude who scarcely satisfied their minimal needs freedom was a luxury beyond reach. Only the poor without aspirations were free, since the chief restraints on freedom were those which limited access to prosperity: the threat of imprisonment; the denial of employment, credit, or social acceptance. Only for the economically secure was such indifference a matter of genuine choice.

The remedy for ambition, avarice, and injustice still lay in the ongoing principle of separation of powers, with its attendant checks and balances, no less than in the principle of federalism which divided power on a geographical basis. It was this diffusion of political authority that guaranteed it proper use. Still the constitution did not fix the relationship of each political entity to the others. There was a constant flux, both in the relative influence of the three branches of government over national policy and in the lines of jurisdiction between federal and state control. But at no time did the ascendency of one constitutional authority endanger the whole. The checks remained intact, even at the price of civil war.

Four years of civil war in America compelled the nation to measure freedom by the standards of national survival. The issue for Abraham Lincoln was the protection of freedom and the American constitutional system within the Union. Yet to achieve this great purpose against the power of the South, he accepted the necessity to restrict the freedom of many in the North who attacked his military and political policies too vociferously. Indeed, he sought to silence many of his fellow Northerners by denying them the right of habeas corpus, holding them in jail without civil trial. Lincoln himself saw his dilemma when he wrote: "The world has never had a good definition of the word liberty, and the American people, just now, are much in want of one. We all declare for liberty; but in using the same *word* we do not all mean the same *thing*. . . . The shepherd drives the wolf from the sheep's throat, for which the sheep thanks the shepherd as a *liberator,* while the wolf denounces him for the same act as the destroyer of liberty. . . ." It was a classic statement. For Lincoln the answer lay clearly on the side of society.

In large measure the eighteenth-century American heritage of freedom remains intact. The early constitutions embodied English common law processes which guaranteed fair jury trials. The First Congress imposed such procedural rights on the federal courts in the Fifth to the Eighth amendments to the Constitution. Congress embodied the right to free expression against the actions of the federal government in the First Amendment. Still the Supreme Court refused to make the Bill of Rights binding on the states. In 1868 the Fourteenth Amendment brought the states under the compulsion of the First Amendment to guarantee all the privileges and immunities of citizenship, but again the Supreme Court failed, in major decisions, to compel the states to eliminate local infringements of individual rights against their citizens. Not until the First World War did freedom of expression become a matter of national controversy. At issue then was the widespread repression of the First Amendment rights among socialists and war critics which sent more than 800 to prison under the wartime espionage and sedition acts. What mattered in the definition of legitimate expression was the fundamental conflict between the individual's right to free speech and the community's right to hear with the latter's right to set limits on what was proper. In the 1925 case of *Gitlow* v. *New York* the Supreme Court took a major step toward the expansion of freedom from public restraint when it at last applied federal restrictions to the states.

Since then the gains for free expression have been substantial. No other branch of government has revealed the expertise and willingness to guard the country's basic rights as has the judiciary. The Supreme Court recognized the diversity in American life and, at least at the level of law, has created an almost totally open society. In practice the judges have rejected the principle of absolutism, for individual liberties too often infringe on the rights and interests of the community. Yet throughout the past quarter century the Supreme Court has adopted an increasingly tolerant view of what comprises acceptable free expression even in matters which involve national security. Justice Stanley F. Reed expressed the majority opinion for the Supreme Court when he wrote in 1946: "Freedom of discussion should be given the widest range compatible with the essential requirement of the fair and orderly administration of justice." Or as Justice William O. Douglas phrased it a year later, "The vehemence of the language used is not alone the measure of the power to punish for contempt. . . . The danger must not be remote or even probable; it must immediately imperil." Spokesmen of the law have insisted that there can be no instance, under the First Amendment, where government can legitimately abridge the right of free speech, even in wartime. For during times of danger the government can best demonstrate what it means by freedom of speech.

On occasion the Court has decided against the press for its disregard of fairness, its public and often unfounded accusations, its pretrial reporting, and its prejudging the facts in criminal proceedings. The case of *The New York Times* v. *United States* (1971) raised the issue of freedom of the press in another form. At issue in this case was the decision of *The New York Times* to publish excerpts of the "Pentagon Papers," released to the press by Daniel Ellsberg, one of the authors. The government sought to stop further publication of the Papers on the ground of national security. Within days, the case reached the Supreme Court, which rendered nine decisions, none of which commanded the Court's majority. Only two justices held that the publication would injure the nation. Although the Court decided in favor of *The Times* and *The Washington Post,* the decision created no clear line between the public interest and the freedom of the press under the First Amendment.

In a wide variety of cases the Supreme Court has increasingly defended the individual against community sentiment and interest. This has been especially true in the free expression of religion. Still in any confrontation between an irate and irresponsible orator and an antagonistic audience, the question of freedom is never clear. When is a speech inflammatory? As Justice Oliver Wendell Holmes declared in his *Gitlow* dissent of 1925, "Every idea is an incitement. . . . The only difference between the expression of an opinion and an incitement in the narrow sense is the speaker's enthusiasm for the result. Eloquence may set fire to reason." Protections against governmental interference, extensive as they are, do not guarantee public tolerance of controversial ideas or limit public restrictions on freedom of speech. Wherever society maintains some claim to homogeneity it will attempt to impose restrictions on those who would question its dominant beliefs, assumptions, or convictions. For Katherine Graham of *The Washington Post* the enemies of freedom would continue to be "the dogmatic perfectionists. These are the demanders of all-or-nothing . . . the pretenders to the possession of all right and all truth." Progress against such restraints lies less in governmental guarantees of freedom than in the influence of time and education. Still the most pervading limitation on free expression rests not in its nature but in the level of its significance. "Americans can say in public what they want," writes Paul Conkin, "but who is listening?" Most voices of dissent have proved to be inconsequential.

In matters relating to obscenity the problem remains one of definition. What is obscene to some is merely realistic to others, and perhaps instructive besides. Justice Potter Stewart, when asked for the meaning of hardcore pornography, replied only, "I know it when I see it. . . ." What renders pornography so unrestrained in both verbal and graphic expression is the fact that it is based on commercialism and not on art. In every form it is confined only by limitations of language, illustration, and advertising, none of which contains any necessary restraint reflective of morality or good taste. After 1960 the Supreme Court ruled against state visual prior censorship laws, or at least the procedures involved. By 1970 few state or city prior censorship ordinances were still in force. Yet obscenity, when of "no redeeming social value," was interdictable and punishable by law.

The courts protected books and other media from unbridled censorship quite as much as they did the movies. The search for a definition of obscene literature remained incomplete, but the Court had decided by 1970 that what occurred in the home lay beyond the reach of government, that hard-core pornography was not totally protected by the First Amendment, and that a double standard which distinguished minors from adults could be enforced. In part public tolerance of eroticism was an expression of powerlessness; in part, of confidence that such freedom of expression would not damage the basic institutions of the country.

In an effort to broaden individual rights, the Supreme Court, under the leadership of Chief Justice Earl Warren, focused in the sixties on "due process of law" and its guarantees against arbitrary, capricious, or unreasonable government action toward the public. Amid the growing complexities of American life, matters of procedure began to overweigh matters of substance in cases before the Supreme Court. The reason is clear. "The history of liberty," wrote Justice Felix Frankfurter in 1943, "has largely been the history of observance of procedural safeguards." Safeguards against what procedures? Stacked juries, delayed or quickie trials, coerced confessions and self-incrimination, denial of counsel and witnesses in criminal cases, arrest without cause, and unreasonable searches and seizures, including the use of electronic surveillance. Unfortunately, what is arbitrary to some is reasonable to others. Still there are standards, judicially tested, which have served as a measure of reasonableness.

By the 1970s the country's black population of some 23 million had achieved equality, at least by law. Still the gains were incomplete. The continued black agitation, including the urban riots of the sixties, demonstrated the continued dissatisfaction of blacks who saw the discrepancy between their hard-won court freedoms and the continuing impediments of race, prejudice, and poverty to the creation of satisfactory and productive lives. As late as 1976 many blacks still wondered whether the system was sufficiently honest and open to give them a chance. Both the national and state governments had made clear that race was no longer an acceptable means of classification in any public sphere. Building on a series of previous cases, the Supreme Court, in the *Brown* decision of 1954, established the legal foundation for school desegregation. Congress assumed the responsibility for extending civil rights to blacks in matters of employment, residence, and voting. The strong Civil Rights Act of 1964 and the Voting Rights Act of 1965 were broad in application and vigorously enforced. Desegregation in education is far from complete, yet the gains, especially in the South, have been significant. Segregation elsewhere—in hotels, restaurants, public transportation and accommodations—has lost the support of law everywhere. Hundreds of blacks hold important public offices as mayors, judges, members of Congress and state legislatures. Expanding economic opportunities created a growing black middle class across the country.

On matters of civil rights the government raised questions of justice not easily resolved. Critics denounced the courts for imposing principles which had no basis in a general moral and intellectual consensus. Many Americans were convinced in their consciences that the civil rights legislation was wrong and unjust. That it created a conflict between the burgeoning power of the blacks and the interests of established society was clear. In the low income neighborhoods of the large cities, often ethnic in composition, the impact was especially severe. Middle class parents, arguing that their children were entitled to whatever schooling their residential status merited, opposed school busing, just as they opposed programs for scatterside housing and equal opportunity employment.

Meanwhile the federal government perfected, at least at the level of law, the country's political freedoms. During the Second World War the United States Supreme Court, in *United States* v. *Classic* and *Smith* v. *Allright,* ruled out the white primary. Subsequent court decisions eliminated poll taxes and other infringements on black voting rights. But not until the Voting Rights Act of 1965 did the federal government remove all remaining impediments to black registration and voting, including all literacy tests. In 1970 Congress extended the franchise in both federal and state elections to eighteen-year-olds. Meanwhile, in March 1962, the Supreme Court, in *Baker* v. *Carr,* terminated the old tradition whereby some states engaged in a deliberate misapportionment of legislative districts to give rural votes far more weight than those of the cities. For a country dedicated to political liberty, such achievements came far too slowly. Still the progress was steady, the results highly laudable.

In any society justice and freedom are elusive. Justice in America insists on rights to the free expression of energy, intelligence, and talent long denied; it requires as well rights to choice, possession, and status that flow from past efforts and achievements. Tragically such fundamental standards of a free society perennially conflict. In any confrontation between individual rights and the established interests of society one must give way, generally at the price of freedom if not of justice.

Nowhere did American society experience the conflict between individual freedom and the public interest more than in the performance of its economy. The general concern for prosperity, goods, and services created some body of mutual interest between businessmen and laborers, producers and consumers. Indeed, the American tradition of economic freedom had always insisted that the individual, in pursuing personal economic interests in a free environment, would simultaneously serve some basic need of society. Adam Smith's *Wealth of Nations* (1776) established the initial defense of economic freedom. The mercantilism which he challenged had sought to maximize national wealth and power through governmental regulation of trade and consumption. Smith accepted the mercantilist goals, but he argued that the removal of governmental restraints would free the force of private initiative. It would matter little if the free individual pursued his own selfish interests rather than the good of society, for as Smith wrote: "By devoting [his] industry in such a manner as its produce may be of the greatest value, he is . . . led by an invisible hand to promote an end which was no part of his intention. . . . By pursuing his own interests, he frequently promotes that of the society more effectively than when he really intends to promote it." Smith lauded private initiative as the prime mover in all human endeavor.

Laissez-faire economics was a rationalization of middle class interests, the economist's answer to the problem of governmental interference. Heralded as a triumph for individual freedom, it soon became acceptable for laborers and the less successful as well. Under the conditions of expanding productivity, it seemed to serve the minimal interests of society better than had any previous system. Whatever the waste, extravagance, and inequality which the system produced, the resulting benefits and the hopes it held out to the able and industrious afforded the system whatever public and governmental support it required. The people would establish the limits of acceptable business behavior through the power to express disapproval in the marketplace and elsewhere. An aroused public would demand political restraints to terminate dishonest, selfish, or illegitimate behavior. Thus the free market and free elections together seemed enough to assure an economic system which would be largely self-regulating and in need of little or no governmental direction. Still for businessmen generally free enterprise was never an end in itself. Far more important for them was the maximization of profits, and if governmental policies would increase their advantages, they would pursue them with remarkable determination.

Increasingly twentieth-century critics recognized the fallacy in the reassuring philosophy that any decline in the power of the state was commensurate with the expansion of individual liberty. Experience demonstrated that for many citizens the retreat of government to the role of policemen did not guarantee the triumph of liberty at all. In production the American system was matchless. But the inflexible pricing structure, reflecting a high degree of monopolization, limited distribution and consumption. The vast concentrations of private power, accumulated under the protection of the state, created a public conscious of its constantly declining freedom of choice. The nominal equality which the law bestowed had little meaning in the face of the actual social, economic, and political conditions which prevailed. The economy, even in boom times, hovered on the precipice of recession, if not depression. It seemed incapable of achieving full employment or lifting millions of citizens above the poverty level. It was not strange that the nation's major political forces eventually called upon the state to limit the control of private and corporate power over other businesses as well as the lives and welfare of the mass of citizens, and thereby restore a greater measure of individual freedom and security.

Those who desired a higher degree of economic equality turned to social and economic planning. Except for such restrained efforts at control as the Interstate Commerce Act, the Sherman Anti-Trust Act, and the Hepburn Act, the concept of planning made little progress before 1914. It required the unprecedented demands for raw materials, transportation, food, and labor during the First World War to move planning to the realm of practice. The War Industries Board set the pattern for controls which served the needs of war. After 1920 federal regulation receded before the new collaboration between government and business in the determination of fiscal and tariff policy. The Great Depression and the New Deal did not terminate government-business cooperation, but they shifted the balance in some important areas toward government planning and regulation. Relief and recovery measures, rural resettlement, social taxation and deficit spending, plus a multitude of federal reform activities, increased the power of government in the economy.

Labor's gains in the 1930s raised serious questions of freedom and restraint. Labor, effectively organized, could impose major limitations on the decisions of business. Even during early New Deal days industry refused to accept a stronger bargaining role for unions. It was not until the formation of the Committee for Industrial Organization (CIO) in

1935, with its invasion of the large mass-production industries, that the union movement, solidly backed by such new federal agencies as the National Labor Relations Board, began to achieve power. Even the United Auto Workers of the CIO required a series of bitter strikes to force recognition from the major automobile companies. Thereafter the American Federation of Labor and the CIO, merging finally into one massive movement, gained enormous influence in American economic and political life. Whereas the big unions managed to secure greater freedom from insecurity for their members, they also created their own large bureaucracies with a momentum that often challenged the broader interests of the nation's citizens.

Since mid-century Americans have lived in a complex society which has made them increasingly dependent on the power and decisions of others. Despite all the claims for "consumer sovereignty" in the market, industry produces goods which serve the interests of investors and not the needs of society. Private corporations continue to pollute the air and water and generate waste at a prodigious rate. The successive waves of new technology, moveover, have reduced individual freedom by placing many of the amenities and necessities of life under the control of few people of great individual or corporate power. Technology grants enormous power to those who control the public services. It contributes to the concentration of power in large national and multinational corporations, and any concentration of power is an infringement on freedom. Population growth merely aggravates the problem of scarcity and assigns ever greater power to those who control the necessary resources and energy.

Washington accepted the obligation to protect the public and business alike from the undesirable externalities of a complicated industrial and economic system. That protective effort created a growing federal superstructure of regulatory agencies. At every step along the way the federal government responded to the demands of organized groups who could not protect their interests in the free market. Whatever its contributions to the nation's welfare, the growing bureaucracy enmeshed the lives of Americans in an increasingly fine net of complex and burdensome regulations. The added costs of government inflicted the public with an ever-heavier burden of taxation. To defend the public from those who wielded dominant power in the nation's highly complex industrial economy, the government moved so steadily and quietly into the body of American life that its full impact was never discernible.

Where the expanding governmental role was most apparent was in the size of the federal government itself. The momentum in bureaucratic and public program expansion carried the total governmental budget—local, state, and federal—from 12 percent of the Gross National Product (GNP) in 1930 to 35 percent in 1975. The number of employees in the executive branch of the federal government alone reached 2.9 million. No other living organism revealed such a lust for life and growth. Established trends would carry the cost of government to 60 percent of the GNP by the year 2000. Any government that taxed away over half of what people earned would essentially dominate their personal lives. The federal budget reached $100 billion in 1962, after 186 years; it reached $200 billion nine years later; it passed $300 billion by 1975. In fiscal 1977 it would exceed $400 billion. At mid-century federal expenditures for domestic services totaled $13.4 billion; during the next twenty years they multiplied ten times. As late as 1952, 81 percent of federal spending went for defense, international relations, postal service, and other traditional expenditures; by 1972, traditional services commanded only 47 percent, with 53 percent for health, welfare, and other forms of social security. In many respects the growth of governmental activity created a welfare state. Still the costs were not reassuring. If the federal government, to assure the country's prosperity, was compelled to deficit spend as much as $50 billion a year when the level of prosperity was high, what would be its obligations in a depression? Massive borrowing under such conditions could destroy the country's entire economic structure.

Despite its growth, the federal government maintained a mixed and often unclear relationship to the public and its needs. Indeed, it was never clear precisely whose interests the vast governmental structure really served. Conservatives as well as economic analysts often questioned its power, its inefficiency, and its alleged abuses. Government programs were so formless, regulations so varied, that no one could master them. So cumbersome and noncommunicative did government become that officials often could not secure needed information from other departments or agencies. Even the White House staff was so large and compartmentalized that some portions worked in isolation from others. It was not strange that programs and guidelines failed to coincide. Public and private institutions, such as hospitals, were often victimized by so many conflicting regulations that they could hardly function at all. Much of the effort appeared wasteful because it was mounted at endless expense against apparently intractable social problems. Some programs with promise suffered from underfunding. Some agencies suffered from huge backlogs of applications or complaints. Despite the multiplicity of bureaus, the self-assigned tasks of government remained increasingly unfulfilled. Whatever its cost, the government could not provide an adequate national health service, an efficient postal system, improved public transportation, or a clean environment. Americans complained that the federal government returned few benefits to the nation's citizens when measured by the vast expenditure of tax money over which they had no control.

Regulatory agencies established to defend the public interests against major industries and carriers did not necessarily serve the public at all. They did little to protect the public welfare against the assaults of impersonal forces or corporate technology. Too often the efforts to regulate American business eliminated rather than enforced competition and thereby increased the costs of products and services, encouraged inefficiency, and stifled innovation. As Lewis A. Engman, chairman of the Federal Trade Commission, expressed it: "The fact of the matter is that most regulated industries have become federal protectorates living in the cozy world of cost-plus, safely protected from the ugly specters of competition, efficiency, and innovation." Subsidies and monopolistic practices masquerading as regulation enabled those with power to restrict the choices of others. Much of the regulation was wasteful, compelling corporations to engage in circuitous practices to maintain some semblance of fairness in their relations with other companies and with the public. Many of the most restrictive federal regulations were instituted to serve some economic constituency, either through special funding or through the removal of competition. Where legal restrictions on business might infringe on profits, federal bureaus often refused to enforce established schedules. Occasionally programs lost their reason for existence. Yet bureaucrats and the beneficiaries of such programs together usually wielded sufficient influence to sustain them.

Thus government became a partner in the processes that determined the nature and direction of national life. That balance between government and business, which supposedly would protect the interests of society, actually served the interests of power far more effectively. The danger to free society in 1976 lay not alone in private and corporate wealth or in the power of government, but in the concentrated power of both working together to create a vast, impersonal, mechanized, and computerized business and governmental bureaucracy that dominated the nation's life, creating despair and feelings of powerlessness that produced total resignation at one extreme and self-assertive violence at the other. No longer did writers even dream of utopias; some anticipated improvement only in destruction. As Bakunin once argued with Marx, "We will become ourselves when the whole world is engulfed in fire." Where the answers lay except in leaner living, reduced private ambitions, and decentralized thinking was not clear.

Through 200 years the American people have sustained the world's longest-lasting democratic government. Repeatedly the American governmental system has demonstrated a remarkable stability and flexibility. As a defense against the tyrannical use of power the federal system of checks and balances, as established by the Constitution, has served the country well. Even in the twentieth century the executive, the Congress, and the judiciary, in turn, have played essential roles in limiting the power and influence of any branch that appeared unmindful of the consequences of its actions. When the Supreme Court defied public sentiment in its attack on New Deal measures, Franklin D. Roosevelt broke its resistance to his program with a political threat to change its personnel. During wartime the executive, at least to its critics, has invariably loomed as a danger to the constitutional system, and no president made claims to executive primacy which equalled those of the Nixon administration in its conduct of the Vietnam War. But in time Congress, supported by the press, reestablished the historic balance. The Watergate scandal demonstrated the power of the judiciary and the Congress to defend the American governmental system against a president who attempted to misuse it. Free institutions—the press, the churches, the universities, the labor unions—have flourished under the Constitution. What contributed to the survival of the Constitution and the entire spectrum of the country's free institutions was the continuing good fortune which permitted and encouraged their original establishment: the country's amazing natural resources, agricultural and industrial; its tremendous physical space; and its general isolation, enhanced by two broad oceans, from the major threats to the peace and stability of the Western Hemisphere.

Unfortunately the prevention of tyranny is not synonymous with good or even adequate government. Free government was never an end in itself. For the Founding Fathers it was the means through which a democratic people would rule themselves wisely. What matters in government is not its form but its capacity to recognize, confront, and resolve issues which endanger the welfare of its citizens. The Republic was above all a political venture in the art of governing, and free government carried a high purpose because it, more assuredly than others, would permit the creation of a society that did justice to human intelligence. But something has gone wrong. The American people have revealed no power to define, much less achieve, a society which assures their health, comfort, security, and satisfaction. For a full decade the nation has experienced the impact of threatening forces beyond its effective control. To protect its physical habitat from pollution and decay, to conserve its energy and resources, to secure a more equitable distribution of the benefits of its economic production, the nation can no longer escape the imperatives of reduced consumption and environmental restrictions. Still it appears incapable of making such decisions.

Whether the United States will in time mobilize its resources against its unanswered challenges depends overwhelmingly on its citizens, for only when they have agreed on a common core of conviction and purpose can they influence the direction of national life. But that needed consensus, thoughtful citizens understand instinctively, cannot generate itself. It requires that leadership which will permit a collection of individuals with many special concerns to act as a civic entity in behalf of public purposes. "Leadership," Benjamin Barber wrote in *Harper's* in April 1975, "is not a surrogate for participation in a representative democracy, it is its necessary condition. Without leaders, a citizenry is unlikely to remain active; without active citizens, responsive leaders are unlikely to emerge, and leaders who do emerge are unlikely to remain responsive." What matters, then, is a public of sufficient awareness to encourage its leaders to design and to act in the public interest. Such an amalgam will come, it is hoped, as the result of intelligent discourse rather than disaster. For nothing less will demonstrate the worth of the country's free democratic institutions.

The Foundations of
American Freedom

Freedom, Revolution, and Resistance to Authority, 1776-1976

Pauline Maier

For most Americans the Revolution is symbolized, if not contained, in certain great documents: the Declaration of Independence, the Constitution, the Bill of Rights. The texts of these fundamental testaments are, however, far less familiar than their names. Citizens of the modern Republic recall isolated sentences, wrenched from their contexts, far more than whole thoughts. Thomas Jefferson's stirring words in the second paragraph of the Declaration of Independence are perhaps best known: "We hold these truths to be self-evident; that all men are created equal; that they are endowed by their Creator with certain unalienable rights; that among these are life, liberty, and the pursuit of happiness." These words are remembered not merely for their rhetorical qualities, but because they support so well our own concern with realizing equality for all Americans, regardless of color or sex, and with individual rights.

What has been forgotten was far more important for the Declaration of Independence than what has been remembered. Thomas Jefferson's affirmation of men's natural equality, of their unalienable rights, was not meant to stand alone. Instead it served as prelude to his assertion of another right more relevant in the context of 1776: the right of revolution. "To secure these rights," he wrote, "governments are instituted among men," and "whenever any form of government becomes destructive of these ends, it is the right of the people to alter or to abolish it, and to institute new government." That, after all, was the point of the Declaration of Independence, to explain and justify what was, quite simply, a massive rejection of established authority.

Why is the Declaration of Independence recalled so selectively? This phenomenon is closely tied to the selective way Americans have recalled the Revolution as a whole. Men who led before 1776, when British authority was resisted and ultimately destroyed, are, for the most part, forgotten. Samuel Adams is a familiar figure, if a not altogether amenable one. His pervasive twentieth-century image is that of a demagogue, a subversive, a violent "left-winger." But his peers in other colonies, such as Christopher Gadsden, Cornelius Harnett, John Lamb, or Isaac Sears, are virtually unknown. Instead our "revolutionaries" are the "Founding Fathers"—those "young men of the revolution," as historians Stanley Elkins and Eric McKitrick called them, who were present at the Constitutional Convention of 1787, or who held prominent national office after 1789. If not Founding Fathers, our revolutionaries are military heroes from the Revolutionary War. Indeed, in popular discourse the revolution *is* the war, not the fundamental transformations that "revolution" suggests.

On one level, this distortion is easy to explain. The new government instituted by Americans, better to secure their rights, lacked the buttresses of time and tradition. It was experimental and insecure, and so naturally, from its desire for survival, it became conservative. The tradition of 1776 held dangers for the infant republic: if the resistance to the Stamp Act or the Tea Act was legitimate, why was it unacceptable to resist the federal excise tax on whiskey, or the federal embargo? To bind the federation more tightly, to reinforce identification with the United States, the country required nationalist symbols. These the early national spokesmen found most logically in the civil and military builders of the new nation, not in the destroyers of the old regime.

In fact, however, the fate of the revolutionary tradition in America is not so simple. An established and articulate Anglo-American revolutionary tradition was fundamental to the earliest stages of the American Revolution. Within its terms colonists understood the meaning of freedom, for which they rejected British authority. If we are to use the Bicentennial as an occasion to reflect on our origins, and on the meaning of freedom in America, it is important to go back to that relatively neglected portion of the Revolution that culminated in the Declaration of Independence, whose two hundredth anniversary we celebrate this year. We must consider the meaning and significance of the right of revolution for Jefferson and his contemporaries in the final years of the colonial era, and reflect upon its fate thereafter—during the later stages of the Revolution, in the nineteenth century, and, finally, in our own day.

Articulate American colonists of the mid-eighteenth century shared a firm and well-reasoned conviction in the rightfulness of revolution. It was part of their English heritage: had not Englishmen of the previous century executed Charles I and forced James II into exile, then refashioned their government, all in the name of freedom and constitutional rule? During the 1770s there were dissenters from the colonists' own implementation of this "fundamental right," but even the Loyalists' objections were, for the most part, phrased within the terms of a cogent body of "Whig" political thought that had emerged from England's own turbulent seventeenth century, and which were often known quite simply as "revolution principles." Human nature, it was said, was deeply flawed: men were avaricious by nature, and would serve their own interests at the cost of others whenever left free to do so. As a result government and laws were necessary to make liberty operative, that is, to free men from the continual depredations of their neighbors. In creating government, however, men established a problem as dangerous as that which government was designed to remedy—the problem of power. Power, to be exercised by magistrates set up to effect the rule of law, was in the hands of men who had in no way escaped the mark of Adam, but who differed from their fellow men mainly in an enhanced ability to satisfy their avarice. For seventeenth-century English Whigs no less than for mid-eighteenth-century Americans, then, the problem of freedom was above all the problem of limiting power. This conception had a strong historical basis, since the establishment of freedom in England had been closely bound up with the limitation of monarchy.

How could power be limited? By institutions, first of all. For Jefferson and other enlightened political writers, governments were but machines designed to protect men's freedom. And at mid-century both Englishmen and Americans congratulated themselves upon their own British constitution, with its "mixed" government of King, Lords, and Commons. These three elements divided and shared power in such a way that no one segment could realize its inclinations toward absolute and malicious power. There was also a second, extra-institutional check on power: the willingness of the people to rise up when magistrates stepped beyond the limits of their legitimate power. Where the people were "jealous" of their freedom and ready to act in defense of it, English Whig writers stressed, rulers were unlikely to infringe their liberty; but where the people were passive and docile, rulers inevitably became tyrants. Indeed, one writer claimed, "the Doctrine of a blind Obedience . . . is the Destruction of the Liberty . . . of any Nation."

The right of the people to oppose wrongful authority was founded upon the contractual nature of authority. On taking office, magistrates bound themselves to act for the common welfare within the limits of the constitution. The people simultaneously agreed to obey so long as those terms were honored. When a ruler stepped beyond the limits of law or of his office, he broke his agreement with the people and forfeited his power. In such cases an insurgent populace confronted not lawful authority but usurpation: the erring rulers were the rebels, not the people who opposed them—an idea repeated continually by American critics of Britain in the decade before the Declaration of Independence. This argument, moreover, was not used only to justify the people's right of revolution, that is, their right to displace rulers or regimes in their entirety. By the eighteenth century it was used to defend a more limited resistance of wrongful government acts so as to avoid the wholesale agony of revolution. If abuses of power were checked on their first appearance, they would never grow to require more drastic action. And of course it was easier for the people to check power, to force rulers to remain "within the bounds of law," before those abuses acquired the force of precedent. Locke was particularly eloquent here. To tell men they must watch submissively until governmental power was wholly misappropriated was, for him, "to bid [men] first to be Slaves, and then to take care of their liberty; and when their Chains are on, tell them they may act like Freemen."

These arguments were used to justify the colonists' nullification of the Stamp Act in 1765 and 1766, their opposition to the Townshend duties and the Tea Act, their militancy against the Coercive or "Intolerable" Acts of 1774, all of which preceded their final espousal of revolution in

1776. English revolutionary tradition served, moreover, to heighten colonial sensitivity to "dangerous" acts of British authority, to help them identify when and where resistance was necessary and appropriate. Would-be tyrants, it was said, sought ways to destroy checks on their power, as the Stuart kings had done in undercutting Parliament. The British attempt to take from colonial legislatures their exclusive right to tax colonists and to act as paymasters for colonial officials seemed to provide a clear parallel. Rulers anxious for despotic power would, moreover, try to raise armies so as to subdue popular resistance by force—which made the despatch of British regulars to Boston in 1768 and 1774 of ominous significance for Britons everywhere. Such rulers would encourage religions that taught submission to authority, such as Catholicism, or Lutheranism, which had supposedly undermined freedom in Denmark, and so undermine their members' willingness to judge and resist erring rulers. Thus when the British government freed Canadian Catholics from the restrictions of the Test Act, allowing them to participate in the government established under the Quebec Act of 1774, its action seemed to betray a sympathy not only for the preferred faith but also for the politics of the Stuart kings, and to mark George III's violation of his coronation oath to maintain the Protestant religion established by law.

English revolutionary tradition also offered colonists guidance as to how and when resistance should be implemented. The thrust of Whiggism was not, after all, for licentiousness and anarchy, but for rule of law: resistance and revolution were but means to prevent or to answer violations of law on the part of rulers. Strict guidelines were defined to prevent any confusion of liberty and licentiousness. Resistance to authority was not justified to terminate casual errors or private immoralities on the part of rulers, or for what Jefferson called "light and transient causes." Nor could private individuals resist the power of their magistrates from malice or for private injuries. Writers such as Locke were adamant here: if private judgment was given full reign, Locke wrote, the prince could be resisted "as often as any one shall find himself aggrieved, and but imagine he has not Right done him." In place of government and order there would then be "Anarchy and Confusion." The victim of private malice on the part of a ruler should perhaps go into exile, or even accept martyrdom, a later writer suggested, rather than deprive his country of a ruler "in the main good."

When, then, was resistance acceptable? Only for provocations so clear and serious that the "Body of the People" adjudged its freedom and security in danger—which suggested a consensus broader than a numerical majority, one involving all ranks of the population. This stipulation was understood as a significant restraint, one fully in keeping with the conservative ends of popular resistance. The people, it was said, were prone far more to submission than to resistance. They would bear "a great deal before they [would] involve themselves in Tumults and Wars," were never turbulent "unless seduced or oppressed," and then bore "a thousand hardships before they returned one." Jefferson repeated these truisms in the Declaration of Independence when he wrote that "all experience hath shewn that mankind are more disposed to suffer, while evils are sufferable, than to right themselves by abolishing the forms to which they are accustomed."

Even when the "body of the people" was alarmed, there were effective limits upon what it could rightly do. The people were not, above all, to use force except as a last resort. "Gentle ways are first to be used," the seventeenth-century Englishman Algernon Sidney wrote, "and it is best if the work can be done by them, but it must not be left undone if they fail." Similarly, John Adams described his cousin Samuel as a man who was always for gentle means—where they would do. When the peaceful means of redress had been exhausted, force might yet be inadvisable because imprudent. If there was little chance of success, uprisings against authority were best not attempted. Should they be repressed militarily, a still more oppressive regime was likely to emerge. Finally, the means of resistance had always to be used in proportion to the evils they acted against, with force limited to what was necessary for effectiveness.

In the works of English writers, these restrictions upon resistance and revolution were often phrased as *descriptive* statements: the people do most often bear rulers' mistakes without mutiny or murmur; they rise only after a long chain of abuses; they use force only after the alternatives have been exhausted. In colonial hands, however, such statements were rapidly transformed into *prescriptive* rules—as by a newspaper writer of 1765 who composed a set of guidelines for the members and leaders of popular assemblies. There was no doubt of the peoples' right to "suspend or dissolve the powers" it had granted its magistrates in forming government, or to "oblige" those in authority "to the performance of their Duty." But participants in such efforts were to remember that "such extraordinary Measures are only taken upon very extraordinary and important Occasions" when "the whole Body of the People concur in Sentiment, unite and determine as One Man." Moreover, such measures "ought to be confined to such weighty Matters of general Concernment and Complaint, as could not be redressed by the ordinary Forms of Proceeding, nor admitted of any other Remedy." The obligation upon "the collective Body of the People" to do justice on such occasions was "no less than it was upon the Magistrates, while the power was in their Hands." As a result, it was imperative that "Men of bad Principles" not be allowed to use the "public Commotions" as an occasion for realizing "villanous Designs," exacting Revenge, or preying upon private property. Moreover, "the greatest Care" was "necessary to keep an undisciplined irregular Multitude from running into mischievous Extravagancies." And as soon as the popular assembly's purpose was "fully answered, and security given that the Stamp Act shall not be executed," it should "immediately . . . dissolve—and let Government go on in its usual Forms."

The restraint that characterized so much colonial resistance to Britain was in part a testament to the stabilizing influence of English revolutionary tradition. After an initial wave of violence, the Stamp Act resistance quickly settled down into an efficient, limited effort to block execution of the act. Uprisings secured the resignation of stamp distributors in the various colonies before the act went into effect, which precluded the distribution of stamps and thus the necessity of more widespread action. The tea resistance was similarly restrained. Often the very landing of East India Company tea was prevented by a timely gathering of crowds. And at Boston, where it proved impossible simply to turn the tea ships back, "Mohawks" threw the leaves overboard only hours before the end of a twenty-day waiting period, when the tea would have become subject to confiscation and sale by customs officers. And then the crowd acted with "very little noise," avoiding damage to property other than tea. One participant tried to steal some tea, but was "stripped of his booty and his clothes together, and sent home naked"—punishment enough, it seems, in eighteenth-century Boston. John Adams was jubilant. "This is the grandest Event which has ever yet happened since the Controversy with Britain opened!" he wrote. "The Sublimity of it, charms me!"

But restraint did not come only from English tradition. To "keep an undisciplined irregular Multitude from running into mischievous Extravagancies" also demanded, it rapidly became clear, that it be organized with some care. The September 1765 Stamp Act uprising in Connecticut, for example, took on a military formation, with "commanders" who carefully fended off all suggestions of unnecessary violence. With the subsequent formation of the Sons of Liberty, organizations became increasingly elaborate. The Albany Sons of Liberty, for example, had a carefully drafted "constitution" or articles of association that set up a committee of thirteen with a president and clerk who were responsible for investigating grievances stemming from the Stamp Act or other matters "thought . . . unconstitutional and oppressive." The Sons condemned "separate and detached" disturbances of the public tranquillity under "colour or pretence of the cause of LIBERTY," along with "the mean practice of dropping Letters on the Streets, setting up scandalous Libels, Verses, or any other thing detractive of any person's Character" so as to bring upon him "public Odium."

In these early attempts to organize the people in order to contain violence and to keep resistance within the bounds of "revolution principles" lay the origins of a protracted effort to involve "the body of the people" in the opposition to Britain and, gradually, as British authority dissolved, in its own self-government. On the local and provincial levels, this manifested itself in the expansion of the Boston Town Meeting into what was called a meeting of the "Body of the People," or, more simply, a "Body" meeting; in the creation of ad hoc town meetings in cities like New York and Charleston, South Carolina, where they had not been part of the colonial heritage; in the formation of nonimportation associations and later of provincial congresses and conventions. From these emerged the first government for the United States—the Continental Congress—which itself encouraged the transformation from royal to elective government.

This development had a long-term effect on American politics: it mobilized groups of persons who had never before exercised governmental responsibilities, such as the tradesmen of urban centers along the Atlantic coast. Moreover, it constituted an unplanned experiment in republicanism, that is, in government founded upon the people and not upon hereditary right. According to traditional wisdom it was impossible for a nation to be ruled successfully without king or nobles: if the people rule, who would be ruled? Anarchy and, in its train, despotism would inevitably follow. As late as 1774 to be called a "republican" was much like being called a Communist in the 1950s. But suddenly republicanism seemed vindicated from the slurs of the past. The people obeyed the committees and congresses they had chosen—more so, it seemed to some, than was true under the old regime. And so the way was opened for one of the greatest of human adventures in the late eighteenth and early nineteenth centuries, an "age of democratic revolutions."

A belief in the right of revolution and resistance to authority was, then, basic not simply to the colonists' dissolution of British authority, which culminated in the Declaration of Independence. It was also critical to the founding of republican government in America. How, then, did it come to be so buried in the revolutionary past? What historical terrain separates it from modern America? How did it become unfamiliar, even unacceptable?

The late stage of the American Revolution, which began with the Declaration of Independence and ended with the ratification of the Federal Constitution, marked a particularly important transformation in American acceptance of the right of revolution. With the establishment of republican government, all political authority became directly or indirectly under the control of the people. Was there, then, any need to step outside the regular, lawful modes of seeking redress? "No people can be more free [than] under a Constitution established by their own voluntary compact, and exercised by men appointed by their own frequent suffrages," Governor Samuel Adams told the Massachusetts legislature in 1794. "What excuse then can there be for forcible opposition to the laws? If any law shall prove oppressive in its operation, the future deliberations of a freely elected Representative, will prove a constitutional remedy." Elections, then, became a peaceful surrogate for resistance and revolution. And so the election that made Jefferson president was known as the "Revolution of 1800," because it set aside an administration whose militarism and repression of dissent were adjudged dangerous to American freedom. Should elections be too far off in time to remedy an urgent threat, the Constitution provided alternatives, above all in the process of impeachment. The House Judiciary Committee's hearings on the impeachment of Richard M. Nixon in 1974 may well, in fact, have been our most authentic Bicentennial "reenactment." Poised, like the Declaration of Independence, against a ruler accused of abusing his power, of attempting to put himself above the law, the impeachment proceedings employed means the Revolution itself defined as a substitute for the more violent traditional responses to similar threats in 1649, 1688, and 1776.

In other ways, too, the late stage of the Revolution undermined the role and legitimacy of direct popular action against constituted authority. The evolution of written constitutions meant that questions of constitutionality could be adjudicated in the courts. Judges, then, replaced the people in deciding when laws were unconstitutional and of no force, so that again formalized procedures replaced the traditional actions of the people "out of doors." If these developments undercut the one-time duty of the people to serve as watchdogs of their freedom, and to rise against rulers oblivious of the public good, that process had a precedent. In England, too, after its seventeenth-century age of revolution, institutions—above all Parliament—gradually took on the active functions accorded the people in Whig tradition.

But the fate of resistance and revolution in the United States was tied to still another important transformation of the late revolutionary period —a changing conception of the locus of danger to liberty. The suspicions shaped by English revolutionary tradition focused upon persons in power, above all upon kings and hereditary magistrates. But was power so dangerous in a republic, where magisterial authority was determined by the people? "There is some consistency in being jealous of power in the hands of those who assume it by birth . . . and over whom we have no control . . . as was the case of the Crown of England over America," one South Carolina writer observed in 1784. "But to be jealous of those whom we choose the instant we have chosen them" seemed absurd. Suspicion of power was, of course, not eradicated. It has remained an important theme throughout American history. But, to a number of thoughtful observers in the 1780s, a greater danger to freedom seemed to come from the people themselves. In traditional terms, that should not have been. If the essence of liberty was the promotion of the public good, how could the public be illiberal? Could it will its own harm? A democratic despotism, John Adams once said, was a contradiction in terms. Yet in the 1780s popularly elected legislatures interfered with Loyalist property despite protective provisions of the Peace Treaty; they were not even scrupulous about honoring the state constitutions by which they were founded. And so observers became aware of a new kind of danger: the tyranny of the majority. This threat to freedom could hardly be checked by "the body of the people." The people were the problem, not the solution. Minority rights might be protected by bills of rights which, as written documents affixed to constitutions, could be enforced in the courts. But their effectiveness demanded a uniform adherence to law and authority —even by disaffected majorities.

This development added a new meaning to freedom. In the past, liberties were understood as preserves against power. Freedom of the press, freedom of speech, even the right to bear arms were traditionally understood as means to assure the people's ability to learn about the wrongful acts of miscreants in power and to resist them. But beginning in the 1780s, and increasingly thereafter, "rights" became separate ends in themselves, goals worthy of pursuing even apart from their older public purpose.

This involved, too, a curious turnabout in the role of the state and the conception of power, although the implications were not realized immediately. If liberty demanded that minority rights be protected, the force of the state might be used against even an unwilling majority, against perhaps "the body of the people," and still contribute to the cause of freedom. An expansion of governmental power need not mean, as it did in the old English Whig tradition, a pursuit of rulers' private interests at the cost of the public. Power and freedom might be reconciled. There were those who remained doubtful, including several surviving "old revolutionaries" of 1776 such as Richard Henry Lee, Patrick Henry, and John Lamb—men who saw in the federal constitution a reincarnation of the Empire rejected in 1776. But the Federalists won the day; and their achievement undercut the more traditional fears of their opponents, whose orientation against the power of kings and magistrates seemed to many hopelessly anachronistic.

To a significant extent, then, the tendency against a continuing and relevant "right of revolution" in nineteenth-century America was built on late revolutionary precedents. Even the North's rejection of Southern secession in 1861 had a revolutionary precedent. In 1777 Vermont had attempted to "dissolve the political bonds" that tied it to New York, and so earned the hearty condemnations of the Continental Congress.

The Declaration of Independence provided no precedent for such efforts against "Order, Stability and good Government," the Congress declared with more rigor than logic. The states had created Congress to secure and defend them in their original boundaries, not to preside over their diminishment. The implications were clear. From the point of view of the nation's high :st authority, the right of a people to "alter or abolish" its government and institute a new one in its place was no longer operative for Americans, though only a year had passed since Jefferson's and the Congress's eloquent assertion of that right.

But did everyone agree? The South's espousal of nullification and secession, the Abolitionists' refusal to recognize the force of laws protecting slavery and their ultimate proposal of "no union with slaveholders"— these suggest, at least, that among some early nineteenth-century Americans the traditions of 1776 were alive and well. Even at the pinnacles of power, and in the man who would preside over the nation during the secession crisis, there was a continuing readiness to defend the right of revolution. Abraham Lincoln in fact asserted that right in terms more permissive than those of 1776. "Any people anywhere, being inclined and having the power, have the *right* to rise up, and shake off the existing government, and form a new one that suits them better," he told the House of Representatives on January 12, 1848. Nor was the right "confined to cases in which the whole people of an existing government, may choose to exercise it. Any portion of such people that *can, may* revolutionize, and make their *own,* of so much of the teritory [*sic*] as they inhabit." Indeed, "a *majority* of any portion of such people may revolutionize, putting down a *minority* . . . near about them," just as the revolutionaries of 1776 had suppressed the Loyalists.

Why this willingness to abet revolution? Because Lincoln was speaking of Texas, which declared its independence of Mexico and sued for annexation to the United States, thus contributing to the growth of republican government. Indeed, revolution was in general approved for parts of the world that had not yet established a republican government after the American model. Thus in January 1852 Lincoln endorsed the right of Hungarians to "revolutionize their existing form of government, and to establish such other in its stead as they may choose," and approved a tribute to "the patriotic efforts of the Irish, the Germans and the French, who have unsuccessfully fought to establish in their several governments the supremacy of the people."

For the people of the United States, where popular self-government was already established, the case was far different. Like Samuel Adams, who in the 1790s had approved the French Revolution but denounced the Whiskey Rebellion in western Pennsylvania, Lincoln's sympathy for revolution stopped at the frontier. The American Revolution obliged citizens of the United States "never to violate in the least particular, the laws of the country; and never to tolerate their violation by others," he argued. "As the patriots of seventy-six did to the support of the Declaration of Independence," he urged, "so to the support of the Constitution and Laws, let every American pledge his life, his property, and his sacred honor":

> —let every man remember that to violate the law, is to trample on the blood of his father, and to tear down the . . . [charter] of his own, and his children's liberty. Let reverence for the laws, be breathed by every American mother, to the lisping babe, that prattles on her lap—let it be taught in schools, in seminaries, and in colleges; . . . in short, let it become the *political religion* of the land. . . .
>
> (January 27, 1838)

And so secessionist Southerners were not the progeny of Jefferson and the Declaration of Independence, but men who would destroy the charter of American freedom established by the nation's revolutionary fathers.

But the distinctions phrased by Samuel Adams and Abraham Lincoln were difficult to maintain. If revolution was a right, how could it be denied to Americans who found their rights and interests inadequately protected under the constitution of 1787? Did the South not represent at least a majority of a portion of the American people, in Lincoln's terms, as the revolutionaries of 1776 had represented a majority of a portion of the British people? There were those who bit the bullet, who proclaimed that the North's decision to block secession denied "the inherent right of any and every great mass of human population . . . to choose and change at will its form of government." It denied "that the only just foundation of government is 'the consent of the governed,' " and so served "to stultify our revolution; to repudiate all our history . . . to sanction all . . . the alien dominations, of other ages and countries." That the South sought independence in defense of a bad cause did not, it seems, affect its right to revolt, for Southerners had a right to choose badly. And in denying that right, the Northern critics of Union policy argued, the evil of political slavery was added to that of chattel slavery.

But those men, the ideological heirs of 1776, were branded "Copperheads" in the 1860s, as Northerners of Southern sympathies, and on at least one occasion published their views, ironically, from exile in England. By contrast, as George Frederickson suggests in *The Inner Civil War*, the heirs of the Loyalists were among the most adamant supporters of the North, and they proved particularly significant in shaping the postwar nation. Men such as Orestes Brownson hoped the war would bring to an end the "wild theories and fancies" of the nation's "morning," when belief in government by consent had led "nearly every American" to assert " 'the sacrid right of insurrection' or revolution" and to sympathize with "insurrectionists, rebels, and revolutionaries, whenever they made their appearance." Loyalty, he claimed, was associated with royalty, treason considered a virtue, and traitors "honored, feasted, and eulogized as patriots, ardent lovers of liberty, and champions of the people." But now, he hoped, in "the fearful struggle of the nation against a rebellion which threatened its very existence," Americans would finally learn that governments must govern, and the people obey.

And so the emphasis upon loyalty and submission in late nineteenth- and twentieth-century thought was itself one mark of a transformation in the "American mind" that Henry James both noted and welcomed. Others predicted the change with foreboding, fearing that war would bring power and dominion "unsought by the free," and that, in the words of Herman Melville,

> the Founder's dream shall flee,
> Age after age shall be
> As age after age has been.

That, in short, the vision of a nation governed by consent would be left among other utopian dreams of the past, and the United States would take its place in the world as a nation no different from all others.

Did the Civil War, then, mark the end of the tradition of 1776? There is much evidence to the contrary. Certainly the Populists of the 1890s thought themselves to be "filled with the spirit of the grand generation that established our independence." In their famous Omaha Platform, passed on July 4, 1892, "the one hundred and sixteenth anniversary of the Declaration of Independence," they announced their intention of restoring "the government of the Republic to the hands of the 'plain people,' with whose class it originated." Others who opposed the concentration of power in an expanding industrial nation also found sustenance in the tradition of the American Revolution, which had poised the people against corrupt power. Eugene Debs, for example, was fascinated with the Revolution of 1776. Thomas Paine and Patrick Henry were his particular "idols." He felt a continuity of cause with the revolutionary fathers who had also believed that "in their time . . . a change was due in the interests of the people," and who had dedicated themselves to "a better form of government, an improved system, a higher social order, a nobler humanity and a grander civilization." Even the uprisings against British authority were relevant for his effort to "do away with the rule of the great body of people by a relatively small class and establish in this country an industrial and social democracy." There was not "a star or a stripe in our national flag," he once argued, "that does not tell of a strike; not one. From Lexington, from Concord, all along the track of gloom and of glory clear down to Yorktown, is one succession of strikes for liberty and independence." The American Left lost its sense of continuity with the American past, it seems, only during World War I, when the country suppressed an indigenous and largely rural socialist movement. The revolutionary tradition fell in the 1920s to urban radicals, often immigrants, who were far more indebted to European critics of industrial capitalism than to Anglo-American traditions of resistance and revolution.

But the revolutionary tradition survived in other ways, above all in the doctrine and practice of civil disobedience. That term derives from Henry David Thoreau's essay "Civil Disobedience," which was written in 1849 but first published in 1866, after the Civil War was over, and which has been increasingly read in modern times as Americans concerned with the limits of civic obligation look back less to the revolution than to the opponents of black slavery for precedent and inspiration.

Yet civil disobedience clearly represents a modern form of the old right of resistance, so integral to the opening stages of the struggle with Britain.

The kinship of civil disobedience and colonial resistance is clear in the very definition of civil disobedience as a limited response to objectionable acts of authority. By definition, it is nonrevolutionary. And because it is and must be limited, restrictions upon civil disobedience have been seriously debated and carefully defined. To a remarkable extent these resemble those articulated by Locke, Sidney, and the American resisters of Britain in the 1760s and 1770s. The spokesmen for civil disobedience consistently stress that legal remedies must be exhausted before an illegal act is undertaken; that if violence or force is to be employed at all—and there are those who insist all civil disobedience must be nonviolent—the least violent means possible must be employed. Moreover, the perpetrators of civil disobedience are enjoined to consider "the appropriateness of the action to its own purpose," much as colonists insisted that acts of resistance be proportional to their provocations. Together such restrictions, or "moral considerations" as one modern writer called them, are meant to manifest the "civil" character of civil disobedience. They signal, that is, that the perpetrator "is, and intends to remain, a responsible member of the community," not "a criminal, a revolutionary, or a social misfit."

There are, of course, striking differences between the revolutionaries' concept of resistance and the "classic" doctrine of civil disobedience as expressed by Thoreau and by dissenting Americans of the 1960s, differences that mark the adaptation of the earlier doctrine to postrevolutionary circumstances. Civil disobedience is not, first of all, an act of the "Body of the People" who, from the founding of the Republic, could act through different, constitutional mechanisms. Instead it is the act of an individual or a minority of the whole, an action specifically condemned by seventeenth- and eighteenth-century writers in the English revolutionary tradition. But individual rights became a more major concern in the course of the American Revolution. Thereafter liberty, understood as an attribute less of the whole body politic than of individuals within it, shifted the just right of opposing authority from the whole to parts of the whole. Thus a second major difference between civil disobedience and eighteenth-century resistance rests in the fact that civil disobedience is a response less to threats to the commonweal than to violations of individual rights or of conscience, which itself has important consequences. As long as resistance met dangerous acts of power, danger could be identified by reference to history. But the violations of conscience are less easy to define; they differ with individuals and change over time, and so cannot be derived from the record of the past as were the signs of despotism so familiar to colonial Americans.

Civil disobedience is, moreover, less an act to direct government than a symbolic act, meant to draw the attention of the majority. The Stamp Act or Tea Act Resistance, like other similar early and mid-eighteenth-century acts, imposed direct limits upon government. They demonstrated what authority could in fact not do. Civil disobedience from its inception was instead an appeal to the majority to effect change, not, for the most part, an effort to effect that change immediately. Acts of civil disobedience manifest injuries to individual rights or to the rights of conscience. This "political" attribute was clear already in Thoreau's essay. "Cast your whole vote, not a strip of paper merely, but your whole influence," he urged. "A minority is powerless while it conforms to the majority; it is not even a minority then; but it is irresistible when it clogs by its whole weight. If the alternative is to keep all just men in prison, or give up war and slavery, the state will not hesitate which to choose."

Political effectiveness remains a major defense of civil disobedience in our own day. Was there no connection between the sit-ins against segregation and the passage of laws against racial discrimination? Were black Americans wrong to disobey segregation laws, even though the Supreme Court had approved them in *Plessy* v. *Ferguson*? Did not the Civil Rights Acts of 1957, 1960, 1964, and 1965 follow from the "determination, the spirit, and the non-violent commitment of the many who continually challenged the constitutionality of racial discrimination and awakened the national conscience"? Because civil disobedience is meant to influence the political responses of others, its defenders have often insisted that acts of civil disobedience must be public, and that the moral purpose of the act be publicized.

A final difference between the colonial concept of resistance and the more modern idea of civil disobedience rests in the frequent insistence that the civilly disobedient must be ready to accept the penalties of law. Eighteenth-century resisters opposed acts of magistrates that were beyond the limits of the law, "unconstitutional," invalid. As a result, it was said, the lawless rulers, not those who resisted their wrongful acts, should be subject to punishment. But the constitutionality of official acts is now determined judicially, not by the people directly. And in an established society, as the defenders of civil disobedience recognize, a willingness to accept the sanctions disobedience entails provides a limit upon its too-frequent implementation. As such, it compensates for the increased permissiveness involved in allowing persons who are far fewer than the "body of the people" to step outside the law.

If civil disobedience is, then, a modern descendant of the colonists' right of resistance, which was itself a variant of the right of revolution applicable in nonrevolutionary situations, it is strange that radicals of the 1960s had so little consciousness of revolutionary precedent. To be sure, some made recurrent symbolic references to the Boston Tea Party. But the theorists of civil disobedience cited Thomas Merton, Gandhi, even Jesus far more than Locke, Sidney, or their English and American Whig colleagues. This in itself testifies to the obfuscation of revolutionary tradition in the first century of the nation's existence. The resulting sense of historic isolation had its toll. Resisters of the 1960s lacked the limits defined by tradition to bind and discipline their numbers; they lacked the sense of historic direction and mission that had so sustained a Samuel Adams two centuries earlier. They lacked, moreover, the support of the past in responding to critics whose arguments had been answered by Whig writers two or three centuries earlier. Like old English Tories, or some Loyalists of the American Revolution, or the most conservative defenders of the Union cause, a majority of the National Commission on the Causes and Prevention of Violence condemned civil disobedience in 1969 as a step toward general lawlessness and anarchy. Danger lay, it seems, not so much in the civilly disobedient, for evidence suggested that they were remarkably free of other "delinquent" behavior, but in the example they set for others less disciplined. But were the adherents of civil disobedience, who both taught and acted within defined limits, responsible for the "uncivil" disobedience of others? Benjamin Hoadly, an eighteenth-century English bishop familiar to many colonists, specifically denied that obligation. Evil men "disposed to public Disturbances" would find excuses in any case, he claimed. And is it possible that civil commotions today continue to be symptoms of official disdain for liberty and constitutional rule far more than they serve as the occasions for popular licentious-ness? If, moreover, the people refused to act directly when the lawful channels of redress proved ineffectual, would their passivity not invite further infringements upon freedom and rule of law?

So at least argued those opponents of the Vietnam War in the late 1960s who found the state itself hopelessly corrupt in its disregard for the right of life on the part of both Americans and Asians. The election of 1964 suggested that Samuel Adams's confidence in the ballot as a check on power was anachronistic at best. The government's use of the Gulf of Tonkin resolution indicated, moreover, that even Congress had lost its ability to check the modern bureaucratic state. And the courts proved too slow and too costly to protect the poor, who were, as Martin Luther King, Jr., recognized, bearing the toll of the war. Only direct interposition by persons engaged in what were increasingly called acts of "resistance" and even "revolution" were appropriate. "In destroying with napalm part of our nation's bureaucratic machinery of con-scription," the "Milwaukee Fourteen" declared, "we declare that the service of life no longer provides any options other than positive con-crete action. . . . [We] are participants in a movement of resistance to slavery."

Persons who take such a stand will always be involved in controversy and danger—as were the colonial revolutionaries who, after all, united in part to avoid "hanging separately" for the crime of treason. That the legitimacy of their tactics has been and will continue to be debated testifies to the seriousness with which thinking Americans regard any principled decision to step outside the laws which, for the most part, serve as the buttresses of freedom. But people like those who provided "links" for the underground railroad or participated in the bus sit-ins of the 1950s or the draft resistance of a decade later have continued to appear in American history, manifesting the conviction of many Amer-icans that devotion to the purposes of law is more important than an un-thinking adherence to its letter, that in certain extraordinary circum-stances the cause of both freedom and law might require persons to step outside the law. And so the continued relevance of the citizen's right and duty to resist authority, articulated by Jefferson in 1776 and endorsed by the United States in its first official act as an indepen-dent nation, the Declaration of Independence.

Freedom and the Constitution

Gordon S. Wood

Americans have a very unusual, if not unique, conception of individual liberty. They enjoy a greater amount of personal freedom from governmental power than any people in the world. Even the English, who share a common legal heritage, do not allow individuals the freedom from governmental restraints that the United States does. One has only to compare the different ways Americans and English treat the question of freedom of the press to realize the extent of the libertarian bias of the United States. Despite repeatedly expressed fears of encroaching governmental power, individual liberty in America still remains paramount, even against the will of legislatures. No other country in the world places such constitutional limits on the power of the whole community to make laws against the rights of individuals. And no other country grants its judiciary such responsibility and power to protect the rights and freedom of individuals from the law-making authorities of the society. Even those countries that have followed the United States in adopting written constitutions have not thereby allowed their judges the power of judicial review.

This high regard for individual freedom is a product of the nation's entire history, but it was first clearly expressed during the Revolutionary era. It was not, however, the controversy with Great Britain or the Declaration of Independence that contributed most to the formulation of this conception of individual liberty. Rather it was the experience of Americans in the decade after the Declaration of Independence, leading up to the formation of the Constitution in 1787, that actually made meaningful the Revolutionaries' concern with personal freedom.

This statement is not easy to understand or accept. After all, Americans are accustomed to thinking of the Declaration of Independence as centrally concerned with liberty and the casting off of the restraints of government. The formation of the Constitution, on the other hand, is usually considered to be something of a reversal of the libertarian impulse of the Revolution and to be involved with the stabilization and consolidation of government. True as this may be, nevertheless, it was the formation of the Constitution, not the Declaration of Independence, that laid the basis for our modern conception of personal freedom. To understand how this meaning of liberty emerged is to understand in microcosm the history of America between 1776 and 1787.

No doubt the Revolution of 1776 was about liberty. But the liberty that most Revolutionaries invoked in 1776 did not as yet have the precise meaning it had later. It is true that liberty in 1776 meant freedom from arbitrary governmental power. There was of course a long English history behind the concern for this freedom. England was famous for its liberty, and the tradition of liberty Englishmen could trace back to Saxon times and its iteration in Magna Carta. The Stuart despotism of the seventeenth century had created new documents protecting these English liberties—the Petition of Right, the Habeas Corpus Act, the Bill of Rights. All of these rights and liberties of Englishmen were very much on the minds of Americans in 1776. Indeed, it was in the name of these liberties that Americans justified their resistance to Great Britain.

Yet the context in which the Revolutionaries viewed these liberties was not one modern Americans would easily understand. The Americans in 1776 still thought of liberty as Englishmen did. For most eighteenth-century Englishmen, even for many of the radical Whigs, liberty meant freedom from arbitrary Crown power. The power of government was identified almost exclusively with the king, or what in America is called the executive. Thoughout English history it had been the ruling power, the king or the executive, that had posed the great threat to the rights of the subject. It was against this ruling power, the Crown, that Englishmen had erected their various barriers—their charters and their bills of rights—to protect their liberties. The Petition of Right, the Habeas Corpus Act, and the Declaration of Rights of 1689 were directed solely at the abuses of power by the Crown or executive. They were not designed to protect the subject from the actions of the legislature or Parliament. In fact, they were the enactments of Parliament. For Englishmen Parliament, or the popular legislature, was the means, the instrument, by which these paper documents were upheld. As Algernon Sidney had written and Americans quoted enthusiastically in 1776, "Peace is seldom made, and never kept, unless the subject retain such a power in his hands as may oblige the prince to stand to what is agreed." For Englishmen that power was their consent expressed in the House of Commons. That representational power was identified with their liberty.

During the debate with Great Britain in the 1760s and 1770s Americans generally conceived of liberty in these traditional English terms, that is, in the way John Locke had defined it: "The liberty of Man, in Society, is to be under no other Legislative Power, but that established by Consent in the Commonwealth." Their quarrel with Britain was that the various acts of Parliament, in which they were not represented, had deprived them of this liberty, their consent. Their property and their personal liberties could be guaranteed only by what they often called their civil or political liberty, the right to participate in the government through representation in the legislature. "Therefore," as one American summed it up in 1773, "the liberty of the people is exactly proportioned to the share the body of the people have in the legislature; and the check placed in the constitution on the executive power." Only the executive, the prince, threatened liberty; the popular legislature protected it, indeed embodied it.

Although some Americans, especially Tories, warned of the threat to individual liberty from public liberty, from the representative bodies of the people, most in 1776 were confident of the popular will. Because the people "as a body," as the Bostonian Josiah Quincy said in 1774, were "never interested to injure themselves," and were "uniformly desirous of the general welfare," there could be no conflict between public and personal liberty. Indeed, the private liberties of individuals depended upon their collective public liberty, that is, their representation in the legislature. Like Locke and other theorists, Americans conceived of the people as a unitary homogeneous body having a single interest when set against the power of the king or the executive. Thus the people represented in the legislature, said Thomas Paine, were the best asylum for individual rights, especially those of property.

In other words, few Americans by 1776 had found it necessary or even intelligible to work out any theoretical defense of individual or minority rights against the collective power of the majority of the people. Tyranny was caused by kings or governors. As John Adams said in 1775, a tyranny by the people or their legislative representatives was illogical: "a democratic despotism is a contradiction in terms." It was necessary to protect the common law liberties of the people, like the rights of habeas corpus and trial by jury, from the power of their rulers, that is, the executive, but not from the people themselves or from their representatives in the legislatures. "For," as one South Carolinian wrote in 1775, "who could be more free than the People who representatively exercise supreme Power over themselves?"

Of course Americans realized that the source of British oppression in the 1760s and 1770s was the enactments of Parliament. Despite this evidence of legislative tyranny, however, the colonists were not compelled to think through the implications of Parliament's assault on their individual liberties. Most Whigs simply fit the parliamentary acts within their inherited Whig theory of politics, which saw only the prince or king as the source of despotism. Most therefore attributed the oppressive actions of the British legislature to their belief that Parliament had become the corrupt and pliant tool of the king and his ministers, that is, the government. When Jefferson came to write the Declaration of Independence he made the king, and the king alone, responsible for all the acts of tyranny that had taken place since 1763.

Most Americans in 1776 were confident they could solve the age-old problem of protecting the liberty of the people from the encroachments of governmental power. Full, fair, and uncorrupted representations of the people in the new state legislatures, together with written constitutions rigidly delimiting the power of the government, that is, the executive, would preserve the people's liberties. So weakened and circumscribed were the governors and so strong were the popular legislatures in the new Revolutionary state constitutions of 1776 that many Americans saw no need to add any bill of rights to their constitutions. After all, a bill of rights was like Magna Carta—a delineation of liberties designed to protect the individual from the executive. With the new executives already so restrained and the people's role in government so strengthened by their newly enlarged representative legislatures, a traditional bill of rights seemed irrelevant. Thus only five states prefaced their constitutions with declarations of rights. Even in most of these the purpose was traditional; most were designed to protect the individual not from the legislature but from the executive.

Yet implicit in the Americans' resort to written constitutions were new ideas about politics. Indeed, perhaps more than anything else, embodying the constitution in a single written document separated Americans from the broad stream of the English constitutional tradition. For the English there is, and can be, no distinction between what is legal, that is, passed by Parliament, and what is constitutional. But for Americans this distinction between legality and constitutionality lies at the heart of the constitutional system. Laws enacted by legislatures are not automatically constitutional, that is, in accord with those fundamental laws expressed in written constitutions. This crucial divergence in the constitutional tradition of the English-speaking world was opened at the Revolution, and it became wider and wider in the decade following Independence. The development was confused and halting, however, for ultimately it required the Revolutionaries to experience what they least expected—violations of liberty by their representative legislatures.

Several of the Revolutionary state constitutions had actually foreseen the possibility of the legislatures' violating individual freedoms and common law liberties. Some even had written into them admonitory statements that such rights "ought never to be violated on any pretence whatsoever," even by the legislatures. During the following decade these rudimentary beginnings were rapidly expanded. New, unanticipated experiences awakened more and more Americans to the potentiality of tyranny from the most unlikely source—the people's representatives. Individual liberty was being threatened by the collective liberty of the people.

During the war with Britain the legislatures inevitably placed all sorts of severe restrictions on the private rights of individuals. Many of these restraints were often no more than what any pre-modern government imposed in the way of mercantile regulation of the economy, justified in terms of the general welfare. But other restraints, including the outright confiscation of private property, were less traditional and could be explained only in terms of the Ciceronian maxim *Salus Populi suprema Lex est.* It was not simply these legislative usurpations occurring under wartime exigency, however, that opened the eyes of many Americans to new kinds of threats to liberty. It was the experience of democratic politics and popular legislation after the war, during the 1780s, that was truly frightening.

The state legislatures of the 1780s, nearly all elected annually, were the most democratic bodies in the eighteenth-century world. So democratic were they that they were extremely sensitive and responsive to shifting conglomerations of interests in the community. To an extent not duplicated earlier in American history, small farmers and debtors were able to capture majority control of these representative bodies and enact legislation protecting their interests at the expense of minority groups within the states, usually merchants and creditors. The legislatures suspended the payment of debts, changed the terms of private contracts, passed other kinds of ex post facto legislation, and printed paper money so profusely that few creditors received back the value of what they had loaned. The legislatures interfered constantly in the judicial process; they remitted fines, set aside jury verdicts, secured defective titles, and dissolved judicially established rights. All in all, the state legislatures in the 1780s enacted more laws, many often simply redressing the minor grievances of individuals, than had been enacted in the entire colonial period.

Twentieth-century historians have not generally been sympathetic with the complaints of those minority business interests hurt by this profuse legislation. These merchant creditors were, after all, just another group in the community, whose special interests had no more legitimacy than any other. Their complaints flowed only from their inability to muster a majority of support in democratically elected legislatures. But whatever we might think of the selfishness and the narrow interests behind these businessmen's complaints, it was largely their experience with what they called tyrannical majorities in the state legislatures that laid the basis for a new appreciation of the meaning of liberty. Their plight attracted the attention of many of the established leaders and best minds of the age—men who usually had no special business interests to protect. Fearful not for their pocketbooks but for the future of America's experiment in democratic government, these enlightened gentry leaders saw the abuses by majorities of the interests and rights of minorities in a wider context. What was needed, they saw, was a new understanding of American politics and a new definition of liberty. The state legislators who embodied the will of the people seemed no less capable of oppression than kings and governors had been. No matter that the leglislatures were the representatives of the people and annually elected by them. "173 despots would surely be as oppressive as one," wrote Jefferson in his *Notes on Virginia.* "An *elective despotism* was not the government we fought for."

Many like Jefferson concluded that the problem stemmed from the undemocratic character of the legislatures, that despite the fullest representation and the broadest suffrage of any country in the world, the American state legislatures were still not accurately expressing the benign will of the people. But others, less dogmatic and ideological, saw that the problem came not from too little democracy but from too much. No one perceived the new situation of the 1780s more clearly than did James Madison, the most astute political thinker of the Revolutionary era and perhaps of all American history. For Madison the difficulties of that decade did not arise because people had been forsaken by their legislatures, "but because their transient and indigested sentiments have been too implicitly adopted." The legislative abuses of individual rights were not violations of democracy but products of it; and they therefore brought "into question the fundamental principle of republican Government, that the majority who rule in such governments are the safest Guardians both of public Good and private rights."

Contrary to what many had thought in 1776, democratic despotism was entirely possible in America. "Wherever the real power in a Government lies," wrote Madison, "there is a danger of oppression. In our Governments the real power lies in the majority of the Community, and the invasion of private rights is chiefly to be apprehended, not from acts of Government contrary to the sense of its constituents, but from acts in which the Government is the mere instrument of the major number of the constituents." The crisis of the 1780s that led to the formation of the federal Constitution in 1787 revolved around this crucial issue: how to maintain democracy and at the same time avoid or mitigate its vices.

Americans know now how the Founders resolved the issue. The new federal Constitution offered new opportunities for diffusing and partitioning power to protect liberty. The expanded sphere of the federal government possessed immense advantages in the dividing of power it could achieve. "In the compound republic of America," wrote Madison in *The Federalist* Number 51, in a clear enunciation of what has come to be called the principle of federalism, "the power surrendered by the people is first divided between two distinct governments, and then the portion allotted to each subdivided among distinct and separate departments."

At the same time the Founders emphasized that the common source of each of these distinct governments and departments lay in the people. By doing away with the formerly exclusive connection between the people and the representative legislature and by making all offices of government, including the chief magistrate or executive, equally representative agents of the people, the Founders were able to justify building up the executive and judiciary at the expense of the legislature. Separating, balancing, and checking these different powers became the foremost doctrine of American constitutionalism. Since tyranny was now defined as the abuse of power by any branch of the government, and not by the executive alone (as Americans in 1776 had thought), it would best be prevented, as Madison put it, "by so contriving the interior structure of the government as that its several constituent parts may, by their mutual relations, be the means of keeping each other in their proper places."

Moreover, continued Madison in *The Federalist* Number 51, perhaps the most significant summary of the political thinking underlying the creation of the Constitution ever written, the partitioning of power in America would be intensified by "the extent of country and number of people comprehended under the same government," so that "the society itself will be broken into so many parts, interests, and classes of citizens, that the rights of individuals, or of the minority, will be in little danger from interested combinations of the majority."

To back up this parceling and dividing of power for the protection of liberty, the idea of a written constitution as fundamental law was expanded and then exploited by judges in the judicial review of legislation. Without such a power of review in the judges, wrote Hamilton in *The Federalist* Number 78, "all the reservations of particular rights or privileges" by the people and the several departments of government "would amount to nothing." Yet it was not easy at the time, nor is it always easy now, for Americans to understand how in a democracy appointive judges could set aside the acts of popularly elected legislatures and uphold the rights of individuals and minorities against the will of the community. "This," even Madison admitted as late as 1788, "makes the Judiciary Department paramount in fact to the Legislature, which was never intended and can never be proper." In a democratic government many thought that the only remedy for bad, unjust, or unconstitutional laws was for the people to elect new legislators to pass new laws. Allowing judges the power to void such laws, critics said, would make them despots more insufferable than any monarch in Europe.

What helped to make denial of popular majority will possible was a new understanding of liberty that emerged from the debates over the federal Constitution. Liberty could no longer be simply the right of the people to participate in government. The liberty now emphasized was personal or private, the protection of individual rights against all governmental encroachments, particularly by the legislature, the body which American Whigs in 1776 had wrongly assumed would be the surest weapon to defend their individual liberties. The aim of republican government was no longer merely to promote the will of the community, but to provide for the security of every individual, even against the will of the community. Unless the private rights of individuals and minorities were protected against the power of majorities, the Founders concluded, no government could be truly free.

These new ideas about private rights eventually came to form the basis for the nineteenth century's conception of individualism and liberalism. As such, they could not be exclusively confined to America. At the same time that Americans were forming their new constitutions and governments, the Swiss commentator on the English constitution, Jean Louis DeLolme, described a similar transformation taking place among Englishmen in their conception of liberty. Liberty, wrote DeLolme, was not, as men used to think, the establishing of a governmental order or the participating in legislation through voting for representatives; for "these are functions, are acts of Government, but not constituent parts of Liberty." "To concur by one's suffrage in enacting laws, is to enjoy a share, whatever it may be, of Power." Liberty, on the other hand, "so far as it is possible for it to exist in a Society of Beings whose interests are almost perpetually opposed to each other, consists in this, that, *every Man, while he respects the persons of others, and allows them quietly to enjoy the produce of their industry, be certain himself likewise to enjoy the produce of his own industry, and that his person be also secure."*

Although these new ideas of personal liberty became increasingly common in nineteenth-century Britain and Europe, it was in America that such ideas achieved their first and fullest expression. By now personal freedom has become equated with democracy. But, as the Founding Fathers realized, such individual freedom is not the inevitable consequence of popular rule. Indeed, the Founders believed not only that liberty was a blessing in itself but that the democracy they valued was more likely to flow from an obsession with individual freedom than the other way round. Whether Americans today can believe that with the same degree of conviction seems doubtful. But at least they should be aware that it is an issue that has been with them from the beginning of their national history.

Freedom and the Crossroads of Politics, 1789-1801

Merrill D. Peterson

It is easier to start a revolution than to end one. The American Revolution offers no exception to this historical truth. The Revolution did not end in 1776 with independence or in 1783 with the treaty of peace, or, indeed, in 1789 with the establishment of government under the Constitution. The Constitution struck a new balance between the claims of liberty and authority, the interests of the states and the union; and although it was vigorously contested during the course of ratification, the Constitution rapidly became the standard of legitimacy for all Americans. But the Constitution neither explained nor executed itself. A "bundle of compromises," it left many difficult questions unresolved. It created a political arena for implementation of the national will but was silent on the processes by which that will might be shaped, collected, and articulated. As the early leaders set about the business of breathing life into the Constitution, their disagreements over matters of policy and principle gave form to two great political parties.

For the better part of a decade the conflict between these parties shook the foundations of the government. The conflict had many sides and sources, but at its core were competing conceptions of freedom in the American republic, still a precarious experiment with an uncertain future. One party, the Federalists, who had brought the government into being, subordinated freedom to its design for order and stability, while the opposition party, the Republicans, believed that the emphasis on order was a betrayal of the experiment itself. The great issue descended from the American Revolution. It was powerfully reinforced, however, by the French Revolution, inaugurated in the same year as the new government. To complete the American Revolution, to secure the principles of freedom and self-government, the Republicans undertook the self-assigned obligation to crush the Federalists. When they did, they called their climactic victory "the revolution of 1800."

It was, therefore, at the crossroads of politics during a turbulent decade that the contest over freedom, opened by the American Revolution, was decisively, if not finally, played out. The cast of characters was much the same, for the American Revolution, unlike so many others, did not "consume its own children." The men who attended its birth lived to become its executors in the 1790s, though they divided on the road it should travel; and there is more than symbolic significance in the fact that the author of the Declaration of Independence, Thomas Jefferson, presided over "the revolution of 1800." This enhances the meaning of the conflict between Federalists and Republicans, for as it had its origins in the Revolution, so did it shape the destiny of the republic.

The new government began auspiciously. It acquired instantaneous prestige because George Washington stood at its head. His person was a point of union—the strongest the country possessed—and Americans, regardless of class, region, or persuasion, extended loyalty to the government out of loyalty to him. Yet Washington's charismatic style of leadership caused uneasiness. The atmosphere of a court surrounded the President, who never went anywhere without his carriage and six attended by liveried servants and outriders, and whose weekly levees possessed all the solemnity of divine worship. John Adams, the Vice President, wanted to confer upon Washington a splendid title, such as "His Majesty" or "His Most Benign Highness," not with the idea of making him a king but of lending authority and dignity to his office. This did not happen, but, as James Madison observed, "the ceremonials of government" were wound up to "a pitch of stateliness" little short of monarchical. Although Washington was surely the innocent dupe of sycophants around him, plain republicans grew suspicious of the forms and ceremonies to which he gave himself. These seemed to betray a lack of confidence in republican government, as though it were necessary to dazzle the people with pomp and splendor or perhaps to prepare them gradually for the adoption of monarchical government itself. Questions of title and ceremony, seemingly trivial, were symbolically important; they focused deeper political fears and preferences. Once anxieties were aroused, of republican feebleness on one side and monarchical grandeur on the other, they could not be stilled but rather pervaded the political discourse of the early years of the Republic.

The first serious division which touched the question of freedom occurred on issues of financial policy. In 1790 Alexander Hamilton, Secretary of Treasury, unveiled his plan for funding the debts inherited from the Revolution. Nearly everyone agreed on the necessity of some scheme of funding to establish the nation's credit, but Hamilton's plan provoked opposition. When Hamilton followed with a plan for a national bank and an elaborate program for aiding American manufactures, the opposition rallied to the defense of the Constitution. Hamilton's political opinions were known to be high-toned. At the Constitutional Convention he had advocated an executive elected for life, an aristocratic senate, and the virtual annihilation of the state governments. He thought the British government "the best in the world and . . . doubted much whether anything short of it would do in America." The Constitution fell far short of his goal. Still, it was a place to begin. Hamilton became its fervent advocate and then labored, as he later said, "to prop up the frail and worthless fabric."

Hamilton's financial system was the central prop. It rested on several assumptions: first, that self-interest is the dominant force in public affairs. In government, Hamilton said, "every man ought to be supposed a knave, and to have no other end, in all his actions, but private interest." This was the reverse of the classical doctrine of republican virtue, which assumed that men were capable of rising above selfish interests. Second, a wise government should "avail itself of the passions [of men], in order to make them subservient to the public good." In Hamilton's statecraft, as in Bernard de Mandeville's, private vices could yield public benefits. Third, as the foundations of both liberty and prosperity were laid in property, the state should mobilize the interests of men of property, particularly of the moneyed class whose capital activates the whole society. Finally, Hamilton believed that both government and property were endangered by democracy—by the power of the people. "All communities," he said, "divide themselves into the few and the many. The first are the rich and well born, the other the mass of the people." The former were steady, capable of enlarged views, and from their own interests friendly to civil order, while the mass of people were ignorant, turbulent, licentious, and given to the invasion of property.

On such assumptions did Hamilton build his financial system. Over the years the debt had depreciated greatly, become an article of speculation, and fallen into comparatively few hands. Funding it at face value enriched the moneyed class, who in the tradeoff identified their interests with the national government. By consolidating the state debts with the national, Hamilton's plan united the creditors and struck a blow for centralization. The aim was not to retire the debt but, by giving it stable value, to use it as a fund for energizing the government and the economy. Servicing the debt required taxes; in fact, the single item of interest on the debt accounted for approximately one-half of the government's budget. Fiscal administration called forth a bank, capitalized on government securities, which disbursed its profits to the holders. This developed the powers of the Constitution. Viewed as a political engine, the fiscal system counteracted the centrifugal tendencies of the federal polity and served as an American substitute for the monarchical and aristocratic establishments of the Old World.

As the Hamiltonian system unfolded, the opposition discerned in it a design to transform the government into something like the cherished British model. The Bank of the United States, after all, copied the Bank of England; the use of the public debt to create "the pretorian band of the Government—at once its tool and its tyrant," in the words of James Madison, mimicked the British practice since Walpole's time; and the plan to subsidize large-scale manufactures aimed to reproduce British industrialism in America. The social and economic effects of this were alarming enough. Leaders of the opposition, men like Madison, who spearheaded the attack in Congress, and Jefferson, who as Secretary of State became Hamilton's antagonist in the cabinet, associated the freedom of American society with its agricultural character. They were spokesmen for the landed interests of the country, not only Southern planters but the mass of small farmers, eastern and western, whose values were threatened by the acquisitive, impersonal, rootless, and speculative values of a new moneyed society. Placing their trust in individual freedom and enterprise, they were shocked by Hamiltonian manipulation of power to force a line of economic development which ran against the course of nature and exploited the many for the benefit of the privileged few. Whereas Hamilton considered the public debt a "public blessing" because it acted as a fund for capitalistic enterprise, Jefferson thought it a contrivance "for withdrawing our citizens from the pursuits of . . . useful industry, to occupy themselves and their capital in a species of gambling, destructive of morality, and . . . introducing its poison into the government itself."

More alarming, and of more immediate danger, were the political effects of the system. It corrupted the Congress, many of whose members had a personal financial stake in the leading measures of the system. It revived anti-federalist fears of the new government, especially in the South and West, where men viewed Hamilton's measures as partial to the commercial interests centered in Eastern cities. The assumption of the state debts presaged the consolidation of power in the national head, eventually reducing the state governments to ciphers. The act incorporating the Bank, in the absence of constitutionally delegated authority to Congress for this purpose, seemed to open, as Jefferson advised Washington, "a boundless field of power, no longer susceptible to definition." Hamilton justified the act on the doctrine of "implied powers." It was a persuasive, even a necessary doctrine, yet it was unknown to the people who ratified the Constitution, and so suggested that the government would be administered on a different set of principles from those pled at its adoption. Madison, a foremost pleader, said that the Constitution had two enemies: "one that would stretch it to death, and one that would squeeze it to death." Death by stretching had become the enemy in his eyes. The process must lead by degrees to Anglicization of the government, for it involved the consolidation of authority, the corrupt influence of the treasury with Congress, and the accumulation of powers in the Executive. In a newspaper essay of 1792 Madison described three species of government: first, a government maintained by permanent military force, as in much of Europe; second, a government operating by corrupt influence, as in Britain; and third, a government deriving its energy from the will of the society. The second, clearly, was the danger he foresaw for America. Such an "imposter" government substituted "the motive of private interest in place of public duty," converted "its pecuniary dispensations into bounties to favorites, or bribes to opponents," accommodated "its measures to the avidity of a part of the nation instead of the benefit of the whole," and thereby established "a real domination of the few under an apparent liberty of the many." The third form, "operating by the reason of its measures, on the understanding and interest of the society," said Madison, was the glory of American republicanism.

Beginning thus in domestic policy, the party conflict assumed added dimension from the diplomatic and ideological issues sent up in the progress of the French Revolution. In large measure the division in domestic policy coincided with the division in foreign policy. One goal of the American Revolution had been the liberation of the nation's commerce from British shackles and an expanding commercial system founded on the liberal tenets of free trade. Commercial freedom was a close ally of political freedom, for the absence of the former would jeopardize the latter. It was also essential to American prosperity which depended on the sale of American raw materials and agricultural surpluses in foreign markets. After the treaty of peace in 1783, Britain rebuffed American overtures, restored its mercantilist restrictions on American trade, and regained its economic ascendancy over the former colonies. To break this bondage Congress sought liberal commercial treaties with European nations, while several of the states retaliated against Britain—a policy that, it was generally expected, would be implemented on a national scale under the Constitution. Until then, certainly, the policy had not been successful. A commercial treaty undergirded the Franco-American alliance; it was the cornerstone of the liberal system, but American trade continued to be dominated by Britain.

In the First Congress Madison, supported by Jefferson, who had recently returned from France, moved to discriminate against British carriers. For five years Jefferson had worked to strengthen the French alliance. The French Revolution, he believed, opened the door to commercial as well as political liberation in Europe; the United States, therefore, should seize the opportunity to further these objectives and at the same time break the British monopoly and influence. Not only did Britain still "colonialize" American trade, but that country continued to occupy military posts in American territory and maintain an intransigent stance on other problems left over from the treaty of peace. Hamilton and his followers, nevertheless, opposed an aggressive policy toward Britain. The Federalist merchants of the coastal cities were tied into the old channels of trade; they were accustomed to trading on British capital, and they objected to any measure tending to excite commercial warfare with the former mother country. To these considerations the fiscal system added others. The treasury coffers were filled with revenue from British trade—revenue mortgaged to servicing the debt. In the undeveloped state of the American economy, Hamilton argued, Britain was the country's surest supplier, its only provider of capital, and its best market. He was reconciled to the subordination required by the British connection and, as Jefferson and Madison soon discovered, effectively countered every move friendly to France and unfriendly to Britain.

It was the ideological controversy growing out of the French Revolution that radicalized the party conflict. As the shockwaves of that Revolution broke across the Atlantic, American opinion, almost uniformly favorable to the Revolution at the outset, began to divide. In 1791 the polemical battle between Edmund Burke and Thomas Paine, in England, sharply defined the issue between tradition and progress, order and liberty, privilege and equality, monarchy and democracy. Americans followed the debate and then gradually duplicated it. For several months John Adams had been filling the columns of the *Gazette of the United States* with rambling reflections on government which, among other things, held up the British constitution as a model and assailed the "levelling" and "fanaticism" unloosed by the French Revolution. Adams sounded vaguely like Burke. The first American edition of Paine's *The Rights of Man* then appeared with a preface which Jefferson inadvertently supplied. Jefferson commended the fiery pamphlet as a reply to "the political heresies" lately advanced and called upon the citizens to "rally again round the standard of Common Sense." The alleged heresies were, of course, those of his old friend Adams, the Vice President.

Journalistic gladiators, "Burkites" and "Painites," with Adams and Jefferson cast in tutelary roles, forced the issue of the French Revolution into the government of the United States. Those who called themselves Republicans perceived their opponents as enemies of the cause of liberty and the disagreements between them as issues of fundamental principle.

In their eyes the French Revolution was the legitimate offspring of the American and entitled to American support. Its triumph over European despotism, moreover, seemed essential to the survival of the American republic, existing perilously in a monarchical world. "I consider," said Jefferson, "the establishment and success of their [the French] government as necessary to stay up our own, and to prevent it from falling back to that kind of half-way house, the English constitution." The Federalists, on the other hand, sharply differentiated the French Revolution from the American, hoped to keep it at bay, and feared the infection of mischievous democratic ideas. What endangered freedom, argued Adams, Hamilton, and their followers, was not wise statesmen who placed a premium on order and stability but visionaries and demagogues who preached liberty and equality until they would turn the people into brutes and conduct them, along the democratic route, back into tyranny. Increasingly, the French Revolution revivified America's own revolutionary heritage, elevated matters of interest to matters of principle, dramatized competing political systems previously perplexing and obscure, and alerted the citizenry everywhere to the stakes in the contest.

The outbreak of general European war in 1792–93 raised the stakes considerably. The National Assembly proclaimed France a republic, executed Louis XVI, declared war on the "conspiracy of kings" against the Revolution, and vowed to light the flames of "liberty, equality and fraternity" throughout Europe. Americans were jubilant. Gratitude to the gallant ally of their own revolution, satisfaction at seeing another republic on the map of the world, hatred of Britain and fear of revenge should the armed despots defeat France—Republicans hastened to convert these feelings into party capital. The Federalists, of course, gravitated to Britain and the First Coalition. They believed that France alone threatened American peace; they denounced the violent course of the revolution and interpreted French decrees as an attack on orderly government everywhere. "The war," Jefferson observed, "has kindled and brought forth the two parties with an ardour which our own interests merely, could never excite."

This "ardour" required cooling if the nation was to remain at peace. The old alliance pledged the United States to defend the French West Indies and extended certain privileges to France in the event of war— privileges denied to its enemies. Hamilton, in the cabinet, argued that the treaties should be suspended because they had been made not with the French nation but with the deposed sovereign, Louis XVI. He advocated only a very qualified reception of the new minister of the republic, Edmond Genêt. Jefferson prevailed upon Washington to uphold the treaties and to receive Genêt unconditionally, but he reacted bitterly to the President's Proclamation of Neutrality, which pledged impartial conduct toward the belligerents. In view of British superiority on the seas and in American trade, Jefferson concluded, such neutrality must redound to Britain's benefit and raise havoc with the French alliance.

Jefferson wished, and he believed the American public demanded, a friendly neutrality toward France. He would force Britain to pay a price for neutrality, a price which included British recognition of the most generous neutral rights, such as the principle of "free ships make free goods." This principle, which Britain had generally refused to recognize, had been embodied in the Franco-American accord. "Freedom of the seas," the modern cry of neutrals seeking to profit from other people's wars, became a fixture of Republican ideology. Again checked by Hamilton, Jefferson was further embarrassed by the firebrand French minister, whose warlike antics spoiled everything. To preserve peace, to preserve the Republican party from the recoil of the threatened explosion, Jefferson was compelled to abandon Genêt. In the prolonged controversy over neutrality, neither side was impartial. Neutrality was a fiction, exploited by both sides, although in the end more effectively by the Federalists than by the Republicans. The real issue was between revolution and reaction in the Atlantic world; and the choice involved a decision on where, between these forces, the balance of freedom lay for the American republic.

The ultimate catalyst in the formation of parties was the Jay Treaty with Great Britain. As Henry Adams observed, it "plunged a sword into the body politic." From the inception of the treaty in 1794 through its implementation by Congress two years later, it confronted the country with an issue that "seemed to require mutually exclusive choices on which the national existence depended, thrust[ing] upon ordinary men the same dramatic necessity as had come to preoccupy the leadership more and more, that of finding a way to preserve the achievements of the Revolution." Americans responded to the treaty's terms with indignation. Even ultra Federalists were dismayed. Some found satisfaction in the British pledge to evacuate the Northwest posts, but other quarrels, if they were settled at all, were settled in Britain's favor. The treaty aimed to resolve a burgeoning crisis over neutral rights in the interest of American peace, but it did so by the sacrifice of American claims, acquiescence in British maritime rule and practice, abandonment of the weapon—the only potent weapon in the nation's armory—of economic coercion, and, finally, at the cost of undermining the old alliance and inviting a crisis with France. For Madison the treaty was the work of "a British party." Jefferson, in retirement at Monticello, viewed it as "nothing more than a treaty of alliance between England and the Anglomen of this country against . . . the people of the United States." Republicans could scarcely find words to express their outrage.

Washington's decision to sign the treaty became the final test of his politics; he proved himself a Federalist president after all. The future of the treaty still depended on the appropriation of funds by the House of Representatives, where the Republican majority attempted to stifle the embryo monster. Many factors contributed to the narrow Republican defeat, but Madison, in his explanation, emphasized the campaign by the Federalist phalanx in the commercial cities to terrify the public. The banks, the mercantile houses, the insurance companies, he said, "were at work in inflaming individuals, beating down the prices of produce, and sounding the tocsin of foreign war, and domestic convulsions." Once the panic invaded Republican ranks, the battle was lost. Hamilton, though gone from the treasury, had orchestrated the campaign. He was still the presiding genius of Federalism, and the Jay Treaty marked the triumph of his British-centered system over the Republican system pegged to peace and friendship with France.

The battle over the treaty set the stage for the presidential election of 1796. Washington's decision to retire lifted the last restraint on partisanship, and two infant political parties, each with its own candidate, Adams for the Federalists, Jefferson for the Republicans, contested the succession. This was a remarkable development, though neither fully understood nor completed in 1796. The Constitution had been intended to work without parties. In every free government, the framers reasoned, various *factions* or *interests* compete for power, but government may be so contrived as "to break the violence of faction," and to prevent any single interest, or coalition in a stable party, from becoming a dominant majority. The Constitution would support this tendency for a number of reasons. As Madison had argued, the system of representation would filter out the baser elements of the public will, and because the jurisdiction of the government extended over such an immense territory, with so many jarring interests, the organization of a majority party would be virtually impossible. Political parties, because they would stir up public opinion in search of support, were anathema to the framers. Parties, they reasoned, fed on the turbulence of the populace, serving the ambitions of demagogues; they caused implacable rivalries in legislative councils, usurping the place of reason and moderation; they introduced whole networks of partisan allegiance at cross-purposes with the national welfare. Foreign nations, drawing the new transatlantic republic into the power balance of the Old World, would seek to subvert these parties to their own uses.

Nevertheless, political parties formed during Washington's two administrations. Pluralistic conflicts of interests became polarized by issues of fundamental principle. The legitimacy of a coalescing opposition party to the party of leaders in control of the government became a fundamental issue itself. The arguments on this issue revealed incompatible conceptions of political parties, of the role of public opinion, of the relationship between leaders and followers, of the process of change in free government; they exposed a wide gulf between two systems of politics, one closed and elitist, the other open and democratic. As men of established property and status, for the most part, the Federalists had a vested interest in social order and were accustomed to clubbing together politically. They had a powerful nucleus—the mercantile community of the coastal cities—to which the measures of the new government made a strong appeal. Conceiving of themselves as a ruling class, as the guardians of the government they had established, the Federalist leaders acknowledged their vulnerability to public opinion. Their political ideal has been described as that of "a speaking aristocracy in the face of a silent democracy." The Federalists sought to mold and manage public opinion, but they distrusted it, felt threatened by it, and spoke of "the people" with a mixture of condescension and fear. The Federalists were conservatives in a country founded in revolution with a set of libertarian and egalitarian values that had reversed the old relationship of rulers and ruled. In the light of the French Revolution the Federalists appeared as counterrevolutionaries.

Republicans, while not lacking notable leaders, were without a nucleus. The party found its strength in the latent power of numbers. The elitism and cohesiveness of the Federalists would be overcome by a heterogeneous party in the electorate. Claiming to be heirs of the revolutionary tradition, Republican leaders sought to keep it alive in the peaceful avenues of the political process. When they went outside the government to build a party in the broad electorate, thus giving voice to the "silent democracy," they set up a new ideal, one that saw in the agitation and mobilization of public opinion the vital principle of American government. Government would be saved by the people, not the people by government; the free criticism of constituted authorities, so long condemned, became a political virtue. Government was no longer to check, control, manipulate, or rise above public opinion, but to enhance it and to base public policy upon it.

To an extent, certainly, the conflict was epitomized in the clash between the two protagonists, Jefferson and Hamilton, who became its personal symbols. One despised, the other idolized rulership. One located the strength of the republic in the diffuse energies of a free society, the other in the consolidation of the government's power. One viewed the Constitution as a superintending rule of political action, the other as a point of departure for heroic statesmanship. One believed that private interest corrupted public good, the other would conscript private interests for the public benefit. In the balance between authority and liberty, Hamilton was an apologist for the former, Jefferson for the latter. Hamilton feared most the ignorance and turbulence of the people, while Jefferson preached trust of the people and feared rulers independent of them. Hamilton labeled his rival a demagogue, Jacobin, and Gallomaniac, while Jefferson named Hamilton a corruptor, monarchist, and Anglophile. Such words may have distorted reality, but they reflected accurately the worst dangers that each man saw in the politics of the other.

Whether partisan opposition based on public opinion was legitimate emerged early as the central issue in the conflict. In 1791, facing the problem of creating a responsive opinion to government measures, Jefferson and Madison founded a newspaper, *The National Gazette,* intended to counteract the "court" newspaper in the capital and to circulate throughout the country as a "Whig vehicle of intelligence." Behind this move was Jefferson's proposition that democratic government required an informed public. As "the people are the only censors of their governors," he said, it was imperative to bring them into the political process; and this could best be accomplished by newspapers penetrating "the whole mass of the people." "The basis of our government being the opinion of the people," said Jefferson, "the very first object should be to keep that right; and were it left to me to decide whether we should have a government without newspapers, or newspapers without a government, I should not hesitate a moment to prefer the latter." Hamilton and his friends reacted to *The National Gazette* by launching a campaign to discredit it as the tool of a faction working to subvert the government.

In 1793 the Republicans seized upon the spontaneous outburst of so-called democratic societies to further their cause. These societies—thirty-eight of them across the country—resembled ‑the corresponding societies before the American Revolution, but their impetus was another revolution, the French, and they channeled popular enthusiasm for the revolution abroad into Republicanism at home. Federalists linked the societies to the notorious Jacobin Clubs of Paris, branded them as seditious, and successfully implicated them in the Whiskey Rebellion of 1794. Washington then delivered the crushing blow, publicly condemning these "self-created societies" as illicit political engines. The Senate concurred wholeheartedly in the President's sentiments. The House debate, however, attempted to define the location of "the censorial power" in the American republic. Madison was emphatic: "the censorial power is in the people over the Government and not in the Government over the people." Jefferson, at Monticello, was shocked by Washington's action: "It is wonderful indeed, that the President should have permitted himself to be the organ of such an attack on the freedom of discussion, the freedom of writing, printing and publishing." Two years later, in his Farewell Address, Washington again betrayed intolerance of political opposition from outside the officially constituted channels of authority. In his view political parties were equally unnecessary and unwanted in a republic; he had attempted to govern independently of them, and he now warned the people against their "baneful" effects. Federalists agreed in principle. Republicans, although they approved of Washington's patriotic sentiments, were coming to see in democratic party organization the appropriate mechanism for wresting the government from the high-handed Federalists who, they believed, were the true bane of the country.

This issue came to a head in the new administration. Adams had been elected President, Jefferson Vice President. Once friends, they were now political foes. They had sought a political *rapprochement* after the election, but partisan pressures on both sides doomed it to failure. Crisis with France, mounting since the Jay Treaty, set the course of the Adams administration. Angrily denouncing French decrees against American commerce, Adams sent a three-man commission to negotiate in Paris under the threat of war. When intriguing agents of the Directory demanded money as the price of negotiation, the Americans indignantly refused. This affair—the XYZ Affair—then exploded in the United States, and the Federalists converted foreign crisis into domestic crisis. Under cover of the whipped-up war hysteria, they assailed the patriotism of the Republicans, portraying them as Jacobin disorganizers in the nation's bowels whose ultimate treachery only awaited the signal of an invading French army. The Republicans argued for keeping the door to peace open, confident that France would not declare war on the United States; but the issue badly damaged their cause and even their survival—perhaps the survival of the republic itself. Adams inflamed the spirit of war and intolerance by his bombastic answers to numerous addresses of loyalty that poured into Philadelphia. He denounced "the rage for innovation" and "the wild philosophy" of the French Revolution, "the delusions and misrepresentations of party," "the profligate spirit of falsehood and malignity" against the government, "the calumnies and contempt against Constituted Authority." He declared that "the degraded and deluded characters may tremble, lest they should be condemned to the severest punishment an American suffers—that of being conveyed in safety within the lines of an invading enemy." It was enough to plunge Madison into melancholy reflection on the old truth "that the loss of liberty at home is to be charged to provisions against dangers real or pretended abroad."

From such political violence came the Alien and Sedition Laws of 1798. Several measures were aimed specifically at aliens. For Republicans the most troublesome of these authorized the President summarily to deport aliens deemed dangerous to the peace and safety of the United States. Federalists believed that two large foreign-born groups, the French and the Irish, constituted a subversive fifth column associated with the Republican party. The law had particularly in view certain prominent philosophers and revolutionaries—Joseph Priestley, Thomas Cooper, C.L. Volney, Thaddeus Kosciusko—friendly to the Republican cause. "It suffices for a man to be a philosopher," Jefferson wrote, "and to believe that human affairs are susceptible to improvement . . . to make him an anarchist, disorganizer, atheist, and enemy of the government." He thought the law "worthy of the eighth or ninth century." The Sedition Law made it a federal crime, punishable by fine and imprisonment, to publish "any false, scandalous and malicious writing" against the government, Congress, or the President. The law rested on the ancient principle that government and governors can be criminally assaulted by opinion, and that government has an inherent right to protect itself, indeed to protect the people whose government it is, by punishing seditious libels. The British ministry, in reaction against revolutionary agitators, had earlier set the example with a wave of prosecutions, and now Congress had introduced this system of terror in the United States.

Amid the hysteria that enveloped the country in the spring of 1798, passage of the Sedition Act was not surprising. The President's addresses invited it; rising intolerance of any opinion critical of the Federalist "war system" demanded it. But Republican leaders stoutly denied that the country was threatened either by France or by the free circulation of opinion. They appealed to the First Amendment guarantee of freedom of speech and press. Liberty and truth went together, as the whole history of the progress of science and religion over the errors of coercive authority demonstrated. And so it must be in government, especially in a republic founded on the reason and consent of the governed. Elections would matter little if one opinion was heard, another silenced; if the ruling party was free, the opposition shackled. Freedom to criticize the government alone would keep it responsible to the people, command public confidence, and secure the avenues of peaceful change.

Behind the smokescreen of war and subversion, the Sedition Law, Republicans believed, aimed at the suppression of their presses and the crippling of their party. Scarcely an opposition newspaper north of the Potomac escaped the "terror of '98." Federal officials arrested twenty-five persons, principally Republican printers and publicists, indicted fourteen, tried and convicted ten. The damage from intimidation cannot be measured, but the effort to coerce opinion proved self-defeating. Jefferson could be philosophical. "A little patience," he wrote in the spring, "and we shall see the reign of witches pass over, their spells dissolved, and the people recovering their true sight, restoring the government to its true principles." But patience eventually deserted him. The Alien and Sedition Laws struck at Jefferson's basic convictions, for they assumed that the human mind could not be trusted with freedom, that it must be awed with "stories of raw-head and bloody bones to a distrust of its own vision, and to repose implicitly on that of others; to go backwards instead of forwards to look for improvement; to believe that government, religion, morality, and every other science were in the highest perfection in the ages of darkest ignorance." If this fraud and these usurpations went unresisted, new repressions, probably involving the use of the army raised to combat an illusory foreign foe, must follow.

Jefferson concluded that "a revolution of opinion" was necessary. But how could it be started? The press was manacled. The Executive, both houses of Congress, the entire judicial establishment were in Federalist hands. There was no official channel for redress. In this situation Jefferson and Madison turned to the state legislatures. The Virginia and Kentucky Resolutions of 1798 interposed the authority of these two states, declared the Alien and Sedition Laws unconstitutional, and appealed to the other states to join in forcing their repeal. By asserting the power of a state to judge the constitutionality of acts of Congress, the resolutions raised the specter of disunion, a cure likely to prove no less fatal than the disease they attacked. But whatever the later significance of these famous resolutions for the issue of states' rights and union—the issue on which the Civil War would be fought—they originated in a desperate struggle for political survival and addressed the fundamental issue of freedom and self-government descending from the American Revolution.

The crisis with France passed in 1799. Adams, seizing the olive branch extended by Talleyrand, the French foreign minister, broke with the Hamiltonian leadership and reopened negotiations with France. The Sedition Act remained in force, however, and ultra Federalists maneuvered to control the outcome of the ensuing presidential election. In January 1800 Senator James Ross of Pennsylvania introduced legislation setting forth congressional procedures to scrutinize the electoral vote cast in the states. A joint committee of the two houses would meet in secret session, throw out votes deemed irregular, and submit its report, which would be final, to Congress. The Federalist majority would control the committee. This blatant party measure passed the Senate, where debates were secret, but failed in the House after the Republican editor in Philadelphia, William Duane, acquired and published the bill. Duane had already been arraigned twice under the Sedition Act only to squirm free each time. Now he was summoned before the bar of the Senate to answer for the publication. (He would finally escape this noose, too.)

Party stratagems looking to the election were not confined to Congress. Under the Constitution a body of electors separated from the people was to choose the president (and vice president), but the rise of political parties made a mockery of this theory. Electoral tickets became party tickets, and every presidential elector became the agent of the majority that elected him. In New York, as in several of the states, the legislature chose the presidential electors. After the Republicans won the state election in April 1800, Hamilton urged Governor John Jay to convene the lame-duck Federalist legislature and thus contrive to nullify the Republican verdict at the polls. Otherwise, he warned, the country faced "a revolution after the manner of Bonaparte." Jay quietly buried the proposal.

The election of 1800 was one of the most bitterly fought in American history. Everyone seemed to understand that its outcome would fix the political destiny of the country for decades to come. Around Jefferson, imaged as "the man of the people," Republicans achieved unprecedented unity of action and feeling. Through the apparatus of party organization they mobilized opinion at the country crossroads and in the city wards. "Every threshing floor, every husking, every party work on a house-frame or raising a building, the very funerals," complained one Federalist, "are infected with bawlers and whisperers against government." Distrusting democracy, the Federalist leaders were ill equipped to conduct a campaign in the electorate. Their "war system," with its engines for terrorizing public opinion, collapsed around them in 1800; and scheming Hamiltonians turned in sullen anger on Adams, who had courageously made peace with France. Divided, dismayed, desperate, the Federalists could nonetheless cordially unite in vilification of Jefferson. Vilify him they did, as a hardhearted infidel, a philosophical visionary, a Jacobin incendiary, an unscrupulous demagogue, and the enemy of Washington, the Union, and the Constitution. Under him the churches would be destroyed and the nation laid waste by revolutionary fanaticism. "Murder, robbery, rape, adultery, and incest will be openly taught and practiced," wrote one pamphleteer, "the air will be rent with the cries of distress, the soil will be soaked with blood, and the nation black[ened] with crimes." In the end, Jefferson won a decisive victory over Adams.

The victory was jeopardized, however, by a treacherous abyss in the electoral system. The Constitution, prior to the Twelfth Amendment (1804), did not provide separate ballots for president and vice president. When the Republican electors cast all their ballots for Jefferson and his running mate, Aaron Burr, giving them an equal number of votes, the final choice fell to the House of Representatives. There the lame-duck Federalist majority plotted to annul the popular verdict either by creating an interregnum or by dealing Burr into the presidency. Burr, if he did not condone the latter scheme, seemed to acquiesce in it. As the crisis mounted, Republican zealots in neighboring states threatened to march on Washington, the infant capital, to put down any man bold enough to offer himself as a usurper. Finally on the thirty-sixth ballot the House broke the stalemate and elected Jefferson. "Thus has ended," Albert Gallatin remarked, "the most wicked . . . attempt ever tried by the Federalists"—their last attempt to control the government in the face of public opinion.

This completed the first democratic transfer of power in the nation's history, indeed in the history of modern politics. Jefferson came to view the Republican ascendancy as "the revolution of 1800." "[It] was as real a revolution in the principles of our government as that of 1776 was in its form; not effected indeed by the sword, as that, but by the rational and peaceable instrument of reform, the suffrage of the people." Many historians have criticized this conception, chiefly because they have looked for revolutionary results in Jefferson's administration and failed to find them. But viewed from the preceding decade of political controversy, or viewed in the longer perspective of the age of democratic revolution which opened in 1776, the conception not only has historical validity but is basic to an understanding of the dynamic ideology of freedom and self-government held by the Republicans.

Jefferson's Inaugural disclosed the nature of this revolution. In one aspect the address was a lofty summation of the Republican creed. Tracing its principles back to the American Revolution, thereby authenticating it for the national consciousness, Jefferson pledged to make this creed the touchstone of government. In another aspect the address was a bold bid for the restoration of harmony and affection. The ship of state, safely on the republican tack at last, might now sail on calmer seas. Believing that the mass of Americans were fundamentally united in their political sentiments, Jefferson sought to quiet the political storms of the past decade, to extinguish hatreds and fanaticism—the insignia of European politics—and thus to enable the country to realize its destiny as "the world's best hope" for freedom. Finally, and above all, the First Inaugural was a commitment to ongoing political change through the democratic process of open debate, popular participation, and free elections. Jefferson named "absolute acquiescence in the decisions of the majority the vital principle of republics, from which there is no appeal but to force." This principle, to be effective, demanded freedom of inquiry and opinion, together with the right of any minority to turn itself into a new majority. "If there be any among us," he said, alluding to the delusions of '98, "who would wish to dissolve this Union or to change its republican form, let them stand undisturbed as monuments of the safety with which error may be tolerated where reason is left free to combat it."

Federalist leaders had reckoned the strength of government on Old World standards: army and navy, the patronage of "the rich, the well born and the able," great treasury, ministerial mastery, central command, the panoply of office and the splendor of state. But Jefferson called the American government, for all its feebleness by these standards, "the strongest government on earth" because it was the only one founded on the energies, the affections, the opinions, and the suffrages of the people. This was the authentic "revolution of 1800." Because of it the Constitution became an instrument of democracy, change became possible without violence or destruction, and government could go forward with the continuing consent of the governed.

It was doubtless fortunate that the Federalists came first to power and with their talent for organization placed the government on firm foundations, permitting the Republicans, in turn, to go about their business of expanding freedom and equality without undermining the foundations. It was also fortunate that, having achieved what even the

Federalists recognized as a revolution, the Republican leadership was generally moderate and conciliatory in power. The reins of power were severed or slackened, but order prevailed. The dangers of foreign influence receded. Rather than remove all Federalists from office, Jefferson converted them to Republicanism with such success that the Federalists soon ceased to be a viable second party. Before a steady stream of defamation and libel emanating from the Federalist press, Jefferson sometimes wavered in his commitment to freedom of opinion, wondering whether some corrective was not in order to save the press from its abominable excesses. But he checked himself and adhered to what he came to call his "experiment" in unmolested political freedom. As he wrote in 1804:

> No experiment can be more interesting than that we are now trying, and which we trust will end in establishing the fact, that man may be governed by reason and truth. Our first object should therefore be, to leave open to him all the avenues of truth. The most effectual hitherto found, is the freedom of the press. It is, therefore, the first shut up by those who fear investigation of their actions.

Jefferson spoke of the demonstrated ability of the people, as in the election of 1800, to sift truth from the mass of error, and of the folly of attempting to dazzle them with pomp and majesty or deceive them with lies. "I hold it, therefore, certain," he declared, "that to open the doors of truth and to fortify the habit of testing everything by reason are the most effectual manacles we can rivet on the hand of our successors to prevent their manacling the people with their own consent."

The experiment, with all that it meant for the future of freedom and self-government in America, proved itself. The manacles were riveted on Jefferson's successors. The first of them, Madison, amid all the provocations produced by the War of 1812, never considered resort to a sedition act or any similar measure. The course of democracy in America had only begun in 1801, but the values, the principles, the basic practices necessary to it were secured, anchored firmly in the nation's revolutionary heritage of freedom.

Freedom, Politics, and the Constitution

The Moral Foundations of American Constitutionalism

Norman A. Graebner

However admirable its constitutional and political structure, the United States could not escape the moral dilemmas which confront all human societies. The true purposes of government do not reflect its forms but rather the needs of its citizens, both as individuals and as a corporate body comprising the state. The test of any government lies in the quality of its performance in judging and defending its interests abroad, in advancing the order, security, prosperity, and welfare of its citizens at home. Normally such challenges demand hard decisions, requiring taxes, regulations, and impositions on some to the advantage of others. Thus democracy and despotism were distinguishable less by their exercise of power than by the processes through which they intended to fulfill their responsibilities. Democracy appeared uniquely promising for human progress because in theory—and it was hoped in practice—it rested on the combined intelligence and virtue of its citizens. Policies democratically formed would of necessity satisfy the broad interests of the majority even while they protected the constitutional rights of the minority.

Still in any society the relationship between governmental action and both public and private welfare is elusive, for the best interests of any people are not necessarily embodied in the clear will of the majority. Alexander Hamilton and James Madison, the two principal authors of *The Federalist*, recognized explicitly the factionalism which would dom-

inate even their comparatively simple society. "In every free and delib-
erating society," agreed Thomas Jefferson, "there must, from the nature
of man, be opposite parties, and violent dissentions and discords. . . ."
Citizens would hold diverse opinions in matters of religion, government,
political leadership, and public policy. But for Madison the most dur-
able source of faction would be the unequal distribution of talent, ambition, and property. He observed in *The Federalist No. 10:* "A landed
interest, a manufacturing interest, a mercantile interest, a moneyed interest, with many lesser interests, grow up of necessity in civilized nations, and divide them into different classes, actuated by different
sentiments and views." The expanding opportunities for profitable employment would merely aggravate the conflicts which already existed.
For the authors of *The Federalist* the regulation of internal conflicts and
the equitable distribution of the benefits of public policy were the overriding burdens of government.

Those who defended the Constitution believed that a government of
power would best secure the varied internal and external interests of the
nation. Yet how it would achieve this noble purpose was not clear.
American society in actuality contained a multitude of major and minor
interests of vastly unequal power, wealth, and influence. Which among
them was to control the immediate and potential power that the Constitution created, and to what end? Some obviously would be the special
beneficiaries of that power, for the policies of government could not reflect the interests of all, at least not in equal measure. What mattered
especially was the extent to which American society could protect the
masses from the ambitions and actions of those who possessed the special
advantages. In a society where economic and political power was distributed unevenly liberty could not be absolute, for its assertion would
result in massive infringements on the freedom and welfare of others.

This posed the central issue of American freedom: how was society
to limit the ambitions and injustices of the powerful? For the problem
of competition in which some wielded power to the disadvantage of
others, there were two possible solutions: a state that curbed the ambitions of some to further the freedom and security of all, or a public
and private virtue of sufficient force to create society's necessary restraints without a massive infringement of public regulation. Edmund
Burke, the eighteenth-century British philosopher and statesman, recognized the issue when he wrote: "Men are qualified for civil liberty in

exact proportion to their disposition to put moral chains upon their own appetites. Society cannot exist unless a controlling power upon will and appetite be placed somewhere, and the less of it there is within, the more there is without. It is ordained in the eternal constitution of things that men of intemperate minds cannot be free. Their passions forge their fetters."

Faced with this inescapable dichotomy, the Founding Fathers, and Jefferson above all, sought to guarantee a maximum of freedom *and* justice in a divided and highly competitive society by formulating a body of principles which would establish a proper relationship between governors and governed as well as among individuals of disparate power and ambition. Jefferson delineated the fundamental rights of all citizens in his initial draft of the Declaration of Independence: "We hold these truths to be sacred and undeniable; that all men are created equal and independent, that from that equal creation they derive rights inherent and unalienable, among which are the preservation of life, liberty, and the pursuit of happiness." Men had a right to existence and to that liberty which would permit them to master their own lives. But central to Jefferson's concept of man and society was the pursuit of happiness; this included such human objects as tranquility, modesty, temperance, order, security, social intercourse, communication, and sustenance. Equality—another essential human right—would not be reflective of origin or economic and social status, but of those opportunities which would enable every man to realize his human nature as fully as possible. For Jefferson the answer to the challenge of inequality lay essentially in treating all members of society as human beings. Equal treatment under the law was the basic principle of justice. For Madison, writing in *The Federalist No. 51,* justice was the end of government and all civil society, protecting the rights, personality, and human dignity of every citizen.

In their defense of these basic moral principles of freedom, equality, and justice the Founding Fathers invoked natural rights, founded on the immutable maxims of reason. Madison referred to these maxims as the "transcendent law of nature and of nature's God." In their appeals to natural law the Founders expressed an unshakable faith in a universal moral order which conferred upon all men a dignity and worth that could not rightly be violated by those who wielded power. Such convictions came easily to men of the Enlightenment, for all had drunk deeply at the fountains of Western civility. Their minds were steeped in the classics of Western political theory from Plato to John Locke. They knew of Solon's evocation of the "unseen measure" of right judgment; of Aristotle's distinction between the right by nature and the right by convention; of Cicero's true and unvarying higher law, knowable by right reason; of Richard Hooker's law of reason which guided those who would consult it and which rightfully ordered even the might of kings; and of Locke's law of nature, or higher moral law, which restrained men even in the state of nature where government and the legal threat of punishment were absent. Freedom for Locke was always accompanied by law; it was not, he wrote in his *Second Treatise,* a "liberty for everyone to do as he lists, to live as he pleases, and not to be tyed by any laws." It was no accident that Jefferson's Resolutions for the Board of Visitors of the University of Virginia concerning the required reading for students of law placed Locke's *Second Treatise* at the head of the list.

Concomitantly with their evocation of the rights of citizens against government, the Founding Fathers stressed the duties of those same persons to make the most of themselves, to live in accordance with the noblest and best that was in them. For Jefferson the foundations of personal morality and civic responsibility lay in nature itself. Jefferson doubted that individual interests, if soundly calculated, could ever become a barrier to social behavior. Nor could a citizen's rights conflict with his obligations to others. As Jefferson wrote in 1787: "He who made us would have been a pitiful bungler, if he had made the rules of our moral conduct a matter of [theory]. . . . Man was destined for society. His morality, therefore, was to be formed to this object. He was endowed with a sense of right and wrong. . . . This sense is as much a part of his nature, as the sense of hearing, seeing, feeling; it is the true foundation of morality. . . ." For Jefferson the evidence of moral law within every individual lay in the conscience which the creator had placed in all. Individual morality, he assured Madison in 1789, would lead to social morality: "If the morality of one man produces a just line of conduct in him, acting individually, why should not the morality of one hundred men produce a just line of conduct in them, acting together?" Jefferson summarized his notions regarding the moral foundations of society in a letter to Du Pont de Nemours in 1816: "I believe

. . . that morality, compassion, and generosity, are innate elements of the human condition. . . ."

Men of the Enlightenment examined religion to determine its possible contribution to civic responsibility. Such eighteenth-century European writers as Jean Jacques Rousseau doubted that religiously inspired activity necessarily contributed to good citizenship. Nor was Rousseau convinced that moral convictions enhanced civic virtue, for the natural rights tradition fostered individualism as well as the ideal of civic harmony. There existed for him no simple, understandable body of moral principles, shared by all citizens, which might guide them in their relations with government and each other.

Jefferson held the moral precepts of Christianity in high regard, but he had little interest in Christian dogma. Pacifism, the proper attitudes of citizens toward the enemy in time of war, and other issues which might force a conflict between religious convictions and the purposes of the state were not his concern, for he asserted, "[O]ur civil rights have no dependence on our religious opinions, more than [on] our opinions in physics or geometry." Civil liberties and the advantages that flowed from them were, for Jefferson, natural rights. But he doubted that religious doctrines determined human behavior. What motivated human action was not the mind but the senses. In formulating national policy Jefferson no less than Madison preferred to rely on observation and experience, not on theoretical arguments, whether in religion, philosophy, or science. For that reason Jefferson did not defend freedom of religion in terms of specific beliefs. "The legitimate powers of government," he wrote, "extend to such acts only as are injurious to others. But it does me no injury for my neighbor to say there are twenty gods, or no God. It neither picks my pocket nor breaks my leg." Religious doctrines, in short, were not relevant to human affairs, and it was largely because Jefferson regarded dogma unimportant in the political life of the nation that he defended religious freedom as an unchallengeable right.

Whether based in religion or not, morality was for Jefferson a powerful force in human affairs. It gave him an implicit faith in the capacity of individuals to direct society harmoniously toward the greatest happiness of all. For Jefferson democracy was a form of government based on self-rule; it could flourish only if the democratic citizen followed his moral instinct or inner check implanted in him by nature. That Jefferson saw no conflict in varying definitions of happiness or in different readings of the moral law he made clear in his noted letter to Thomas Law in 1814: "[N]ature has constituted utility to man, the standard and test of virtue. Men living in different countries, under different circumstances, different habits and regimens, may have different utilities; the same act, therefore, may be useful, and consequently virtuous in one country which is injurious and vicious in another differently circumstanced. I sincerely, then, believe with you in the general existence of a moral instinct. I think it the brightest gem with which the human character is studded, and the want of it as more degrading than the most hideous of the bodily deformities."

Here Jefferson argued that the general moral instinct conformed to the prevailing views of happiness in every society. But this rendered moral law considerably less than universal. Perhaps even within one society the standards of what comprised a moral order were subject to disagreement. It was not certain in Jefferson's day that the pursuit of happiness assured the common good of society. Even then individual and group interests were more powerful determinants of public and private action than was the moral sense which Jefferson attributed to all men. As society became more complex the moral certainties on questions of public policy became increasingly elusive.

Amid the moral uncertainties which existed in the early Republic, the Founders agreed that freedom and justice necessitated a variety of public and private restraints on individual behavior which flowed from the constitutional system itself. For them the powers granted to the federal government in combination with the limitations which the Constitution imposed provided the means for maximizing both the freedom and the security of the nation's citizens from the assertions of public and private power. John Adams especially feared that villainy and corruption were interwoven in all human affairs, and that both increased where the stakes were highest. For him a republic was no guarantee of good behavior in government or society. Democratic procedures would not necessarily prevent those in power from depriving others of property, opportunity, or liberty. For that reason, he argued, the only defense against the power of some was the countering power of others, exerted generally through constitutional procedures. For Madison the danger to society lay in the possibility that government itself would fall to the ambitious and self-seeking, causing it to become the chief reflection of human avarice. "If men were angels," he wrote, "no government would be necessary. If angels were to govern men, neither external nor internal controls on government would be necessary. In framing a government which is to be administered by men over men, the difficulty lies in this: you must first enable the government to control the governed; and in the next place oblige it to control itself."

Such a government required close public scrutiny, for only an attentive populace could enforce the general welfare. Madison discovered the defense of the public interest against the power of individuals or the state in a general will which, on major issues, might encompass much of society; moreover, he believed the wide separation of geographic and economic interests within the nation would render an injurious combination of power improbable. Madison warned the readers of *The National Gazette* in 1792 that any government would respond to an apathetic and voiceless public by consolidating the interests of those who controlled it. Only an alert citizenry, actively participating in local and state affairs, could counter such consolidation by expressing "the sense of the people" on important public questions. Madison believed that men and groups, even as they pursued interests of their own, would respond to more enduring concerns when an aroused opposition denied them success.

Jefferson like Madison placed his faith in the public and the presence of a civic virtue. He hoped to square individual ambition with the precepts of freedom and justice by sustaining a simple agrarian society in which freedom would not war on the generally equal status of its citizens. Virtue—the necessary limitation on individual behavior—would survive, he believed, as long as agriculture remained the nation's principal object. Manufacturing, he feared, would not only magnify the opportunities for profit and thereby increase the power and wealth of the few at the expense of the many, but also establish materialism as the dominant force in American culture. Men, Jefferson once complained, did not become more honest as they increased in riches. Industry would, moreover, bring to America the complexities and tensions of urban life. "When we get piled upon one another in large cities, as in Europe," he wrote to Madison, "we shall become corrupt as in Europe, and go to eating one another as they do there."

Ultimately both Adams and Jefferson found the assurance of virtuous government in the principle of republicanism and the conviction that the American people would accept and sustain the leadership of those uniquely prepared for the role. Both men recognized a natural aristocracy among men based on differences in education, ability, moral discipline, and practical genius. Jefferson argued that such an aristocracy, as long as it reflected superior human qualities rather than wealth, should govern the country. He wrote to Adams on October 28, 1813:

> For I agree with you that there is a natural aristocracy among men. The grounds for this are virtue and talents. . . . There is also an artificial aristocracy founded on wealth and birth, without either virtue or talents. . . . The natural aristocracy I consider as the most precious gift of nature for the instruction, the trusts, and the government of society, and indeed it would have been inconsistent in creation to have formed man for the social state, and not to have provided virtue and wisdom enough to manage the concerns of the society. May we not even say that that form of government is best which provides the most effectually for a pure selection of these natural aristoi into the offices of government? The artificial aristocracy is a mischievous ingredient in government, and provision should be made to prevent its ascendancy. . . .
>
> I think the best remedy is exactly that provided by all our constitutions, to leave to the citizens the free election and separation of the aristoi from the pseudo-aristoi, of the wheat from the chaff. In general they will elect the real good and wise. In some instances, wealth may corrupt, and birth blind them; but not in sufficient degree to endanger the society.

Later John Stuart Mill, in his noted defense of liberalism, argued even more forcefully that the quality of democratic government depended on the capacity of the people to recognize and follow its natural leadership:

> No government by a democracy or a numerous aristocracy, neither in its political acts or in the opinion, qualities, and tone of mind which it fosters, ever did or could rise above mediocrity except in so far as the sovereign may have let themselves be guided (which in their best times they always

have done) by the counsels and influence of a more gifted and instructed *one* or few. . . . The honor and glory of the average man is that he is capable of following that initiative; that he can respond internally to wise and noble things, and be led to them with his eyes open.

Constitutionalism, then, would combine the superior virtue of the country's leadership with the promise of an increasingly virtuous society and a body of public policy characterized by wisdom and fairness. American constitutionalism, in its defense of freedom, did not seek the overthrow of all restraints but built the idea of restraint into the fabric of government itself. It anchored its hopes for justice and civility in society to the existence of a moral order ordained by the laws of nature. In the constitutionalist understanding, freedom and morality—fundamentally a restraint on freedom—were complementary, not antithetical. Moral restraint, as Burke suggested, enhanced the freedom and security of all. The moral order served as a standard for both governors and governed; the man who formed his life in accordance with reason, the noblest of his possessions, joined the ranks of the natural aristocracy and thus helped to enrich and elevate the entire society.

Unfortunately, to cite such possibilities for republicanism is not to describe the society which evolved. If Jefferson's vision of a moral order had any chance of implementation, it had long since vanished. The notion that a free society required a moral foundation to constrain the operation of individualism in the interests of society and the general welfare demonstrated its validity in the excesses of American industrialism. Still the nation never lost its conscience and often set limits to ignoble behavior in all of its forms. Gross profiteering and the limitless exertion of special advantages, such as that displayed by the industrial and business leaders at the turn of the century or later by the Nixon White House, did eventually produce some form of public retribution. American constitutionalism had provided a government with the power to define and enforce good behavior, at least to the extent that those in power believed some form of restraint required by public sentiment or minimum standards of fairness. Through time the federal government accepted the obligation to protect the public and business alike from the undesirable externalities of a complicated industrial and economic system. That protective effort created a growing federal superstructure of regulatory agencies. Thus the bureaucracy did not grow by accident. At every step along the way the United States government responded to the demands (and influence) of organized groups who could not protect their interests in the free market. The growth of federal power is one measure of the relative absence of virtue and common concern in American life.

This effort to assign to government the burden of maintaining order and fairness in the nation's individual and business relationships has been expensive. It has achieved no more than limited success. Madison warned that the ultimate problem of government is its inability to control itself. Furthermore, the process of defending society through public action is one that has no end. However large the federal bureaucracy, however pervading its encroachment on American freedom and initiative, there remain countless elements in society who require additional protections from those with the power to infringe upon their rights and interests. Only a more virtuous society, as men of the Enlightenment made clear, can regulate itself without the massive infusion of public power and the dangers to freedom and democracy that such power entails.

No one in recent years saw the moral dilemma of contemporary American society more clearly than did historian Carl Becker in his essay, *Freedom and Responsibility in the American Way of Life,* published posthumously in 1945. "We need," he said, "more integrity—less dishonesty and less of the feeling that, in private and in public life, our conscience is clear if we keep, with whatever slick maneuvering, within the letter of the law. But what we need most of all is a heightened sense of individual and collective responsibility—less insistence on negative rights and the unrestrained pursuit of individual self-interest, and a more united and resolute determination to concern ourselves with the public good and to make the sacrifices that are necessary for it. This is only to say that the preservation of our freedom depends less upon the precise nature of our constitutions and laws than it does upon the character of the people."

If character is the issue, where is Jefferson's natural aristocracy of leadership—for him the essential element in American constitutionalism —capable of inspiring commitment to a higher moral order? Perhaps in this year of the Bicentennial such leadership exists in greater profusion than ever before in the history of the country. But it is still limited in numbers and in the strength of its appeal; thus it continues to face the resistance of an apathetic public which seems willing to tolerate the partiality in federal legislation and bureaucratic behavior, if not actual corruption. Madison reminds us that an apathetic public will encourage government to consolidate the interests of those who control it. The result of that consolidation has been almost daily revelations of misbehavior in the huge Executive branch of government. So negligible has been the evidence of genuine public concern in government, so low the public estimation of both Congress and the Executive, that morality in government emerged as the central issue in the nation's Bicentennial election.

Many members of Congress are as capable and as troubled by matters of fairness in public policy as any that have graced its chambers. Still too often congressional majorities fail to distinguish between the public and the private interests. As a body the Congress could do more to elevate the level of civic virtue in the nation. Beyond that some of its members are perennially subject to charges of immorality and criminality. They have permitted conflicts of interest to lead them into questionable practices. Some members in 1976 stand accused of bribery. Some take junkets which contribute nothing to the nation's welfare but which do provide excellent free vacations. Some fill their staffs with relatives and friends at salaries which far exceed the needs of Congress or the competence of those who receive them. This has occurred in a reform-minded Congress which has sought to improve its public image. James Reston of *The New York Times* offered another measure of intellectual and moral failure when he declared recently that none of the tragedies in national life from Vietnam to Watergate produced one memorable speech by a national leader which defined the essential issues.

No government, whatever the perfection of its design, can transcend in performance the character of those who control it. The guarantees of freedom and justice based on natural law and embodied with care in the American constitutional system have served those Americans well who otherwise have been able to sustain those aspects of life loosely contained in the Jeffersonian notion of human happiness. But the major challenges of American society have confronted the Constitution far less than the human qualities of those who govern. If the government has failed to achieve the high standards set for it long ago, much less eliminate even the most glaring aspects of the country's human and environmental degradation, the problem has centered in the dual failure of the natural aristocracy to elevate the tastes and standards of the public and to rule itself in accordance with the essential principles of fairness and impartiality. Those who have governed the nation have scarcely comprised an aristocracy of virtue. Some would insist that as a governing elite they are finished.

Still the problems which face a democratic society are unique, for a people incapable of understanding their nation's deepest interests cannot compel those whom they elect to fulfill the responsibilities which befall them as leaders. Nothing less than an informed and engaged public, as Jefferson and Madison knew so well, would elevate an aristocracy of virtue and thereafter hold it to account. Yet there is not—nor was there in Jefferson's day—any sufficient common core of conviction, purpose, and moral judgment to establish that full sense of civic responsibility which the Founders believed necessary for the satisfactory performance of the American constitutional system. Notions of civic virtue respond to wide variations of interest, wealth, and status. Some leaders and members of the professions have become self-serving, using their advantages of scarcity to maximize their incomes and conveniences at the expense of the public and the ethical standards which should guide them. Even among Americans generally there has been a tendency for many, operating through business or labor organizations, to extract far more from society than their achievements or contributions merit. Equality and justice defy simple judgments in a society produced by generations of individual effort. The ambiguities in what comprises decency and humaneness in contemporary American society are profound. Yet those responsible for the highly consequential decisions of business and government can remove some of the barriers to a higher level of response in facing the country's inescapable challenges by contemplating more thoughtfully than in the past the meaning of freedom and fairness in an intricately complex society.

Lincoln and the
Paradoxes of Freedom

Don E. Fehrenbacher

On April 18, 1864, Abraham Lincoln boarded a train for Baltimore to
participate in the opening of the Maryland Sanitary Commission Fair,
a fund-raising project for the Civil War equivalent of the Red Cross.
This was the city through which Lincoln as president-elect had passed
surreptitiously late at night in order to thwart a reported assassination
plot—the city in which arbitrary arrest and imprisonment of Confederate sympathizers had been exceedingly common, and in which
Chief Justice Roger B. Taney had issued a stern rebuke to the Lincoln
administration for its suspension of the writ of habeas corpus. It is
therefore not surprising that in Baltimore the President's thoughts should
have turned to the nature of liberty. In his short speech during the
opening ceremonies he said:

> The world has never had a good definition of the word liberty,
> and the American people, just now, are much in want of one.
> We all declare for liberty; but in using the same *word* we do
> not all mean *the same thing*. . . . The shepherd drives the
> wolf from the sheep's throat, for which the sheep thanks the
> shepherd as a *liberator,* while the wolf denounces him for the
> same act as the destroyer of liberty.

The shepherd in this little parable was obviously Lincoln himself.
The sheep was black and one of a great many that the shepherd had

rescued. The wolf, not yet on anyone's list of endangered species, represented the slaveholding South. There is no mistaking the hero, the victim, and the villain here, for Lincoln was making no pretense of impartiality. He did acknowledge, however, that the parable embodied a disturbing paradox: any act of liberation may also be, for someone, an act of oppression. The emancipation of four million slaves was a confiscation of property on an enormous scale, to the amount of several billions of dollars. And the famous proclamation with which it began was viewed by the people of the Confederacy as a monstrous, bloodthirsty effort to incite servile insurrection.

For Southerners, therefore, emancipation was but the "crowning act of tyranny." They had been calling Lincoln a despot ever since the onset of hostilities. He was their George III, implacably denying them the very right of self-government for which Americans of 1776 had risked their lives, fortunes, and sacred honor. A powerful sense of being engaged in reenacting the heroic roles of the Founding Fathers lent the Confederacy much of its élan during the early months of the conflict. Yet Lincoln, from the beginning of the war, had insisted that it was the defenders of the Union who were fighting for the principle of self-government. Long before his thoughts turned seriously to emancipation, he characterized the struggle as one for human freedom generally. It was, he believed, the last great test in the American experiment of popular government and thus a kind of sequel to the Revolution. To members of Congress assembling on the Fourth of July he declared: "Surely each man has as strong a motive *now*, to *preserve* our liberties, as each had *then* to *establish* them."

It is scarcely surprising, to be sure, that Northerners and Southerners should have disagreed about which side was fighting for freedom. The real paradox in Lincoln's case is that so many Northerners likewise called him despot and that so many historians have at least partly confirmed their judgment. Late in 1862, the distinguished Benjamin R. Curtis of Massachusetts, one of the dissenting justices in the Dred Scott case, published a pamphlet virtually accusing Lincoln of assuming dictatorial power. Shortly thereafter, the Democratic governor of New York publicly attributed to the Lincoln administration the "new and strange doctrine . . . that the loyal North lost their constitutional rights when the South rebelled, and all are now governed by a military dictation." The London *Times,* in denouncing what it called the "gigantic wickedness" of the Emancipation Proclamation, referred to the "absolute despotism of the present Government in Washington." And on the eve of the Battle of Gettysburg, a group of New York Democrats, while pledging their continued support of the war effort, at the same time accused the President of "pretensions to more than regal authority," and of claiming to have found "within the Constitution, a principle or germ of arbitrary power, which in time of war expands at once into an absolute sovereignty, wielded by one man; so that liberty perishes, or is dependent on his will, his discretion or his caprice."

A generation later, Lord Bryce, in his classic study, *The American Commonwealth*, compared Lincoln's powers to those of a Roman dictator and said that he wielded more authority than any Englishman since Cromwell. The historian James Ford Rhodes, a great admirer of Lincoln, acknowledged that in the months following the fall of Fort Sumter, the acts of the President were those "of a Tudor rather than those of a constitutional ruler." "The country attorney of Illinois," Rhodes added, "had assumed the power of a dictator." Samuel Eliot Morison agreed, saying that "Lincoln came near to being the ideal tyrant of whom Plato dreamed." Other scholars wrote in similar vein of the presidential decrees, arbitrary arrests, military trials, and various other bold employments of executive power which contributed so much to the emergence of that astonishing modern phenomenon that Arthur M. Schlesinger has called "the imperial presidency."

In the history of freedom, then, Abraham Lincoln is a somewhat ambiguous figure. He liberated slaves but suppressed the movement for Southern independence. He epitomized democracy but assumed a considerable measure of autocratic power. He preserved the structure of American popular government but in the process impaired some of the substance of American liberty.

The ambiguity, beyond any doubt, inheres partly in the character of Abraham Lincoln himself. He was a complex man and, in some respects, a remote one, seldom indulging in self-revelation. There were profound depths in him and strange contrasts of light and shadow that have made him elusive and puzzling for his biographers, as he was for even his closest friends. It appears that he had no strong appetite for power; yet he was at times almost arrogant in his readiness to grasp and exercise power. His tender-heartedness—no mere legend—is visible in numerous acts of kindness and clemency, but not in the grim determination with which he supported Grant's bloody progress toward Richmond. The transcendent humaneness of the man lent the Civil War much of its luster, but it was his inveterate toughness that helped determine the outcome. The terrible human cost of the conflict nevertheless wore him down and perhaps made him less sympathetic to the complaints of dissidents who suffered only some temporary abridgment of their liberties. Commenting on the most notorious political arrest of the war, he asked: "Must I shoot a simple-minded soldier boy who deserts, while I must not touch a hair of a wily agitator who induces him to desert?"

If, however, the ambiguity of Lincoln's record in the history of freedom reflects certain characteristics of the man, it also reflects the anomalous character of civil war. The paramount purpose in any war is to defeat the enemy, but the first major task in a civil war is to distinguish enemies from friends. A nation breaking apart seldom does so cleanly; the fracture is usually jagged, ugly, and, in places, indistinct. The outcome of the struggle may depend upon which side can persuade or coerce uncommitted intermediate elements to its support. Thus in every civil war a certain amount of repression may be one of the unavoidable costs of victory.

The state of the nation on March 4, 1861, is difficult to recapture subjectively because it was an alien experience, unique in American history. Within a period of three months, seven states had held special elections, assembled conventions, seceded from the Union, established a new federal republic, drafted its constitution, and elected its first president and vice president. The movement proceeded with such efficiency and speed because Southerners had often rehearsed it in their minds, with the example of the Founding Fathers serving virtually as a script. In the North, meanwhile, there was confusion, discord, and irresolution. Disunion had been predicted often enough, but no one was rehearsed in procedures for dealing with the emergency when it came. The retiring President, a strict constitutionalist, turned the problem over to Congress, which tried to meet a new kind of crisis by imitating the compromisers of 1850.

Some Southerners in Congress and in the Buchanan cabinet acted virtually as Confederate intelligence agents while continuing to draw their federal salaries. A Texas senator remained in his seat long after Texas had seceded, carrying on a program of military recruitment for the Confederacy from an office in Baltimore. The Southerner commanding the Department of Texas first surrendered to state officials all military posts and federal property within his control, *then* resigned from the Army of the United States and accepted a Confederate commission. The Chief Justice of the United States, who detested the incoming Republican Party and gave all of his sympathy to the Southern cause, nevertheless clung to the office until his death in 1864—the highest placed copperhead in the wartime Union government.

Many Northern Democrats insisted that the federal government had no constitutional authority to use force against the seceding states; some abolitionists and Republicans favored peaceable separation as a policy of good riddance to slavery; and it was obvious that any military movement against the Confederacy would set off another round of secession activity in the still uncommitted upper South. In any case, all the talk about "coercion" was for the time being academic, given the smallness of the regular army and the divided loyalties of its officer corps.

Northern confusion and disunity did not end on March 4. The policy of drifting inaction continued, as Lincoln and his cabinet devoted much of their attention to filling offices and to the other managerial tasks facing a new administration. Then time ran out for the garrison at Fort Sumter, and after it surrendered under fire, Lincoln, in a series of decisive actions, gave authoritative definition to a crisis that had not yet been defined. By these actions—which included declaring that an insurrection was in progress, calling for volunteers, increasing the size of the regular Army and Navy, proclaiming a blockade of Southern ports, and suspending the writ of habeas corpus in certain areas—he also defined the role that he expected to play in meeting the crisis.

Ordinarily, the Thirty-Seventh Congress would not have assembled until December 1861. Immediately after the fall of Fort Sumter in April, however, Lincoln summoned it to meet in special session on July 4. This was five months early, but still some two months later than what might seem to have been appropriate in the circumstances. Without any disposition to establish a dictatorship, he nevertheless wanted a breathing spell and a free hand before legislative activity began—an interval in which to assert presidential leadership and set the course of national policy. The initiative seized with this strategy was never lost.

In subsequent years, for example, Lincoln on his own authority introduced conscription, proclaimed emancipation, and inaugurated a program of reconstruction.

The Lincoln administration also dealt vigorously and sometimes melodramatically with the problem of disloyalty inside Northern lines. In the process, it infringed upon the authority of Congress, the federal judiciary, and various state governments. Antiwar behavior verging on treason was nothing new in American history, but it posed an especially dangerous threat in 1861, when allegiances were still being sorted out. The secession of Virginia and three more states of the upper South in April and May put intense pressures on Maryland, Kentucky, and Missouri. The struggle for this "great border" was fought in a variety of ways, including movement of troops, political intrigue, mob action, guerrilla raids, and military arrests. Maryland was a particularly critical area at first because a violent upsurge of pro-Confederate sentiment in Baltimore blocked off the most direct access to Washington, which for a time seemed extremely vulnerable to capture.

In the circumstances, it probably was unrealistic to insist, as Chief Justice Taney did in *Ex parte Merryman,* that the administration should rely upon the normal processes of government to deal with rioting, sabotage, and other echoes of rebellion north of the national capital. Units of Maryland militia and Baltimore police participated in the burning of bridges, destruction of railroad track, and cutting of telegraph wires. The police marshal of Baltimore, a secessionist sympathizer, himself directed some of these activities. Even if offenders had been arrested by civil authorities, it was unlikely that any Maryland jury would have convicted them. Lincoln, accordingly, took a step unprecedented in American history. He authorized military commanders to suspend the privilege of the writ of habeas corpus if such action should appear necessary for protection of troop movements or for suppression of legislative efforts to align Maryland on the side of the rebellion. Later he extended these orders geographically, and in 1862 he made them nationwide for specified offenses tending to impede prosecution of the war.

Such suspension made it possible to throw thousands of persons into prison and keep them there for months at a time. Lincoln and his generals also imposed martial law in certain critical areas, caused civilians to be tried before military commissions, and temporarily suppressed a number of newspapers. But the principal weapon against disloyalty continued to be arbitrary arrest (often for reasons that would not have stood up in court), followed eventually in most cases by release without trial.

It is true, as Lincoln himself asserted, that the purpose of these summary detentions was not punitive but preventative, and that the effect was in some respects more humane than trial and conviction would have been. It is also true that the worst excesses were committed by subordinates without presidential approval, and that Lincoln never contemplated a systematic effort to suppress dissent. In fact, he suffered more abuse than any other president, despite having more power to stifle abuse than any other president.

Nevertheless, the security system established by his authority, with its secret police, paid informers, *agents provocateurs,* midnight arrests, and dank prisons had an ominous, alien ring for most Democrats, and even for some Republicans. It was Illinois Republican Senator Lyman Trumbull who denounced the system as a usurpation of power which might set "precedents for the destruction of Constitutional liberty." A Democratic pamphlet published in 1863 pictured Lincoln standing trial before great Americans of the past, with Washington presenting the list of charges. After extensive argument, the Spirit of the Constitution passes judgment: "You were born in the freest country under the sun, but you have converted it to a despotism. . . . I now leave you with the brand 'tyrant' on your brow." That the brand was partisan and undeserved need scarcely be said; the striking thing is that Lincoln of all men should have been the target of such an accusation.

The President vigorously defended his course of action. He had a sworn obligation to protect the Constitution of the United States, and that in turn meant preserving, *by all necessary means,* the government and nation for which the document had been written as organic law. The Constitution, he argued, plainly authorized the use of extraordinary justice in specified circumstances, but even if this were not the case, must "all the laws *but one* . . . go unexecuted, and the government itself go to pieces, lest that one be violated"? His answer to the question was eventually cast in Lincolnian metaphor: "By general law," he wrote, "life *and* limb must be protected; yet often a limb must be amputated to save a life; but a life is never wisely given to save a limb."

Lincoln's conviction was not shaken by the acknowledged fact that an indeterminate number of innocent persons had suffered arrest and imprisonment at his hands. He seems to have regarded such mistakes as more or less equivalent to battle casualties—both being part of the total human cost of the war. Lincoln, indeed, was rejecting one of the oldest and most honored maxims of jurisprudence: *fiat justitia ruat coelum*— "let justice be done though the heavens fall." He believed that as chief magistrate his first duty was to keep the heavens from falling, if possible.

All of this might seem to place Lincoln on the side of authority against liberty, but he certainly thought otherwise. For him, it was a matter of temporarily diminishing the rights of some individuals so that an entire structure of freedom might be preserved. Thus, while critics persisted in calling him despot, he persisted in describing the Civil War as a struggle for human liberty, affecting not only his own generation but the "vast future." The contradictions, already suggested, reflect the character of the man and the nature of civil war as a social phenomenon, but one must add that they also derive from the exceedingly complex nature of freedom itself.

The proliferated meanings of this familiar word have been studied most exhaustively by Mortimer J. Adler in a work of some fourteen hundred pages titled *The Idea of Freedom*. It is a word that readily inspires paradox, such as the complaint of George Bernard Shaw: "Our liberties destroy all freedom." Such as the facetious apostrophe: "O Freedom, what liberties are taken in thy name!" Such as the gloomy cynicism: "Men rattle their chains to show that they are free." And such as the definition offered by Walter Lippmann: "A way of life which requires authority, discipline, and government of its own kind." Adler points out that according to one school of thought, freedom means *exemption* from legal restraint, while to another school it consists in *obedience* to law. The appearance of disagreement is deceptive, however, for the two groups are talking about two fundamentally different categories of freedom. Thus debate on the subject can easily become the mere repetition of variant definitions.

Perhaps the primary distinction to be made is between freedom as the condition of an individual and freedom as the ruling principle of a society. And no doubt the most elemental definition of individual freedom is exemption from physical coercion and forcible restraint. The prisoner sitting in his cell has a fairly clear and simple conception of freedom, but it is one that will prove inadequate as soon as he is released. For people who possess a considerable measure of freedom, the word is likely to have a more complex and extensive meaning, with the emphasis tending to shift from avoidance of restraint to enjoyment of opportunity, from a state of personal independence to a process of self-realization. John Dewey, for instance, defined liberty as power—"the effective power to do specific things." Lincoln stressed this positive version of individual freedom when he talked to soldiers about the purpose of the war. The struggle must continue, he told one group, "in order that each of you may have through this free government which we have enjoyed, an open field and a fair chance for your industry, enterprise and intelligence."

The central paradox of freedom is the extent to which it originates in social control. Samuel Johnson once said to Boswell, "Every man has a right to utter what he thinks truth, and every other man has a right to knock him down for it." Now this scarcely summarizes true freedom of speech, which means not only that government will refrain from interfering with a speaker, but that it will intervene, if necessary, to prevent others from interfering. Even when conceived of strictly as the absence of restraint and coercion, liberty, in the words of Edmund Burke, "must be limited in order to be possessed." And liberty conceived of as opportunity for self-realization is even more completely a function of organized social effort. In short, except for the limited negative freedom that a few persons can still acquire through isolation, individual liberties in the modern Western world are essentially the output of free society, and the prime input of such a society is power, properly conferred, organized, and applied.

There are two principal measures of a free society. One is the extent to which it optimizes individual liberty of all kinds. The other is the extent to which its decision-making processes are controlled ultimately by the people; for freedom held at the will of others is too precarious to provide a full sense of being free. Self-government, in Lincoln's view, is the foundation of freedom. The Civil War, he insisted again and again, was being fought to save the world's best example of a free society and to vindicate the very principle of self-government. It was a fiery test of "whether any government, not too strong for the liberties of its people, can be strong enough to maintain its existence in great emergencies."

One can therefore readily perceive that Lincoln and his libertarian critics were looking at freedom from opposite directions and in some degree talking past each other. The critics gave priority to individual liberty in its classic form of immunity from arbitrary restraint and coercion. Lincoln gave priority to maintaining the institutional structure of a free society within which individual liberty had flourished. The two commitments were far from being essentially incompatible, but the pressures of national crisis brought them frequently into conflict.

For example, the former congressman Clement Vallandigham was arrested in 1863 and swiftly convicted by a military commission for making an antiwar speech. Lincoln regretted the action but was reluctant to overrule the general in command. Ohio Democrats soon made things more embarrassing by nominating Vallandigham for governor. But Lincoln, using a light touch and unorthodox tactics, succeeded not only in overcoming the difficulty but in trivializing it. He changed the sentence from imprisonment for the duration of the war to banishment behind Confederate lines. A large delegation of Ohio Democratic leaders called on Lincoln at the White House to demand that Vallandigham be restored to his home and freedom. In the course of their written presentation they asked:

> If a man . . . believes that from the inherent nature of the federal compact, the war . . . cannot be used as a means of restoring the Union . . . but would inevitably result in the final destruction of both the constitution and the Union, is he not to be allowed the right . . . to appeal to the judgment of the people, for a change of policy, by the constitutional remedy of the ballot box?

Lincoln's answer, written on June 29, with Lee's invading army well north of Washington in the vicinity of Gettysburg, was, in effect, *no*, not when that man's speeches had the effect and probably the intent of encouraging military desertion, resistance to conscription, and violent interference with prosecution of the war. In practice, Lincoln's views prevailed, but ideologically there was deadlock.

To the argument of some critics that constitutional liberties remained ever exactly the same in peace and in war, Lincoln replied that the Constitution itself plainly indicated otherwise by permitting the privilege of the writ of habeas corpus to be suspended "when in cases of rebellion or invasion the public safety may require it." To the argument of certain Albany Democrats that his policies were in any case setting a dangerous precedent, he responded with another of his analogies:

> Nor am I able to appreciate the danger, apprehended by the meeting, that the American people will, by means of military arrests during the rebellion, lose the right of public discussion, the liberty of speech and the press, the law of evidence, trial by jury, and habeas corpus, throughout the indefinite peaceful future . . . any more than I am able to believe that a man could contract so strong an appetite for emetics during temporary illness, as to persist in feeding upon them through the remainder of his healthful life.

Although Lincoln, in a general sense, proved to be right, the history of the United States in the twentieth century suggests that he brushed aside too lightly the problem of the example that he might be setting for future presidents. The concept of emergency executive power is firmly, if somewhat obscurely, fixed in the Lockean political tradition, and even such a confirmed libertarian as John Stuart Mill acknowledged that an "extreme exigency" might require that constitutional government give way to temporary dictatorship.

The limits of such emergency power (if it exists) must be determined by the nature of the emergency itself and are therefore undefinable in specific terms. But what kind of "exigency" is extreme enough to justify suspending constitutional forms? Here, the Founding Fathers offered some guidance by designating rebellion and invasion as the two circumstances in which the privilege of the writ of habeas corpus might be suspended. Not *war* of any kind, it should be noted; not economic depression, or famine, or plague, or flood, or presidential election. Just rebellion and invasion. Lincoln assumed enormous emergency powers and perhaps went beyond necessity, but at least he was acting within the limited definition of national emergency that had been provided by the framers of the Constitution. Furthermore, he made it plain that he regarded his extraordinary authority as temporary. In December 1864, with the conflict grinding to its close, he said to Congress. "The Executive power itself would be greatly diminished by the cessation of actual war."

The modern imperial presidency was built to a considerable extent upon the concept of emergency power which Lincoln was the first to use on a significant scale, and this in spite of the fact that there has been no real instance of rebellion or invasion since 1865. Franklin Roosevelt in 1941 declared an "unlimited national emergency" more than six months before the attack on Pearl Harbor b ought the United States into a war fought far from home. Under the authority of his Executive Order 9066, issued in February 1942, some 112,000 Japanese-Americans were removed from their homes and virtually imprisoned, although they, unlike most persons suffering arbitrary arrest during the Civil War, had done nothing to justify a charge of impeding the war effort. At the hands of various twentieth-century presidents, the meaning of "emergency" and "national security" expanded greatly, and the use of the terms to explain extraordinary executive action became so frequent as to be almost routine. Finally there came the Watergate affair as a sick parody of presidential power responding to grave crisis. It is possible to conclude that Lincoln's judgment was eminently sound in the unique context of the Civil War, and yet not entirely fortunate as an example to be cited by other men acting in different circumstances.

At the same time, there is good reason to remember Lincoln's warning that in moments of crisis an excessive perfectionism may be as dangerous as an excessive use of power. "No small matter," he said, "should divert us from our great purpose."

> There may be some irregularities in the practical application of our system. It is fair that each man shall pay taxes in exact proportion to the value of his property; but if we should wait before collecting a tax to adjust the taxes upon each man in exact proportion with every other man, we should never collect any tax at all. . . . In no administration can there be perfect equality of action and uniform satisfaction rendered by all. But this government must be preserved in spite of the acts of any man or set of men. It is worthy of your every effort.

How valid was Lincoln's contention that the Civil War, from its beginning, constituted a struggle for freedom having universal significance? Surely, one might argue, a smaller United States could have continued to function as a free society made even freer by disengagement from the states most heavily committed to slavery. Perhaps so, and yet such an alternative may never really have existed. For one thing, Fort Sumter was by no means the last barrier to peaceable separation. The corrosive problem of fugitive slaves would have remained; ownership of the Western territories would have been difficult to settle without violence; and the people of the upper Mississippi Valley were belligerently opposed to surrendering control of the mouth of that great river. Moreover, division of the United States into two independent nations would have meant the intrusion of European balance-of-power politics into North America, and further divisions in one or both republics might even have balkanized the continent. The old free security behind ocean ramparts would have come prematurely to an end, and with it the special environment in which freedom had flourished.

The heart of the matter for Lincoln, however, was the threat that secession posed to democratic government and its core principle, majority rule. He believed that few Southerners really wanted to secede, and that the primary purpose of secessionism had always been to extort concessions from the North and thus enhance Southern power *within* the Union. The critical issue, accordingly, was not whether a state possessed the constitutional right to secede, but how a constitutional majority should respond to the coercive action of a minority. Put in those terms, the problem sounds very familiar to the modern ear; for we live in an age of proliferating coercive minorities—some legal, such as transportation workers on strike; some mildly illegal, such as demonstrators staging a "sit-in"; and some criminal, such as terrorists threatening to kill a hostage unless their demands are met. In many of these situations there is overwhelming pressure on persons in authority to yield or compromise in order to save life, protect property, or maintain public order. But Lincoln in his crisis stood firm, well aware that an historic example was being set. "No compromise, by public servants, could, in this case, be a cure," he told Congress; "not that compromises are not often proper, but that no popular government can long survive a marked precedent, that those who carry an election can only save the government from immediate destruction by giving up the main point upon which the people gave the election." In other words, coercion of government by a minority is incompatible with the principle of majority rule and thus ultimately with the preservation of individual freedom.

We today tend to associate minority rights with liberty and majority rule with the bureaucratic establishment that stifles liberty. This is a reflection, perhaps, of the modern consumer mentality; for one ordinarily visualizes rights as in the process of being *exercised* by individuals and minority groups. The only right possessed by a majority, as such, is the right to rule. One can scarcely disagree with the statement of an English historian, Lord Acton, that "the most certain test by which we judge whether a country is really free is the amount of security enjoyed by minorities." What he failed to add, however, is that the provision of such security requires the exercise of sovereign power; and the quality, extent, and durability of such security will depend very much upon who holds that sovereign power and on what terms. Majority rule and minority rights, as Lincoln perceived, are interlocking parts of one structure of freedom.

In his famous utilitarian defense of liberty, John Stuart Mill argued that the ultimate justification for toleration of dissent lies not in the minority's right to speak but in the majority's need to be challenged. In a sense, Lincoln's words and acts during the crisis of civil war offer testimony to the validity of an obverse proposition: The ultimate reason for acquiescence in the decision of a majority lies not in the majority's right to rule but in the minority's need to be secure. For, as Lincoln wrote in the first draft of his First Inaugural, "A Constitutional majority is the only true sovereign of a free people."

Freedom and the American Constitutional System

Robert K. Murray

What is astonishing about the United States of America is that it is governed by the same document and operates under the same system with which it began almost two hundred years ago. The Constitution has seen the American people through five declared wars and several police actions. It has helped them withstand sectionalism and regionalism, class and economic divisions, racial discrimination and segregation, and the siren call of imperialism. It has survived a bloody civil war, numerous depressions, and the atomic bomb. Under it they have transformed themselves from thirteen insignificant colonies with a population of four million to the most powerful nation on earth, with a citizenry of over two hundred million. Germany during the same time progressed from a congerie of diverse entities to a monarchy, to a republic, to a dictatorship, and back to a republic, while France moved through a monarchy, five republics, and two empires.

The American Constitution was a product of the Age of Reason. It grew out of the belief that reason was a faculty of man and that reason underlay the proper conduct of human affairs. Similarly expressive of this belief was the Declaration of Independence which set in place many of the foundation stones upon which the Constitution later rested. Sometimes called "the most noble document ever conceived by the mind of man," the Declaration contained four basic assumptions: all men were created equal; they were endowed by their Creator with unalienable rights; governments were established for the purpose of protecting those rights; and the powers of such governments were derived solely from the consent of the governed.

It probably comes as a surprise to the average twentieth-century American how much the Founding Fathers based their political beliefs on the existence of "a higher law," on a God who was the author of a cosmic constitutionalism which man should strive to emulate. The right to life, liberty, and the pursuit of happiness was assumed to be part of this cosmic plan, and man was seen as a creature of God who was both good and bad, with the bad often in the ascendancy. Such beliefs were common during the era which produced the Declaration of Independence and the Constitution. Their expression, of course, received its initial impetus from American colonial difficulties with the British Crown and Parliament after 1763. But their roots were embedded in the Judeo-Christian tradition and were nourished by such diverse sources as the Magna Carta, John Locke's *Second Treatise on Government,* Sir Edward Coke's *Institutes,* and Montesquieu's *Spirit of the Laws.*

Despite their frequent clashes of opinion on structural details, the Founding Fathers displayed broad agreement on the fundamentals required in any government. They believed that government should preserve maximum liberty and equality for all persons under it, preventing some men from rising to tyranny and others from falling to slavery. Government should be kept as near as possible to the people through rotations in office and frequent elections. Rulers had to be made servants of the people, and the powers of government had to be separated and balanced. Government needed to be constitutional, reflecting the dictates of law and not of men.

The post-Declaration constitutions of the new American states put many of these assumptions to immediate use. But only a few of those assumptions influenced the creation of the first national government after 1776—the Articles of Confederation. The reason was simple. The Confederation government was conceived only as a creature of the states. The Declaration of Independence had not mentioned a *single* nation but "the *thirteen* United States of America." The Articles were therefore little more than a temporary means for cooperative state action to conclude the Revolutionary War and establish peace with Great Britain. Under them each state zealously retained its sovereignty. There was no executive, no judiciary. The Confederation's unicameral legislative body had no power to regulate commerce or to tax. Voting on all issues was by state, with each state casting one vote.

The weaknesses of the Articles and the increasing chauvinism of the states soon caused a number of leaders to argue for revision. Both Thomas Jefferson and James Madison complained that the Articles allowed the states to ignore their collective financial obligations, trespass on the rights of their neighbors, violate treaties made by the Confederation congress, and create a jungle of competing and conflicting laws. Their crusade for change ultimately resulted in the Constitutional convention.

Within a week of the opening of this convention in Philadelphia in May 1787, the delegates despaired of patching up the Articles and instead turned their attention to writing a new document. For the remainder of the hot summer they labored, finishing their task in late September when thirty-nine of the forty-two members present signed it. Altogether there were fifty-five delegates to the convention, but seldom were there more than thirty present and no more than eleven states were represented. The delegates from New Hampshire did not arrive until the very end, and Rhode Island sent no representatives at all. Jefferson was not there; he was an ocean away as minister to France. John Adams was similarly occupied in London. Virginia elected Patrick Henry as a delegate, but he refused to serve because he feared that the convention would undermine states' rights. Sam Adams and John Hancock were not named. Otherwise the gathering was a Revolutionary *Who's Who*. Washington was present. So was Madison, Hamilton, the two Morrises (Robert and Gouverneur), the two Pinckneys (C.C. and Charles), James Wilson, and Benjamin Franklin, who, because of an aggravated case of gout, was carried in on a sedan chair.

The convention was hardly an open democratic meeting. Troopers guarded the doors while it was in session; a strict secrecy oath was imposed. No press credentials were honored. All attendees were men of substance and advantage, of property and education. There were no blacks, no Jews, no Indians, no women, and no representatives of the laboring classes. More than sixty percent were lawyers. The major work of the convention was done by about twelve men, foremost being Madison, who was thereafter called "the Father of the Constitution." Arguing earnestly and sometimes violently, these men wrestled with such divisive matters as states' rights versus centralization, the privileges of the large states as opposed to the small, the powers of the various branches of government, and the continuation of slavery. All of them had reservations about the result. Even the thirty-nine who finally signed the document did so with misgivings. As someone later quipped, the United States Constitution was a child of chance, conceived illegitimately and brought into this world unwanted by many members of its own family.

During the ensuing ratification struggle, which raged from October 1787 to August 1788, the opposing forces debated the precise meaning of almost every word and phrase. A skeptical electorate called upon the framers, in particular, to defend their creation, and at the height of the battle eighty-five essays, carefully analyzing the proposed Constitution, appeared in the New York press. Signed with the nom de plume Publius, the papers became known collectively as *The Federalist* and were penned largely by Madison and Hamilton. Expanding on natural law and human freedom as they related to governmental structure, these essays sought to educate the public in all the thirteen states in the theory of balanced government, the diffusion and separation of political power, and the delineation and limitation of that power. When New Hampshire, Virginia, and New York (the ninth, tenth, and eleventh states) agreed to the document in late summer of 1788, it was evident that the framers had won the ratification struggle.

In creating this new structure the Founding Fathers built far better than they suspected. Although they had relied heavily on European thought and history for their theories, they had constructed something entirely new. Here was a complex and complicated political system sustained by a colossal balancing act—a government strong enough to achieve the common purposes demanded by the majority, yet weak enough to be defied by a minority when those purposes were thought to be seriously mistaken or arbitrary. It was a dynamic equilibrium maintained by a divided, limited, constitutionally restrained federalism. Convinced that the nature of power is to expand and seek its own enlargement, the authors of the Constitution wisely distributed that power among counterbalancing branches and levels of government. As Madison described it: "In the compound republic of America, the Power surrendered by the people is first divided between two distinct governments [state and federal], and then the portion allotted to each subdivided among distinct and separate departments [legislative, executive, and judicial]."

Jefferson immediately detected a flaw in the system. After reading the draft of the proposed Constitution, he questioned the omission of residual rights and, from Paris, suggested additions similar to those he had written earlier into Virginia's state constitution as a Declaration of Rights. Such rights, he contended, citizens were entitled to "against every government on earth." Madison, Hamilton, and Washington thought this inclusion superfluous since the Constitution dealt only with delegated powers. However, to secure Jefferson's support, the drafting fathers agreed to the submission of ten amendments covering these rights as soon as the original document was implemented. Congress proposed these amendments to the state legislatures in September 1789. The necessary ratification came two years later. In essence, the Bill of Rights was a protest against the original Constitution. By incorporating it, the Constitution not only passed its first test but also demonstrated that it possessed great flexibility.

The so-called Bill of Rights fell into two main categories. The first category embraced the First through the Fourth amendments and highlighted certain universal liberties. The First Amendment established freedom of religion, speech, press, petition, and assemblage. Clearly designed to protect the thought and expression of some men from being restrained by others, this basic amendment, according to Jefferson, would prevent half the citizenry from being fools, the other half, hypocrites. The Second, Third, and Fourth amendments permitted the people to keep and bear arms, forbade the quartering of soldiers with the populace in times of peace, and prohibited unreasonable searches and seizures.

The second category of rights comprised the Fifth through the Eighth amendments which, taken together, provided for the fair administration of justice in the belief that the first step of the tyrant is to use the criminal law to eliminate opposition. The Fifth Amendment stated that no person could be held for crime without a grand jury indictment, nor could he be compelled to be a witness against himself or "be deprived of life, liberty or property, without due process of law." The Sixth and Seventh amendments protected the accused in his right to a jury trial, to counsel, and to be confronted by witnesses against him. The Eighth Amendment prohibited excessive bail, fines, and sentences. The final two amendments, the Ninth and Tenth, restated unequivocally what many framers automatically assumed—that *all* rights and powers not mentioned in the Constitution were reserved either to the states or to the people.

These ten amendments underwrote American freedoms within the constitutional system. Added almost as an afterthought, they marked a major difference between the American arrangement and every other existing government. They limited not only the powers of the executive but even those of the legislature. The First Amendment, which was pure Jefferson, underlined the basic theme: *"Congress* shall make no law. . . ." The Bill of Rights, however, did far more than this. As Justice Joseph Story said, they offered an "important protection against unjust and oppressive conduct on the part of the people themselves." These amendments were designed not only to prevent executive and legislative tyranny, but *popular* tyranny as well. They were inserted to protect the American people from the worst of all enemies—themselves. They harkened back to the basic premise contained in the Declaration of Independence that certain rights belonged to *all* men and could be contravened by *none*. It is little wonder that these amendments were later called the "soul of the Constitution." Some claimed that the document was a corpse until the amendments breathed life into it.

The original document has been amended sixteen more times. Eight of these amendments involve procedural changes in the election process or in the taxing function, and two relate solely to prohibition. However, six, like the original ten, concern fundamental freedoms. In each of these six instances Congress made an attempt to expand liberty and to bring contemporary practice more in harmony with the idealistic sentiments expressed at the dawn of the American experiment. Addressing a problem which had distressed a number of the Founding Fathers, the Thirteenth Amendment, ratified shortly after the Civil War in 1865, abolished slavery. Three years later, the Fourteenth Amendment made blacks citizens, offered to all equal protection of the laws, and prohibited to the states what the Fifth Amendment had already forbidden to the federal government—no person could be deprived of life, liberty, or property without due process of law. In 1869 the Fifteenth Amendment declared voting no longer affected by the race, color, or previous servitude. A century later, in 1964, the Twenty-Fourth Amendment outlawed the poll tax and any other kind of tax designed to prevent the exercise of the franchise. The Twenty-Sixth Amendment, ratified in 1971, extended voting privileges to eighteen-year-olds. Already, in 1920, the Nineteenth

Amendment had stated that the right to vote could not be abridged on account of sex. Wherever she was, Abigail Adams must have savored that particular moment. In 1785, while her husband, John, was a member of the Confederation congress, she had warned him: "In the new code of laws which I suppose will be necessary, I desire that you would remember the ladies. . . . If attention is not paid to the ladies, we are determined to foment a rebellion and will not be bound by laws in which we have no voice." John had replied somewhat condescendingly: "I cannot but laugh. You are so saucy!" Abigail had the last laugh.

From the outset one fact was clear: the Founding Fathers had assumed correctly that power is toxic to all who wield it and that only a balance of forces and a separation of functions could adequately preserve freedom and protect the whole scheme from collapse. But even these safeguards faced a serious challenge in the bitter struggle for supremacy between the states and the federal government which punctuated the nation's first seventy years. Possessing geographic, economic, cultural, and social ramifications, this persistent and escalating battle for dominance first appeared in the acrimonious debates in the Constitutional Convention involving states' rights versus centralization. This struggle ultimately centered on the moral issue of slavery which served as the catalytic agent that precipitated the most serious crisis the Constitution ever faced—the Civil War. The final victory of the North at Appomattox Courthouse in 1865, after four years of internecine fighting, preserved the Union, a result the founders undoubtedly would have applauded. But it also modified the original design envisioned by them by markedly increasing federal authority at the expense of the states.

With respect to the internal functioning of the federal government itself, no sooner was that government formed in 1789 than complaints arose about its performance. In the pre-Civil War era the executive branch, whether headed by John Adams, Thomas Jefferson, or Andrew Jackson, was constantly denounced as dictatorial. John Marshall, an early chief justice of the Supreme Court, was charged with unconscionably expanding the power of the federal judiciary and with seeking judicial dominance. Immediately after the Civil War, the Reconstruction congresses were condemned for attempting to destroy both the presidency and the courts. So it has gone. Throughout our history each branch has attempted to aggrandize itself at the expense of the others, and the alleged usurpation of power by one branch or another has created a continual concern for the vigor of the Constitution.

Ironically, that branch of government in which the Founders placed the greatest faith has in many respects proved to be the least reliable and the least effective. Of the three branches, the legislature was thought to be the safest because it was nearest the people. Hence the framers assigned it far-reaching powers. However, its size, its organizational complexity, its cumbersome and archaic rules and regulations, and the need of its members to satisfy the demands of their local constituents have frequently militated against Congress's ability to react sensibly to crises or solve many national problems. The Congress, after all, has been a composite microcosm of the nation as a whole. At those times when public opinion has been in agreement a unified Congress has been able to act with vigor and show real power. But when the public mind has been badly divided by the conflict between heterogeneous life styles or by differing moral and social attitudes, the Congress has faltered. At such moments the Congress has required a direction and a leadership which it could not itself supply. And when such leadership was missing, the Congress was unable to manufacture a censensus. The crucial issue of slavery, for instance, rendered it impotent. With respect to most moral, social, and cultural matters it has usually played an unsatisfactory or ambiguous role.

The area of greatest congressional effectiveness has been in the economic realm, especially in harmonizing individual economic freedom of action with the broader public interest. The regulation and protection of the public welfare, the encouragement of business expansion, the granting of economic assistance to various groups, and the prevention of economic instability have been matters in which Congress has assumed an increasingly vital task. Particularly has this congressional function expanded since the outburst of economic activity in the United States in the late nineteenth century, which saw the creation of the railroads and large-scale manufacturing establishments. But the even more complex technological revolutions of the twentieth century, together with the economic demands of the Great Depression and of two world wars, have heightened Congress's involvement in this important area. Fortunately, the Constitution endorsed no specific kind of economic system—capitalism, for example, was not mentioned—although competitive

profit-making in a relatively free market created the economic atmosphere which existed at the time of the Constitutional Convention. This
has provided for great latitude, and the Congress has wisely endorsed
a process of economic experimentation that has aided the movement of
American society from a simple nation of pioneering farmers, craftsmen,
and slaves to the present mixed economy which is both regulated and
unregulated, private and governmental, free and controlled, large and
small, singly owned and corporate.

In the area of civil liberties, where Congress might have been expected
to write an illustrious chapter, it has failed miserably, thereby confirm-
ing Jefferson's wisdom in seeking a Bill of Rights. The nation was
scarcely nine years old before an anxious Congress passed the infamous
Alien and Sedition Acts in the hope of preventing French revolutionary
ideas from infiltrating the American scene. In World War I it endorsed
severe restrictions on freedom of speech and action. Its sanity collapsed
completely during the anti-red hysteria of 1919–1920. It became an ally
of Joseph McCarthy in the anti-communist crusade of 1950–1954.
Meanwhile, legislatures at the local level performed no better. There
criminal syndicalist, red flag, and teacher loyalty oath legislation were
often the rule rather than the exception. And state legislatures, not the
executive or the judiciary, were responsible for all the Jim Crow laws
and poll taxes that existed in the United States' history. In times of
peril or social and racial unrest the legislative branch has proven to be
a poor defender of freedom, since it becomes infected with the same
emotional anti-libertarian virus that makes the general public feverish.

It is doubly ironic that in the practical operation of the American
system, the branch which caused the most worry at the outset should
have become the most effective—and the most revered. The founders
at no time envisioned the president as a world leader or, as Clinton
Rossiter put it, "a kind of magnificent lion who can roam widely and
do great deeds." Those sections of the Constitution which dealt with
the executive branch were left somewhat vague. From the beginning,
however, the presidency developed as the focal point of the American
system. Washington set the image and the tone. Although he demonstrated that the presidency was compatible with republican government,
he also indicated that the presidency was an office possessing great res-
ervoirs of power. When in 1793 he unilaterally issued a Proclamation
of Neutrality in the war between England and France, Madison de-

nounced the action as illegal. Washington countered that the president's obligation to conduct the foreign affairs of the country *made* it legal.

Since that time the power of the president has grown. Through frequent altercations with Congress, the issuing of executive orders, and the threat or the actual use of the veto, the president has carved out an increasingly important role for himself. Further, the emergence of the president as head of a political party dispensing patronage and other political largesse has added to his significance. Before 1865 Jackson, Polk, and Lincoln, especially, enlarged presidential powers. Presidential authority declined in the Reconstruction years, but with the advent of the present century presidential power again burgeoned. Two world wars and a severe depression, coupled with the personalities of Theodore Roosevelt, Woodrow Wilson, and Franklin Roosevelt, resulted in the White House finally becoming the pulpit of the country and the president serving as chaplain. A quick succession of other strong presidents—Truman, Kennedy, Johnson, and Nixon—solidly entrenched the executive as the bellwether of the nation. Ranging over both domestic and foreign policy, the president increasingly assumed the responsibility of speaking for all the people. By 1974 Woodrow Wilson's earlier observation about the presidency was essentially correct: "His office is anything he has the sagacity and force to make it. . . . His capacity will set the limit."

The emergence of the United States as a world power, the constancy of the threat of nuclear war, the requirements of national security, and the growing complexity of domestic issues added to presidential opportunities as well as responsibilities. The Great Depression, the Korean police action, the Suez Crisis, the Cuban Missile Crisis, and the Vietnam conflict were steps in this development. In the process, the frequent ineffectiveness of Congress to deal with severe internal problems and foreign crises became clear. It was the president, not the legislature, which provided the leadership during the Great Depression. It was the president, not Congress, who first acted to block the post-World War II Communist surge. It was the executive branch, not the legislative, which first saw the need for desegregation, a national health program, and proper energy planning. It is a sobering fact that throughout this entire period the representatives of the people consistently granted to the executive all the power that he requested—from Franklin Roosevelt and his emergency powers during the Depression to Lyndon Johnson and the Gulf of Tonkin Resolution. Congress has pretended that the president obtained this imperial power by chicanery and sly ruses, but this was not the case. Congress was aware of what it was doing. When Senator John Sherman Cooper, for example, asked Senator J. William Fulbright, the manager of the Gulf of Tonkin Resolution in 1964, if its passage meant the president could commit the nation to war in the Vietnam situation, Fulbright replied: "That is the way I would interpret it."

The tragic case of Richard Nixon is a final, sad commentary on both the rise and the current low state of the American presidency. Yet it is also a glowing tribute to the Founding Fathers. No matter how powerful or how arrogant any one of the separate branches might become, there were always remedies at hand within the constitutional system to rectify the situation. In this case a combination of the fundamental rights contained in the First Amendment (especially freedom of the press) and the review power of the judiciary helped to redress the balance. The symbolic Armageddon of the modern president occurred on July 24, 1974, in *Nixon* v. *U.S.* when the Supreme Court by an 8-0 decision ordered the president to surrender certain secret tapes. Galvanized into action at last by a crusading press and by an increasingly unified public opinion, the Congress also began to move, and on July 30 the House Judiciary Committee voted three articles of impeachment against the president because of the misuse of his powers. When, on the night of August 8, President Nixon resigned, it was a personal tragedy; but it was also a vindication of the Constitutional system. Art Buchwald, who was at the White House on that fateful evening, declared that the thing which impressed him most was that he saw not one tank, not one helmeted soldier. Two hundred million Americans had changed their chief executive and not one bomb had burst, not one bayonet had been unsheathed. Said he, "I believe that any country in the world that can still do that, can't be all bad." The next morning, shortly after Gerald Ford was sworn in as the new president, Senator Hugh Scott of Pennsylvania sat down at his desk and composed this letter.

> August 9, 1974
> The Honorable James Madison
> Sir:
>   It worked.
>   Sincerely,
>   Hugh Scott
>   U.S. Senator

The judicial branch, an entity not given much attention in the original Constitution, has been in many ways the most aggressive protector and expander of American liberties since the founding. This has happened more by chance than by design. Article III of the Constitution left the final arrangement of the federal courts to Congress, which in 1789 passed the first of many acts dealing with the judiciary. The original law created district and circuit courts and set the number of justices on the Supreme Court at six. Because of the political infighting among the branches, this number subsequently varied between five and ten, but in 1869 it was finally pegged at nine.

The Constitution made no mention of the "powers" of the courts or of the doctrine of judicial review, although it stated that the federal courts were to interpret the fundamental law. It was John Marshall, the fourth chief justice of the Supreme Court, who by a series of important decisions from 1803 (*Marbury* v. *Madison*) to 1819 (*McCulloch* v. *Maryland*) converted the federal judiciary from being the least considered branch to one of full authority. In these cases Marshall established the Court's right of judicial review not only over congressional legislation but also over the acts of state legislatures and the decisions of state courts.

No less than the other two branches, the judiciary has precipitated controversy by its exercise of power. Beginning with Marshall's zealousness, the other branches watched the Supreme Court with suspicion. President Jackson once said in a moment of defiance: "John Marshall has made his decision; now let him enforce it." Other presidents have tried to bully the Court or change its composition. Even the Congress has at times harrassed the Court and passed highly dubious laws striving to circumvent its decisions. The most celebrated confrontation came in 1937 when the Supreme Court's opposition to certain New Deal legislation prompted Franklin Roosevelt to attempt to place more sympathetic judges on the bench. Only its own sudden about-face in endorsing all subsequent New Deal laws as constitutional permitted the Court to thwart Roosevelt's packing plan.

From time to time the Court has created its own problems. The justices, being human, have made erroneous or untimely decisions. Moreover, attitudes on the Court have ranged from liberal to conservative and back again, causing a fluctuation in the way in which it has interpreted the Constitution. Certainly Chief Justice Roger Taney wrote the Supreme Court's most controversial single decision in *Dred Scott* v.

Sanford (1857). By deciding that the Missouri Compromise of 1820 was unconstitutional and that the slave, Dred Scott, was not a free man simply because he had moved with his master into free territory, the Court precipitated a national crisis. This was a decision that required a civil war and two amendments (the Thirteenth and Fourteenth) to undo and cast a shadow over the reputation of the Court for more than a generation.

The Supreme Court in the pre-Civil War and immediate post-Civil War periods was basically property-conscious; it did little to protect fundamental freedoms. But its strong defense of property rights under the due process clauses of both the Fifth and the Fourteenth amendments unquestionably encouraged it to examine other rights later on and set a pattern whereby the Court ultimately became a sanctuary for the defense of all freedoms. Gradually the Court's interpretation of the due process clauses shifted from primarily protecting the property rights of businesses to restricting individuals or businesses from acquiring property at the expense of others. Since the Great Depression, the Court has consistently applied the due process clauses to the protection of personal economic freedom. Its endorsement of maximum hour and minimum wage legislation, its outlawing of yellow-dog contracts, and its approval of the right to strike and bargain collectively have been symptomatic of this development.

More significant, the Court has come to view other freedoms, not related to economic matters, as also covered by the due process clauses of the Fifth and the Fourteenth amendments. Before World War II most civil liberties were either protected or not protected by the action of the states. The states possessed a variety of laws, some of which condoned open discrimination. The Supreme Court traditionally upheld such laws on the narrow basis of states' rights. It set this pattern in 1883 in the so-called Civil Rights cases when the Supreme Court declared unconstitutional an act of Congress which would have made equal accommodations mandatory for all citizens everywhere in inns, theaters, public conveyances, and places of amusement. In this manner most of the supposed gains of the Civil War embodied in the Thirteenth, Fourteenth, and Fifteenth amendments were actually nullified. Not long thereafter, in *Plessy* v. *Ferguson* (1896), the Court specifically endorsed a two-track racial arrangement which permitted public and educational facilities to be "separate" if presumably "equal."

Times and attitudes changed. By the 1920s the Court was beginning to use the due process and the equal protection of the laws clauses of the Fourteenth Amendment to prevent state action against free speech (*Gitlow* v. *New York,* 1925). By the end of World War II it was also employing these same clauses to preserve, against state action, *all* the basic rights of citizens enumerated in the First Amendment. It was on this basis that in 1954 the Court, in the famous *Brown* decision, overturned the old *Plessy* "separate but equal" doctrine. With respect to speech and press, specifically, the Court has attempted to apply broadly Justice Oliver Wendell Holmes's "clear and present danger" principle, that all opinions must be tolerated until they "so imminently threaten immediate interference with the lawful and pressing purposes of the law that an immediate check is required to save the country." Similarly, the Court has recently moved into other, even more controversial, areas of rights, such as those relating to illegal arrest and the invasion of privacy contained in the Fourth Amendment. Whatever one chooses to think of such recent decisions, it is clear that the Supreme Court, representing the judicial branch, has served an important function in protecting and expanding American freedoms under the constitutional system.

Thomas Jefferson once stated that the price of freedom is eternal vigilance. Thomas Paine observed that those who would reap the benefits of freedom must undergo the fatigue of supporting it. Today the American people are involved in the same struggle to maintain their freedoms that their ancestors fought. The vantage point has changed as have the combatants and the weapons. But the fundamental issues remain the same.

Along with the Founding Fathers, most Americans have made the assumption that a constitutionally created government of separate branches operating under a system of checks and balances is best. But will that system continue to function properly? Some think that popular democracy has already gone too far, that the electorate is saturated with the poor and illiterate, and that Congress cannot be expected to remain responsible under such conditions. In 1787 Madison worried about power sliding into the hands of those who had nothing as contrasted with those who had something. Fisher Ames, a New England conservative, complained when Jefferson became President: "Our disease is democracy—our very bones are carious and their marrow blackens with gangrene." When Jackson took office in 1829 many said that the government was in the hands of "men who gambled, haunted taverns, drank, swore, were uncouth—men who wanted to manage the affairs of the nation but couldn't handle their own." But the challenge to American democracy does not rest with such charges. What troubles Congress and renders it ineffective is the total absence of consensus on almost every important issue confronting the nation among the wealthiest citizens, the best educated, the most civic-minded. Working without consensus, Congress can scarcely face, much less resolve, such divisive issues as monetary solvency, energy control, and welfare reform.

In a day when the president has immediate access to the nation through television and can "manage" a favorable public opinion, there is a natural concern that this office will remain a grave danger to the stability of the constitutional system. The restraints on presidential powers are presently not so much legal as they are proportional to his ability to capture both the congressional and the public mind. International crises and internal alarms give the president special advantages in his quest for public support. Beyond that, in a highly complex society only the Executive is capable of offering the leadership which the country requires. Despite Watergate and the political demise of Richard Nixon, the presidency remains the focal point of the American system. Can a government of balanced powers survive repeated presidential assaults?

The federal judiciary has admittedly been a servitor of the people in expanding and protecting fundamental rights, but has its crusade lately erred in the opposite direction? The charge is made that the courts have so protected the rights of the accused that they now allow crime to go unpunished, that they have made the Fifth and the Fourteenth amendments the refuge of scoundrels, and that they have twisted the laudable desire for racial reform into a death knell for local self-rule. Pornography and obscenity have become the new yardstick by which free speech is measured, and their existence has become standard practice. It is also said that minority rights now mean minority veto and that American society is slowly being forced to accept the premise that all men are equal not only in their fundamental rights but in ability, character, intelligence, and ambition as well. Many conclude that the "nationalization" of our fundamental liberties by the federal courts has not resulted in progress but in centralized oppression to protect the inferior.

Other disturbing questions arise. The Founding Fathers in 1787 had no idea when they were writing the Constitution that they were also underwriting "big" government. In 1970 there were thirteen million citizens employed in government at all levels, many of them in the local communities attempting to translate federal programs into practice. This represented almost one out of every six persons in the entire labor force. Such expansion has been particularly staggering in the executive branch of the federal government. In 1939 there were six administrative assistants assigned to Franklin Roosevelt. In 1973 Henry Kissinger, as only one of more than twenty presidential assistants, had more persons on his payroll than Roosevelt's total White House staff in World War II, including cooks and gardeners. What this portends for the future is alarming. Not only does such a bureaucracy mean a tremendous drain on the taxpayer, but it perpetuates a potentially irresponsible fourth branch of government which is unusually resistant to change. Congress does not control it, and there is fear that the president at times may be more its hostage than its administrator.

Further, there are mounting suspicions concerning sections of this executive bureaucracy and their impact on fundamental freedoms. Agencies such as the FBI, the CIA, and NASA frequently seem to be in mortal conflict with the purposes of democracy. The need for such organizations often comes perilously close to being canceled by the dangers which they create. Similarly, the obvious demands for secrecy and loyalty in the modern state pose serious problems for the retention of an open society. The increasing involvement of the military in foreign policy making and in domestic economic planning has been and will remain worrisome.

The problem of national security is not new. Freedom in revolutionary America did not include the right to be pro-British. Nevertheless, even at that time, Benjamin Franklin flatly claimed that "those who would give up essential liberty, to purchase a little temporary safety, deserve neither liberty nor safety." The modern version of the problem, however, is not quite so simple. As Franklin's comment implied, most of the security restrictions imposed on liberty in the past were associated with emergencies of a transient nature. It was assumed that their rapid passing would allow an immediate restoration of the *status quo ante*. But we no longer can be certain that our emergencies are merely temporary, and history has shown that fundamental freedoms are endangered less by sudden overthrow than by the process of gradual barter for something in which the public places a higher current value. Other dangers to the American constitutional system abound. One still pertinent question is whether economic security and individual freedom can be maintained at the same time. Much of the history of our political liberty has been the story of the separation and distribution of governmental power and the progressive limitation on the arbitrary exercise of that power. Yet our economic development has moved us consistently toward the concentration and the consolidation of power. The continued expansion of the large corporations and their effect on domestic and foreign policy, the constant drive to curtail and eliminate competition, and the arrogance and corruption of some of the large labor unions are not encouraging signs for the future. Moreover, one can only guess what the energy crunch and the decline in the nation's natural resources will mean for the maintenance of American liberties. And only the sheerest speculation exists on the impact a concerted drive to clean up the environment would have on traditional freedoms.

Even more disquieting is the fact that we find ourselves troubled in an area in which the Founding Fathers had absolute confidence—freedom of expression. The growth of the media has radically changed our view of freedom of speech and freedom of the press. Currently the problem is not only how to protect them, but how to guard against those who would acquire a monopoly on collecting and disseminating information. The Founding Fathers never conceived of a CBS news program reaching twenty million viewers. Yet they did speak of a "free press" along with "freedom of the press." Jefferson quite correctly told Washington in 1792: "No government ought to be without censors, and while the press is free none will." There is presently a serious need to assure American society that its press is indeed *free*. Only then can the public be expected to accept, as the Founding Fathers were willing to accept, all the frustrations that an aggressive press causes, the harassment of public officials that it permits, and the worries to the security-conscious that it brings.

Finally, there is a deep concern regarding the recent growth in general violence and in public apathy toward it. We can put a man on the moon but we can no longer walk freely in Central Park. The Founding Fathers assumed that man was part of a moral order and that he relied on reason to conduct his life. Unlike many citizens today, the Founders did not conceive of American life, let alone American constitutionalism, apart from a moral order. Indeed, they believed that popular government would not survive unless a basic morality existed and unless personal restraints against intemperate actions and violence were exercised. As for morality, they considered religion its primary safeguard and hence enshrined freedom of religion as the very first right under the First Amendment. Moreover, they never spoke of rights without speaking of responsibilities. They called it a Bill of Rights not a Bill of Privileges; to them rights involved responsibilities. In our present situation, petty tyrannies and lawlessness can be expected to grow unless the Founders' appreciation of civil responsibilities and their belief in a moral order are revived.

As we celebrate our Bicentennial and as we face our manifold problems, it is not meaningless rhetoric to say that the future of America depends directly upon how much faith of the Founders we retain. Because democracy is rooted in the principle that more than half the people are right more than half the time, the American public, more than its executive leaders or its jurists or its Congressmen, will finally determine the fate of this nation. Naturally, our concept of American freedoms and how they relate to the contemporary environment will be different from that held in the past. Such freedoms are not in the same relative position today as they were in colonial America, or even in the industrialized America of the early twentieth century. That older America saw liberty as a by-product of conflict in a multipolar, pluralistic society in which the primary ingredient was the absence of arbitrary governmental power. Modern America views liberty more as a by-product of an institutionalized and governmentally nurtured due process of law. Clearly each generation of Americans has been forced to reevaluate and vindicate its freedoms anew for itself. The American system with its counterbalancing branches of government has been a continuing imperfection, but it is an imperfection which encourages perpetual revision so that it can burn up its past errors in constant search for the light of truth.

But some things do not change. The United States is, as the Founding Fathers planned, a government of laws instead of men, and the purpose of its government—executive, legislative, and judicial—is to expand and protect the fundamental freedoms enumerated in the Constitution and its amendments. Many Americans still believe that a government which most carefully protects and promotes freedom of thought, expression, action, and criticism has the best chance for survival and for achieving progress, security, and happiness. Freedom in such a society is not a luxury; it is a necessity. After two hundred years this primary truth is still self-evident, for modern history is full of examples of the practical consequences of denying freedom—Nazi Germany, Red China, the Soviet Union.

Admittedly there is room for pessimism. But there is also much room for hope. The constitutional system as designed by its original architects still survives. Like a runner in motion when viewed through the lens of split-second photography, this system seen by the contemporary observer always seems to be off-balance and falling. First one and then another of its parts appears faulty, autocratic, insensitive to liberty, and out of phase. But when the whole is placed in its historical continuum it is seen to be in rhythm and remarkably stable. Flexible yet resting on rigid doctrine, complicated yet strangely simple, the American constitutional system is a corpus of living usages which have proven to be infinitely applicable to new and untried situations. The Constitution itself has provided us with elastic grooves in which the life of the nation could run. For modern Americans the key problem, therefore, is not the continued validity of this system or its ability to protect traditional freedoms, but the nation's wisdom and ingenuity in applying it to modern circumstances. Whether it can do this in the next twenty years may be shrouded in doubt. That it accomplished this feat to the benefit of the majority of the nation's citizens in the past two hundred years is beyond question.

The Future of Political Freedom

Hans J. Morgenthau

Political freedom has two different and incompatible meanings according to whether we think of the holder or the subject of political power.
Freedom for the holder of political power signifies the opportunity to
exercise political domination; freedom for the subject means the absence
of such domination. Not only are these two conceptions of freedom
mutually exclusive in logic, but they are also incapable of coexisting in
fact within any particular sphere of action. One can be realized only at
the expense of the other, and the more there is of the one the less there is
bound to be of the other.

The concept of freedom is contradictory whether seen from the vantage point of the political master or his subject. It is also ambivalent in
that most members of society are not simply one or the other, master or
subject, but both at the same time. When they claim freedom for themselves, what do they mean: their freedom to dominate others or their
freedom from domination by others? Perhaps they mean one; perhaps
they mean the other; perhaps they mean both. This ambivalence makes
inevitably for continuous confusion, manifesting itself typically in ideologies which rationalize and justify the freedom to dominate in terms
of the freedom from domination. It follows that universal and absolute
freedom is a contradiction in terms. In the political realm, the freedom
of one is always paid for by the lack of freedom of somebody else. The
political master can have his freedom only at the price of the freedom of
those who are subject to him; the latter can be free only if the master
is made to sacrifice his freedom as a master.

What applies to the freedom to exercise political power also reveals itself in the profession and application of the political truth which justifies and informs the exercise of political power. He who believes that he has a monopoly of truth in matters political is free to propound his "truth," which to him appears to be all the truth there is, and to act upon it only if the nonbelievers are not free to oppose their "truth" to his, for freedom for error to corrupt thought and action is incompatible with the freedom of the truth to prevail. On the other hand, the freedom of the many to compete in the market place for acceptance of their different truths requires the abrogation of the freedom of the one to impose his conception of truth upon all. In any given society not everyone can be as free as everyone else. Every society must decide for itself who shall have what freedom. The kind of freedom a particular society is able to realize in a particular period of its history, then, depends upon the kind of political order under which it lives. The nature of that particular order, in turn, is determined by the fundamental values with which that society identifies itself and which it attempts to realize through the medium of politics. In short, the kind of liberty a society enjoys is determined by the kind of political justice it seeks. Liberty cannot be defined without justice, and it can be realized only by a particular political order informed by a particular sense of justice.

All attempts at realizing freedom have, throughout history, derived from one of two incompatible conceptions of justice: one, minoritarian; the other, equalitarian. The minoritarian conception of justice assumes that only a minority, determined by birth, supernatural charisma, or qualifications of achievement, is capable of finding and understanding the truth about matters political and of acting successfully on it. The majority, not so endowed, is subject to the will of the minority, both for its own sake and for the sake of the whole commonwealth. From Plato and Aristotle to the modern justifications of aristocratic and totalitarian government, the denial of political freedom for the majority has derived from a conception of political justice which limits to a minority the ability and hence the right to enjoy political freedom. This conception determines not only the over-all character of political society but also the specific nature of its institutions. It claims for these institutions the attribute of freedom, if not in good faith, at least in good logic.

Communist theory claims that the government monopoly of information and control over the mass media of communication means freedom of the press and the only freedom of the press there is, while what we call freedom of the press is but a sham. The absurdity of the argument does not lie in the claim itself but in the underlying assumption of a government monopoly of political truth, from which the claim follows with logical necessity. For since we have all the political truth there is, so the Communist argument runs, how can we allow freedom of expression to those who refuse to recognize the political truth and hence are by definition enemies of the truth, that is, criminals, saboteurs, or foreign agents? And what the West calls freedom of the press is nothing but the license to sow confusion by propounding error as truth.

The decisive argument against the Communist idea of freedom and against all political philosophies reserving political freedom to a minority, however defined, must come to terms with the philosophic assumption from which those political philosophies derive. The argument is two-pronged.

It opposes the monistic assumption of a monopoly of political truth vested in a minority with the pluralistic assumption that, while no member of society has a monopoly of political truth or can even be certain what action political truth requires in a given situation, all members of society as rational beings have access to a measure of political truth, however dimly seen. From this equalitarian political ontology and anthropology evolves an equalitarian conception of political justice which postulates equality of political rights and equal treatment of equal situations. Since no conception of political truth, or any political philosophy and program of action derived from it, is necessarily and demonstrably superior to any other, they must all have an equal chance to prevail; but none of them must be given an a priori chance to prevail once and for all. The mechanism through which this equal chance materializes is the periodical majority vote, which decides the issue temporarily either through popular elections or through the enactments of legislative assemblies.

Equalitarianism, then, attacks the minoritarian conception of political justice on the grounds that no minority can be politically so wise in comparison with the majority as to possess a monopoly of political wisdom. No minority can be trusted with absolute power on the assumption that it possesses absolute wisdom. When Cromwell appealed to the representatives of the Church of Scotland, "I beseech you, in the bowels of

Christ, to think it possible you may be mistaken," he expressed in the religious sphere the equalitarian mood.

Yet equalitarianism not only refuses to accept the explicit minoritarian claim of infallibility but also rejects its implicit claim to incorruptibility. Here is the other prong of the equalitarian argument. The minoritarian claim to a monopoly of political freedom derives from the overt assumption of a monopoly of political wisdom and of necessity implies a monopoly of political goodness, for the minoritarian claim can be defended by the minority and accepted by the majority only on the assumption that the minority will not abuse its absolute power. The nature of man, as it reveals itself to introspection and through the evidence of history, militates against the correctness of that assumption. The inevitable corruptiveness of power is the political manifestation of the inevitability of sin. Equalitarianism attempts to limit the opportunities for the abuse of power by limiting the political freedom of the holders of the power. Western constitutionalism is an elaborate device to subject the political freedom of the holders of political power to institutional limitations and legal controls.

The decisive safeguard against the abuse of political power, however, is the institution of periodical popular elections. The very fact that political power is subject to recall and can be taken for granted only for stated periods of time limits the duration of political power with mechanical sharpness. But it also limits the freedom with which political power can be used as long as it lasts. Since the holders of political power have a natural tendency to keep themselves in power by having themselves reelected, they must use their political freedom in view of winning the ever impending elections. Thus the preferences of the electorate, real or fancied, are an ever-present limitation on the freedom of the holders of political power to use that power as they would like to. The absolute ruler is free to govern as he sees fit, subject only to the limits of physical nature. The freedom of constitutional government is hemmed in not only by institutional devices and, insofar as it is democratic, by the mechanical limits of popular elections, but also by the political dynamics of the democratic process. It is this contrast between the complete freedom of the absolute ruler to exercise the authority of government at his discretion and the limits within which constitutional government must operate which Theodore Roosevelt had in mind when he expressed the wish to be, for twenty-four hours, President, Congress, and Supreme Court at the same time.

The democratic processes, in order to be able to delimit the freedom of the rulers to govern, must themselves be free to bring the will of the majority to bear upon the personnel and policies of the government. The freedom of the government to control and replace the rulers and the limitations upon the rulers' freedom to govern are the two sides of the same coin, the latter being a function of the former. Without that freedom of the governed, democracy loses its substance; for it no longer provides the people with the freedom of choosing rulers and, through them, policies. A democracy that loses that freedom can survive only as the periodical plebiscitarian approval of the personnel and the policies of the government. This is the totalitarian type of democracy.

One would misunderstand the nature of democracy and of totalitarianism as well as their relationship were one to suggest that totalitarian elections are necessarily and always a sham and that they never reflect the true will of the people. They may well reflect that will, as elections in Nazi Germany and Fascist Italy undoubtedly did, expressing a consensus between the popular will and the government. Here lies the decisive difference between traditional autocracy and modern totalitarianism. Autocracy imposes its will upon an indifferent or hostile people; totalitarianism aims at, and may succeed in, governing with the consent of the governed.

However, what sets totalitarianism apart from genuine democracy is the manner in which the government attains the consent of the governed. Totalitarianism creates that consent through the monopolistic manipulation of the mass media of communication; the consent of the people does not set limits for the government but is a function of its unlimited freedom. In a genuine democracy, on the other hand, the consent of the governed is the temporary result of the interplay of antagonistic forces, competing freely with each other for popular support. The government enters this contest essentially as an equal; whatever advantages it may have by virtue of prestige, influence, and information do not substantially affect the principle of free competition. Thus a genuinely democratic government can never be certain whether it will survive the next election to be replaced by another which, in turn, must subject its personnel and policies to the popular judgment in still another election to come.

Genuine democracy must forever guard against the temptation to transform itself into an imperfect type and then to degenerate into totalitarianism. While democracy requires that the will of the people limit the freedom of the government, it also requires that the freedom of the popular will be limited. A popular will not so limited becomes the tyranny of the majority, which destroys the freedom of political competition and thus uses the powers of the government to prevent a new majority from forming and to, intrench itself permanently in the seat of power. There is only a small step from the destruction of the freedom of competition, that is, imperfect democracy, to the destruction of competition itself, that is, totalitarianism.

The freedom of political competition essential to democracy can be impaired in two different ways. The people are being deprived of their freedom of choosing among alternative policies by choosing among different candidates for office if the different candidates for office are not identified with different policies but compete for power as an end in itself, not as a means to achieve a particular policy. The people may still be able to choose in terms of the personal qualities of the candidates, such as competence and trustworthiness; their choice has no meaning for the substance of the policies to be pursued. The people, if they do not vote for the person of a candidate as such, will then vote out of habit or not at all, and in the measure in which this happens democratic elections will have lost their ability to protect the freedom of the people by limiting the freedom of action of the government.

The other—and more insidious—threat to freedom of political competition stems from the tendency of all majorities to act upon the assumption that they are more—at best—than temporary approximations to political truth, that is, the repositories of all the political truth there is. They tend to think and act, as long as they last as majorities, as though their will provided the ultimate standard of thought and action and as though there were no higher law to limit their freedom. The majority, as long as it lasts, tends to become the absolute master, the tyrant, of the body politic, stifling in that body the vital spirit of questioning and initiative and evoking instead the submissiveness of conformity. Yet since there is no higher standard for thought and action than the will of the majority, in theory at least each successive majority may produce a new tyrant with a political truth of its own. One political orthodoxy may be succeeded by another, calling forth a new conformity, and the very relativism which is the philosophic mainspring of the supremacy of the majority will produce not only the tyranny of the majority but also a succession of tyrannies, all justified by the will of the majority.

While this is possible in theory, it is, however, not likely to occur for any length of time in practice, for the majority, by making itself the supreme arbiter of matters political, must at least implicitly deny to the minority the right to make itself the majority of tomorrow. Since the majority of today tends to claim a monopoly of political truth, it must also tend to claim a monopoly of political power, freezing the existing distribution of power. In one word, the majority of today tends to transform itself into a permanent majority and, by the same token, to reduce the minority of today to a permanent one.

This development not only reduces the minority to a permanent one but also deprives it of its democratic reason to exist. That reason is its ability, equal in principle to that of the majority, to have access to political truth and act upon it; hence its claim to compete freely for majority status tomorrow. The assumption that the majority has a monopoly of political truth destroys the minority's political function and gives the respect for its existence an anachronistic quality. Since its continuing existence implicitly challenges the majority's monopolistic claims, it is a living reminder of alternative rulers and policies, and may, by virtue of these attributes, become a political nuisance to the majority, the minority cannot for long survive the destruction of its philosophic justification and political function. With its destruction, democracy itself comes to an end. The unlimited freedom, that is, the tyranny, of the rulers corresponds to the unlimited lack of freedom of the ruled.

Thus decadent democracy goes through three stages before it transforms itself into its opposite: totalitarian tyranny. It starts out by emptying itself of part of its substance; it destroys the freedom of choosing policies by choosing men. Then it substitutes for the spirit of free political competition, which derives from a pluralistic conception of political truth, the monistic assumption that only the majority possesses that truth. Then it subjects the minority to restrictions which put it at a decisive disadvantage in the competition for intellectual influence and political power, thus transforming the majority into a permanent one, existing side by side with a permanent minority. The process of degeneration is consummated with the majority becoming the sole legitimate political organization, which combines the claim to a monopoly of political truth with a monopoly of political power.

Against these tendencies toward self-destruction, inherent in the dynamics of democracy, the institutions and the spirit of liberalism stand guard. Liberalism has erected two kinds of safeguard, one in the realm of philosophic principle, the other in the sphere of political action.

Liberalism holds certain truths to be self-evident which no majority has the right to abrogate and from which, in turn, the legitimacy of majority rule derives. These truths, however formulated in a particular historic epoch, can be subsumed under the proposition that the individual—his integrity and self-development—is the ultimate point of reference for the political order and, as such, owes nothing to any secular order or human institution.

It is on this absolute and transcendent foundation that the philosophy of genuine democracy rests, and it is within this immutable framework that the processes of genuine democracy take place. The pluralism of these processes is subordinated to, and oriented toward, those absolute and transcendent truths. It is this subordination and orientation that distinguishes the pluralism of the genuine type of democracy from the relativism of its corrupted types. For in the latter the will of the majority is the ultimate point of reference of the political order and the ultimate test of what is politically true. Whatever group gains the support of the majority for its point of view gains thereby also the attributes of political truth, and the content of political truth changes with every change in the majority. Out of this relativism which makes political truth a function of political power develops, as we have seen, first the tyranny, and then the totalitarianism, of the majority, unlimited as it is by an absolute, transcendent conception of political truth. Thus the relativism of majority rule, denying the existence of absolute, transcendent truth independent of the majority will, tends toward the immanent absolutism of a tyrannical or totalitarian majority, while the pluralism of genuine democracy assumes as its corollary the existence of such truth limiting the will of the majority.

As a matter of philosophic principle, the political order is oriented toward the individual; the political order is the means to the individual's end. Yet as a matter of political fact, as we have seen, it is the very earmark of politics that men use other men as means to their ends. That this cannot be otherwise is one of the paradoxes of the politics of liberalism; for political reality disavows, and does so continuously and drastically, the postulates of liberal philosophy. Liberalism believes in the truth of man's freedom, but it finds man everywhere a slave. Thus it adds another paradox—more shocking than the first for being the result of liberalism's own efforts—by creating political institutions which limit the freedom of some in order to preserve the freedom of others. Constitutional guaranties of civil rights and their legislative and judicial implementation are the liberal defenses of freedom of political competition. While the will of the majority decides how these guaranties are to be implemented, the existence of the guaranties themselves is not subject to that will. Quite to the contrary, these guaranties set the conditions under which the will of the majority is to be formed and exercised. They establish the framework of democratic legitimacy for the rule of the majority.

Yet the very need for these safeguards limiting the freedom of the majority points up the dilemma that liberalism faces. If the majority could be trusted with its power, the liberal safeguards would be unnecessary. Since it cannot be so trusted, its freedom must be curtailed for the very sake of freedom. The dilemma of freedom manifests itself typically in the concrete terms of the antinomy between individual rights and some collective good, such as general welfare, administrative efficiency, national security. The liberal concern for individual rights may stand in the way of the maximization of such a collective good, and the greater the need for the full realization of a collective good appears to be, the greater is the temptation to sacrifice individual rights for its sake. Is individual freedom more important than national security, without which there will be no freedom at all? What benefits does a man draw from the Bill of Rights if, in the absence of measures of general welfare, it guarantees him the right to sleep under bridges and sell apples in the street? This dilemma lies outside the purview of liberal philosophy, which inclined to identify itself in the nineteenth century with the individualistic prong of the dilemma and shifted in the twentieth to the other, collectivist, one. Thus the philosophy of liberalism can provide no intellectual tools with which to master this dilemma. The decline, in our time, of liberalism as theory and practice is the result.

Liberalism conceived of the problem of freedom in terms of a simple juxtaposition between society and the state. It saw the sole threat to individual freedom in the state, conceived either as an aristocratic minority or a democratic majority. Liberal policy, then, had a twofold aim: to erect a wall between the government and the people, behind which the citizens would be secure, and to confine the government behind that wall in as narrow a space as possible. The smaller the sphere of the state, the larger the sphere of individual freedom, in theory, was bound to be.

However, the aspirations for power, and the struggle for power resulting for them, could not be so neatly confined; for these aspirations are not the exclusive property of any group but common to all men, ruler and ruled, oligarchs and democrats. The autonomous forces of society, left to themselves, engendered new accumulations of power as dangerous to the freedom of the individual as the power of the government had ever been. And while liberalism had assumed that the weakness of the government assured the freedom of the individual, it now became obvious that it also assured the unhindered growth of private power, destructive of individual freedom. Against these concentrations of private power, which derived primarily from economic controls, the state was called back from the corner in which it had been confined to do battle. The state, which had just been relegated to the inconspicuous and relatively innocuous role of a night watchman by a society fearful of its power, was now restored to power as the protector of individual rights. Thus the modern state bears a Janus head: one face that of a monster lusting for power over the individual, the other with the benevolent mien of the individual's defender against his fellows' infringements of his freedom.

The struggle for freedom in the modern state has thus become a three-cornered fight, and the old dilemma reappears in a new and intricate configuration. A new feudalism of giant concentrations of economic power in the form of corporations and labor unions vies with the old tyranny of the state for limiting the freedom of the individual, subjecting ever new spheres of formerly free individual action to ever more stringent restrictions. That new feudalism calls into being the "new despotism" of the administrative state, which, for the sake of individual freedom, superimposes its restrictions on those who control concentrations of economic power. From the latter's vantage point, this is but the old tyranny in modern garb. Yet the mass of individual citizens welcomes the administrative state as the champion of freedom.

It is the measure of the inadequacy of the simple juxtapositions of nineteenth-century liberal philosophy and the measure of the inner contradictions and ambivalences of freedom as it actually operates in the modern state that both sides have a point. The administrative state can become a new despot to some and a new liberator to others, as majority rule can be both the nearest approximation to freedom in a mass society and a many-headed and hence unassailable destroyer of freedom.

If free government is defined as the choice by the people at large, according to preestablished rational procedures, of the personnel and, through it, of the policies of the government, then the decline of free government throughout the world is an observable fact. Most of the nations that still comply with the procedure of periodic elections are one-party states, where elections do not provide the electorate with a choice among different persons, and hence policies. Rather they are in the nature of plebiscites through which the electorate, as a matter of course, confirms the rulers in their power and gives them a mandate for whatever policies they wish to pursue.

Many of the nations that once offered the people a genuine democratic choice or at least paid their respects to democratic legitimacy through plebiscitarian elections are governed by military dictatorships. Of the new African states only one, Gambia, can still be said to have a multiparty system offering the people a genuine choice of men and policies; close to half of them are governed by military dictatorships. In Latin America the number of military dictatorships has steadily increased at the expense of genuine democracies; more particularly the few attempts at return to democratic rule have met with seemingly insuperable difficulties. Even in countries such as France, Italy, Great Britain, and the United States, where democratic procedures appear to be unimpaired, the substance of democratic rule has been diminished. France and Italy for a quarter of a century have, as a matter of principle, deprived one-quarter and close to one-third of the electorate, respectively, of any direct influence upon the personnel and the policies of the government by excluding the Communist party from it. In Great Britain a general political malaise has begun to crystallize in calls for nondemocratic solutions to problems parliamentary democracy appears to be unable to solve.

Finally and most importantly, the United States has experienced two presidencies in succession whose arbitrary, illegal, and unconstitutional rule tended to reduce democratic choice to exercises in futility. Those who voted in 1964 for one candidate because they preferred the policies for which he campaigned, found him, when he was elected, to pursue the policies of his defeated opponent with a ruthlessness and deception the latter might not have found possible. Lyndon B. Johnson, whom I called in March 1966 "the Julius Caesar of the American Republic," was followed by Richard M. Nixon, who bids fair to be its Caligula. Nixon introduced into the American system of government four practices of a distinctly Fascist character: the deprivation of the minority of an equal chance to compete with the majority in the next elections; the establishment of the "dual state" in which the official statutory agencies of the government, subject to legal restraints, are duplicated by agencies performing parallel functions, which are organized by the ruling party and responsive only to the will of the leader; the invocation of "national security" as justification for any government action, however arbitrary, unconstitutional, or illegal; and, finally, a nihilistic destructiveness, only thinly disguised by the invocation of conservative principles and patriotic and religious slogans.

Aside from the intangible damage these two presidencies have done to the practices of the American government and to the relations between that government and the people, they have given the United States it first president who owes his position not to a popular election but primarily to the choice by his predecessor (congressional approval having been a foregone conclusion), who had to leave office in order to escape impeachment for "high crimes and misdemeanors." These procedures have given America a vice president, next in line to succeed to the presidency, through the present incumbent's choice (congressional approval being in the nature of ratification rather than genuine choice). Thus at the very least with regard to the incumbent president and vice president the democratic processes of choosing among a number of candidates have been attenuated to the point of virtual disappearance. If one wants to give free rein to one's morbid imagination, one can visualize the incumbent vice president ascending to the presidency, then appointing a new vice president, and so forth. But it requires nothing more than some knowledge of ancient history to be reminded of the Roman emperors appointing their successors with the approval of the Senate, given either as a matter of course or under the threat of physical violence.

To understand the reasons for the decline of the democratic order throughout the world and, more particularly, in the United States, it is necessary to consider the fundamentals of government, regardless of type, and its relations with the people over whom it rules. We leave out of consideration only the theocratic type of government, which derives its justification from divine origin or grace.

Men expect their governments to perform for them three basic functions: to protect them from themselves and from their fellow men, that is, to protect them from violent death; to give them the opportunity to put their abilities to the test of performance, that is, to protect a sphere of freedom, however defined; to satisfy at least some of their basic aspirations, that is, to fulfill the requirements of substantive justice, however defined. It is these expectations that the Declaration of Independence referred to as "Life, Liberty and the pursuit of Happiness." Not all men will expect at all times their governments to live up in the same measure to all these requirements. Yet it can be said that a government that consistently falls short of one or the other of these requirements loses its legitimacy in the eyes of its citizens: its rule will be suffered since it cannot be changed, let alone eliminated, but it will not be spontaneously supported.

Applying these standards to contemporary governments, one realizes that the crisis of democratic governments is but a special case of the crisis of government as such. That is to say, contemporary governments—regardless of their type, composition, program, ideology—are unable to govern in accord with the three requirements of legitimate government. They are no longer able to protect the lives, to guarantee the liberty, and to facilitate the pursuit of happiness of their citizens. Governments are thus incapacitated because their operations are hopelessly at odds with the requirements or potentialities of modern technology and the organization it permits and requires.

It has become trivial to say—because it is so obvious and has been said so often—that the modern technologies of transportation, communication, and warfare have made the nation-state, as principle of political organization, as obsolete as the first industrial revolution of the steam engine did feudalism. While the official governments of the nation-states go through the constitutional motions of governing, most of the decisions that affect the vital concerns of the citizens are rendered by those who control these technologies, their production, their distribution, their operation, their price. The official governments can at best marginally influence these controls, but by and large they are compelled to accommodate themselves to them. They are helpless in the face of steel companies raising the price of steel or a union's striking for and receiving higher wages. Thus governments, regardless of their individual peculiarities, are helpless in the face of inflation; for the relevant substantive decisions are made not by them but by private governments whom the official governments are unwilling or unable to control. Thus we live, as was pointed out long ago, under the rule of a "new feudalism" whose private governments reduce the official ones to a largely marginal and ceremonial existence.

The global corporation (misnamed "multinational") is the most striking manifestation of this supercession of national governments not only in their functional but also in their territorial manifestations. While the territorial limits of the private governments of the "new feudalism," as first perceived about two decades ago, still in great measure coincided with those of the nation-state, it is a distinctive characteristic of the global corporation that its very operations tend to reduce those territorial limits to a functional irrelevancy.

The governments of the modern states are not only, in good measure, unable to govern, but where they still appear to govern (and appearances can be deceptive) they are perceived as a threat to the welfare and very existence of their citizens. National governments, once hailed as the expression of the common will, the mainstays of national existence, and the promoters of the common good, are now widely perceived as the enemy of the people, a threat to the citizen's freedom and welfare and to his survival. That is, the fear that governments have always inspired as a potential threat to the concerns of the citizens (*vide* the philosophy of *The Federalist Papers*) has now become not only a reality of everyday life, but a reality that the citizen can neither counter nor escape. It is the great political paradox of our time that a government too weak to control the concentrations of private power that have usurped much of the substance of its power has grown so powerful as to reduce the citizens to impotence.

That reduction, by an unchallengeable government, of the citizen to an impotent atom is, of course, most strikingly evident in authoritarian and totalitarian societies; Mandelstam and Solzhenitsyn bear eloquent testimony to the individual's helpless plight in such societies. Yet in liberal democracies, too, the capacity to maintain oneself and find redress against the government is markedly reduced. How many of the innocent public officials who were ruined socially and professionally by the government during the McCarthy era were able to restore their good name and recover their livelihood? What effective redress does a citizen have whose income tax returns are audited year after year for suspected but unprovable political reasons and with results both destructive and absurd?

Most important, that drastic shift of power from the citizen to the government has rendered obsolete the ultimate remedy for the government's abuses—popular revolution. It is not by accident that the last major popular revolutions occurred in Russia and China, then technologically backward nations, and that this is the age of the coup d'etat, especially its military variety, that is, the takeover of the government by an elite enjoying a monopoly of the modern technologies of transportation, communication, and warfare. But a modern government that can count on the loyalty of the technological elites is immune to displacement by the wrath of the people, not only for technological but also moral and intellectual reasons. The political consequences of Watergate are a case in point.

While the United States has a new president, the country is still governed by the same people who governed before Nixon's downfall. While the power of the Nixon administration was not sufficient to conceal all its misdeeds—thwarted by its own incompetence, scrutinized by a free press, and subject to the rule of independent courts—the individual citizen cannot help but wonder how many secrets will remain hidden forever; he cannot but marvel at the generosity of some of the judgments and sentences. In ancient Athens politicians dangerous to the state were ostracized without any charge being brought against them. In America an adminstration whose prominent members are accused or convicted of common crimes and guilty of subverting the public order blends easily into its honorable successor without a drastic change in personnel.

Shame—the public acknowledgment of a moral or political failing— is virtually extinct. The members of the intellectual and political elite whose judgments on Vietnam proved to be consistently wrong and whose policies were a disaster for the country remain members of the elite in good standing; a disgraced president moves easily into the position of an elder statesman receiving confidential information and giving advice on affairs of state. Thus the line of demarcation between right and wrong, both morally and intellectually, is blurred. It becomes a distinction without lasting moral or political consequences. To be wrong morally or politically is rather like a minor accident, temporarily embarrassing and better forgotten. That vice of moral and intellectual indifference is presented and accepted as the virtue of mercy, which, however, as forgiveness and dispensation with the usual reaction to vice, supposes a clear awareness of the difference between vice and virtue.

The people are not only deprived of the traditional effective means of stopping the abuses of government, they are also helpless in the face of the ultimate abuse, their own destruction. A government armed with the modern weapons of warfare, even of a nonnuclear kind, holds the life of the citizens in its hands. The weapons acquired for the purpose of defense or deterrence also serve as a provocation to a prospective enemy similarly armed, and that dialectic of defense-deterrence, threat and counterthreat, seeks and assures the destruction of all concerned. The universal destructiveness of that dialectic is of course pushed to its ultimate effectiveness in the nuclear field where effectiveness is the equivalent of total destruction, obliterating the conventional distinction between defense and offense, victory and defeat.

The individual faces this prospect in complete helplessness. He cannot forestall it; he cannot hide from it; he cannot escape from it. He can only wait for the ultimate disaster. Looking, as is his wont, to the government for protection, he realizes that he continues to be alive only because his government and a hostile government threaten each other with total destruction and have thus far found the threats plausible. Thus his life is for all practical purposes the function of the will of two unprecedentedly mighty governments who have the power and proclaim to have the will to destroy utterly their respective populations.

Man throughout the world has reacted to his attrition as the center of political concern—according to Aristotle, individual happiness is the purpose of politics—by political apathy, political violence, and the search for new communities outside the official political structure.

Apathy can be a comprehensive reaction all by itself. It then manifests itself simply as a retreat from politics, nonparticipation in political activities and a contemptuous unconcern with traditional political procedures. Since the individual has no influence upon the policies of the government and his vote appears to be meaningless, providing normally only a choice between Tweedledee and Tweedledum, since, more particularly, political corruption appears to be endemic, regardless of the individuals and the parties in power and of the policies they embrace, the individual turns his back upon politics altogether and tends his own garden, trying to get as much advantage as possible for himself at the expense of his fellows and his government.

While this apathy as a self-contained attitude is widespread throughout the world, as expressed by popular political attitudes and, more particularly, large-scale abstention from voting, it can also form a backdrop for political activism, seeking by violence the destruction of the existing political order or the substitution of a new and radically different one for the existing one. The violence that we witness in the form of hijacking, kidnapping, torture, indiscriminate killing, differs from traditional violence in the form of political assassinations and the destruction of political institutions in that it is in general politically aimless. Rather than being a rational means to a rational end, it is an end in itself, as such devoid of political rationality.

One could argue that while this kind of violence, as isolated and sporadic acts, is indeed devoid of political rationality, it becomes endowed with that quality when it is part of a concerted action seeking a clearly defined political change. Yet it is a common characteristic of individual violence throughout the world—Argentina, France, Germany, Great Britain, Italy, Japan, the United States—that it does not serve a rationally defined political aim but finds its fulfillment in the act of destruction itself. It is an act born not of political concern but of political frustration and despair. Unable to change the political order from within through the procedures made available by that political order, unable likewise to overthrow that political order through concerted acts of violence, that is, revolution, the political activist finds in indiscriminate destruction a substitute for the meaningful political act. For the revolution which aims at changing the world he substitutes the revolutionary tantrum, which for a fleeting moment satisfies him psychologically and frightens the supporters of the status quo without having any lasting effect upon the character and the distribution of power within society.

The individual, frustrated by his own loss of power and threatened by the unchallengeable power of the state, has still another avenue of escape. He can turn his back upon the existing social order and its institutions and search for and build a new society that makes him at home by giving meaning to his life and a chance for his abilities to prove themselves. Throughout long periods of history other-worldly religions have offered this alternative, and the monastery became the refuge of frustrated political man. In our period of history man thus frustrated must build his own monastery in the form of communes for living, political cooperation, esthetic pursuits, and manual labor, searching for a "counterculture" of some kind that in time will fill the void left by the disintegration of the old one.

It is against this background of general political decay and disintegration, affecting democratic and nondemocratic societies alike (but in different ways), that one must consider the decline of democratic government. Democracy suffers from what ails all governments, but it does so in a specific way. Democratic government is sustained by two forces: consensus upon the political fundamentals of society, and government with the consent of the governed through the people's ability to choose from among several policies by choosing among different men. These two forces must be sharply distinguished both for diagnostic and therapeutic purposes.

All democratic societies take for granted that the fundamental issues bearing upon the nature and distribution of power in society have been settled once and for all. Such settlements are typically the result of revolutions and civil or international wars. They are generally codified in written constitutions and, as such, they are not subject to public debate, let alone change by majority rule. They are the stable foundation upon which democratic institutions are erected, and the framework within which democratic processes operate. In other words, men, if they can help themselves, will not allow the issues that are most important to them to be subjected to the vagaries of parliamentary or popular vote. They willingly submit to the vote of the majority only those issues that are not vital to them, that is, those issues on which they can afford to be outvoted. The really vital issues, which are, as it were, issues of political or economic life and death, are not susceptible to democratic settlement. Rather the viability of the democratic processes is predicated upon their settlement by the free interplay of military, economic, and political forces.

It is the common character of the great issues, which have either wrecked or paralyzed democratic governments, that by their nature they are not susceptible to democratic settlement. They concern basically the distribution of economic and, through it, political power within the state. Thus it is that democratic elections appear not to settle anything of vital importance; for what needs to be settled cannot be settled by democratic procedures. In consequence, democratic elections tend to resemble more and more charades, which at best result in adjustments within the status quo without even raising the fundamental issues of the distribution of economic and political power. Democratic challenges to the economic and political status quo are staved off by the manipulation of the electoral and parliamentary procedures, as in France and Italy or, where that manipulation appears to be insufficient, by military force, as in Argentina, Brazil, or Chile. Considering the attempts at changing the basic distribution of economic and political power in the United States from Populism to the Great Society, one cannot but marvel at the staying power of the status quo, which has not only maintained itself against attempts at radical reform but also has coopted its main enemies by transforming the main body of the labor movement into its defenders.

Insofar as the popular challenge to the status quo is feeble, the democratic procedures are irrelevant to the fundamental issues that agitate society. Insofar as that challenge is perceived as a genuine threat by the ruling elite, the democratic procedures will be shunted aside if it appears to be necessary for the defense of the status quo. Thus the lack of consensus on the fundamentals of power in society renders government with the consent of the governed, that is, democracy, either irrelevant or obsolete. The opposition turns its back on democracy because democracy withholds the chance to get what it wants. The powers that be dispense with democratic procedures because they fear to lose what they have. Thus frustration causes political apathy in all its forms, and fear reduces democratic procedures to means to be used or discarded on pragmatic grounds.

However, as concerns the weakness of democracy, frustration and fear are not distinct social phenomena. They are organically connected, one stimulating the other and both cooperating in weakening democracy. Each manifestation of alienation in the form of violence and competitive social structures of counterculture increases the fear for the viability of the status quo. That fear, in turn, translates itself into measures of defense which are chosen primarily in view of their service to the status quo and without regard for the requirements of democracy. Thus democratic government, by dint of its political dynamics, comes to resemble more and more the plebiscitarian type of pseudo-democracy. The people have still the legal opportunity of registering their dissent, and the government still observes the more conspicuous restrictions of its power; but neither provides a genuine choice. The relevant decisions are made neither by the people at large nor by the official government, but by the private governments where effective power rests, and they are made not in deference to democratic procedures but in order to serve the economic and social status quo.

The decline of official government, both in general and in its democratic form, has still another consequence, transcending the confines of politics. In a secular age men all over the world have expected and worked for salvation through the democratic republic or the classless society of socialism rather than through the kingdom of God. Their expectations have been disappointed. The charisma of democracy, with its faith in the rationality and virtue of the masses, has no more survived the historic experience of mass irrationality and the excesses of fascism and of the impotence and corruption of democratic government than the charisma of Marxism-Leninism has survived the revelations of the true nature of Communist government and the falsity of its eschatological expectations. No new political faith has replaced the ones lost. There exists then a broad and deep vacuum where there was once a firm belief and expectation, presumably derived from rational analysis.

No civilized government that is not founded on such a faith and rational expectation can endure in the long run. This vacuum will either be filled by a new faith carried by new social forces that will create new political institutions and procedures commensurate with the new tasks, or the forces of the status quo threatened with disintegration will use their vast material powers to try to reintegrate society through totalitarian manipulation of the citizens' minds and the terror of physical compulsion. The former alternative permits us at least the hope of preservation and renewal of the spirit of democracy. Neither alternative promises us the renewal of the kind of democratic institutions and procedures whose two-hundredth anniversary we celebrate.

Freedom and the Human Condition

Contemporary Issues in Freedom

Societal and Individual Rights and Obligations

Henry J. Abraham

That the status of our basic freedoms, our civil rights and liberties, today is generally healthy—however one may differ on perceptions of degree or emphasis—is due in overriding measure to the efforts of the Supreme Court of the United States. For it was the Court, at the apex of the judicial branch, acting practically single-handedly, that so memorably addressed itself to the great line-drawing issues in the realm of civil rights and liberties in the fifties and sixties—issues that had pinpointed the need for dramatic change along the path of the attainment of justice, issues that had been veritably crying out for redress, yet issues that were ignored—when they were not rejected—with mordant consistency by the two branches of the government politically charged with their resolution, the executive and legislative. True, on the federal level at least, there had been certain attempts to deal with some of them—notably the race issue, which President Franklin D. Roosevelt and especially the president from the border state of Missouri, Harry S. Truman, attempted to tackle in the face of overwhelming congressional lassitude and/or hostility. But it remained to the Supreme Court—to be precise, the Warren Court of 1953–1969—to mark and walk the trail for change. It did so amid a chorus of a good many cheers, but far more jeers, the latter often centered in the legislature—that very branch which, above any other, should have concerned itself with these pressing matters of policy, but which preferred to play the old "buck-passing" game while publicly flaying, even vilifying, the Court in often intemperate language.

Most notable and most crucial among those major issues were race, legislative apportionment, and criminal justice. (They remain crucial, but to a lesser degree, and now frequently in a rather different framework.) The Court's activities have not been confined to these three, of course; there were—and remain—many other areas of note and controversy, such as the prevalent egalitarian syndromes of sex, alienage, and nationality; the range and extent of freedom of expression in its manifold aspects (demonstrations, libel, symbolism, press versus fair trial, national security, obscenity—the latter remaining contentious and unsettled to this day); that emotion-charged, and never entirely dormant, issue of separation of Church and State; and the potentially burgeoning issue of privacy. Yet race, legislative apportionment, and criminal justice unquestionably represent, historically and sociopolitically, the three issues that stood most in need of both public and private recognition and of responsive change by orderly process. In the face of congressional unwillingness to face that need, and of executive failure to possess or exercise the requisite range of power (in all but marginal areas), it thus fell to the Court to pick up what was the "passed buck," once it reached the high tribunal by way of the judicial process. It is to the enduring credit of the institution of the Supreme Court—and to the lower federal courts—that it did so, no matter what one may think of specific cases and situations. And lest we forget that human beings comprise courts—as well as that ubiquitous concept of "government" generally—it is of course a tribute to the membership of the United States Supreme Court, led by the remarkable former attorney-general and governor of California, who was the vice-presidential nominee on the 1948 Republican (Dewey) ticket, Earl Warren, appointed by President Eisenhower, who later referred to this choice as "my biggest mistake."

In the spring of 1969, the then retiring chief justice of the United States looked back upon his sixteen-year record on the Court and identified the three decisions that he regarded as having been most instrumental in bringing about widely perceived, much-needed changes in the law and custom of the America of the 1950s and 1960s. As he saw and evaluated those three in a valedictory interview, they were in his assigned order of importance:

1. *Baker* v. *Carr,* 369 U.S. 186 (1962), the monumental 6–2 acceptance of the principle of justiciability in instances of alleged mis-, mal- or non-apportionment of state (later federal, and still later local) legislative representative districts.

2. *Brown* v. *Board of Education,* 347 U.S. 483 (1954), the most far-reaching sociopolitical decision of the century (still, Warren listed it second rather than first, for he contended that it might not have been needed had the *Baker* principle been on the books fifty years earlier), which held unconstitutional, as a violation of the equal protection of the laws clause of the Fourteenth Amendment, the compulsory segregation of public school children on the basis of race.

3. *Gideon* v. *Wainwright,* 372 U.S. 335 (1963), in which the Court held that the due process of law clause of Admendment Fourteen mandated the application of the Sixth Amendment's guarantee to a right of counsel in *all* criminal cases—not merely in capital cases, as had been the law—by the *states* as well as by the federal government. It was a decision that proved to be the bellwether in a string of highly contentious Supreme Court holdings broadening the right to assigned counsel in a number of diverse circumstances at various levels of criminal procedure.

In these three leading decisions the Supreme Court of the United States demonstrated to the body politic and its representatives that even if the two other branches—inexorably, if understandably, consensus-oriented as they are—were unwilling and/or unable to come to grips with clamor for change that clearly appeared to be mandated by the letter and the spirit of the Constitution, it was prepared to do so, however hesitatingly, and, of course, only within the confines of the walls of its own assigned role in the governmental process of America's constitutional democracy. To be certain, those judicial walls are but dimly perceived by the layman, and may well be of questionable substance in the eyes of the Court's critics; but they are solid walls surrounding the prerogatives of the judicial role under our system, walls built of our noble heritage of the Anglo-Saxon law. The Court's role is necessarily one of a "line-drawing" nature, the appropriate role of the arbiter between conflicting constitutional and legal demands. It is a tripartite role that is not always duly recognized and acknowledged by the average observer: it embraces legal, governmental, and political responsibility. In that role the Court functions and, ultimately, hands down its judgments, judgments that in their authority and finality not only do not—or at least should not—take a back seat to those of the other two branches of the government involved, but judgments—as even Richard M. Nixon finally had to accept, however reluctantly and angrily—that represent the duly pronounced law of the land. Any other course would lead to anarchy.

Inevitably, this recognition raises a very basic, fascinatingly complex, timeless question: is the Court not, has the Court not been, guilty of overstepping its proper role and mandate in engaging in the kind of far-reaching, wide-lensed policy decisions that characterized so much of the era of the Warren Court (and of course that of others, including the Burger Court's rulings on abortion, capital punishment, busing, school financing, and sex discrimination)? In effect, is the Court thereby not engaging in "legislating" rather than "judging"? If so, what is the constitutional justification, if any? Although there remain a few court detractors who would even now deny to the Court its basic power of judicial review—its ultimate weapon—even those few acknowledge, however reluctantly, that the Court must possess the authority to adjudicate, to interpret, to draw lines, to "arbitrate" between and among conflicting constitutional claims. Yet many more students of the Court are concerned lest, in drawing its lines, it "legislate"—a function presumably reserved to those who represent the people by virtue of having been *elected* by them for that purpose (regardless of how faithfully that representative notion may or may not be effectuated). The overridingly difficult problem, of course, is one that is so crucial to any understanding of the continuous controversy that has embroiled all echelons of the judicial branch since the dawn of the Republic: *where* to draw the line between "judging" and "legislating," especially since there is no agreement—nor is there ever likely to be one—on these definitions.

Each of the aforementioned three landmark civil libertarian decisions, as identified by Mr. Chief Justice Warren, has quite naturally been the recipient of charges of judicial "legislating," albeit, significantly, not always or even predominantly by the same protesting groups. Does it perhaps depend on "whose ox is gored," in Al Smith's felicitous phrase? It is undoubtedly regrettable that such basically political and social issues as legislative apportionment and racial segregation had to be adjudicated, if not necessarily settled, by the Supreme Court of the United States and, in response to the latter's "It Is So Ordered," by the lower federal courts. It is also regrettable, although perhaps somewhat less so in terms of the subject matter involved, that it fell to the same body to force the hand of the several states—and, to a lesser extent, that of the federal government—in closely scrutinizing the procedures of criminal law, in bringing more into line with the literal commands of the Constitution the practices and the processes of criminal justice. Yet in all three of these areas the other two branches of government, for a variety of reasons, had either failed to act or, in some instances, while acting did so *in violation* of the fundamental law of the land, as the Court would see it. Ultimately the Court, embracing President Truman's famous exhortation that "the buck stops here," chose to accept the challenge. In one of the last public statements he rendered as Chief Justice of the United States, Earl Warren reaffirmed his deep conviction that the Court "must always stand ready to advance the rights of . . . minorities if the executive and legislative branches falter."

In a sense, of course, all judging is "legislating" and all legislating is "judging," particularly since there is no agreement on the substantive meaning of either of these participles. What the anti-judicial "legislating" protagonists protest fundamentally is the alleged "lawmaking" by jurists who have the presumed duty to "judge" and do nothing else than "judge." The making of laws, so goes their argument, is a function reserved exclusively to legislative bodies, save when aspects of that legislative power may be validly delegated to executives and administrators under carefully circumscribed formulas, and emphatically not a function of the judiciary. With that basic argument no jurists will quarrel. Yet the difficulty arises at that point when the men of the robe render decisions, particularly at the appellate level where, at least in theory, only questions of "law," not those of "fact," are being adjudicated. And, of course, what appears to be nothing more than a *bona fide* judicial decision to some will appear as rank assumption of legislative authority to others.

Thus, to return to the three key areas of constitutional law in the realm of civil rights and liberties pronounced by the Supreme Court of the 1950s and 1960s—racial segregation, apportionment, and criminal justice—charges of "legislating" have been flung with abandon in each of them, sometimes even by justices of the Court themselves. To wit, writing his last major dissenting opinion in the *Baker* case, a 68-page valedictory exhortation of judicial self-restraint, Mr. Justice Frankfurter, that consistent adherent to judicial self-abnegation (he was fond of being referred to as a "humilitarian"), flayed his brothers on the bench for what he regarded as a rank immersion in a "political thicket," compounded by a "mathematical quagmire." In short—if that is the appropriate description here—the lifelong devotee of deference to what he viewed as the necessities of the separation of powers was entirely willing to sanction (although he did not of course support) a continuation of deliberate mis-, mal-, and non-apportionment, for he regarded the matter as a "political question," to be settled by, as he put it characteristically, a "searing of the conscience" of the people's representatives. It is precisely that kind of reasoning, no matter how "humilitarian" it may be jurisprudentially, that saps the hope of those suffering from an unjust *status quo.* Those who suffered here most often, although not exclusively, were the rather considerable numbers of disadvantaged in the cities and, surprisingly, in the suburbs, who had so long faced discrimination at the ballot box vis-à-vis rural minorities often grossly overrepresented in state (and federal) legislatures. Those disadvantaged found their champion in the Warren Court, whose sizable majority here held, in Mr. Justice Brennan's opinion, that the "allegations of a denial of [the] equal protection [of the laws clause of Amendment Fourteen] present a justiciable constitutional cause of action. . . ." And from this landmark pronouncement of the justiciability of the issue there grew in short order the "one man one vote" doctrine, which has gone so far to redress ancient representation aberrations. Had the Court "legislated" or "judged"? It had called its interpretative shots as it saw them under the Constitution, which is its rightful task.

There was no public quarrel whatsoever—although the recorded passage of time has since made us aware of some private reservations—among the nine members of the Court who, on that May day in 1954, handed down their historic desegregation decision in *Brown* v. *Board of Education,* the then still fledgling Chief Justice speaking for his unanimous colleagues in a relatively short opinion of which, as he put it proudly later, he had written "every blessed word." But probably no case in the Court's annals witnessed such denunciation from the outside in terms of "sociological legislating" than *Brown*, with the ironic exception of *Dred Scott* v. *Sanford*, almost a century earlier (1857). There the ancestors of the 1954 opponents of *Brown* eagerly lauded Mr. Chief Justice Taney's controversial decision for his Court, whereas the ancestors of the proponents of *Brown* lashed the Taney decision in language not at all unsimilar to the 1954 opponents of *Brown*. Now which Court "legislated" and which "judged"? Whatever the view, the 1954 Court had ventured forth where the other branches of government had feared or were impotent to tread—and the implementation children of *Brown* are still very much with us, plagued by problems of maturation.

Much controversy continues to abound, of course, in the still very much unfinished and still litigation-prone criminal justice sector. While the *Gideon* decision was rather widely and readily accepted with but a minimum of charges of "legislating," such more or less applicable and inevitable follow-up Fifth and Sixth amendment decisions as *Malloy* v. *Hogan* (self-incrimination clause), *Escobedo* v. *Illinois* (counsel at the interrogation state), and *Miranda* v. *Arizona* (warning and counsel at the arrest stage) met with withering criticism from both within and without the Court. This criticism has not only continued but has accelerated against the backdrop of the "law and order" syndrome which has permeated—and frequently justifiably so—our contemporary scene and, indeed, has resulted in some significant amendatory Supreme Court decisions by the Burger Court. Thus Mr. Justice White, strongly dissenting in *Escobedo*, suggested that as a result of the five-man 1964 majority's holding, law enforcement "will be crippled," police cars would now need to be "equipped with public defenders and undercover agents," and police informants would require "defense counsel at their side." And Mr. Justice Harlan, dissenting from the 5–4 majority decision in *Miranda* two years later, lectured to his colleagues as follows:

> Nothing in the letter or the spirit of the Constitution or in the precedents squares with the heavy handed and one-sided action that is so precipitously taken by the Court in the name of fulfilling its constitutional responsibilities.

Yet it was precisely these "constitutional responsibilities," as the five justices in the majority saw them, that prompted those controversial holdings which were based upon the fundamental democratic concept, initially phrased by Mr. Justice Cardozo and frequently reiterated by later jurists, that "the interest of the United States [and that of several states] is not that it shall win a case, but that justice shall be done." Yet lest we forget, we ought to note that it was the same distinguished champion of civil liberties, Cardozo, who had asked the hauntingly pertinent question of whether the "criminal [is] to go free because the constable has blundered." In any event, unquestionably the main rationale underlying President Nixon's nomination of Judge Warren Earl Burger to succeed Earl Warren as chief justice of the United States had been the chief executive's confident belief, based on Judge Burger's on-the-record public assertions and lower court decisions, that he would be a "tough" law-and-order jurist, a "strict constructionist," a nonlegislating member of the highest bench of the land. In general, the new chief justice has lived up to these expectations in the "law-and-order" realm (though with some noteworthy exceptions such as warrantless, nonjudicially sanctioned wiretapping in domestic cases and capital punishment) and, to a somewhat lesser extent, in that of apportionment, but certainly not in the egalitarian sectors of race, sex, nationality, and alienage. Quite the contrary! Nor could Nixon have been pleased with the Burger Court's seminal decision in the 1973 *Abortion Cases,* a matter that, ironically, the Warren Court had consistently refused to adjudicate. Hence we must beware of oversimplifications. The Court is a complex mechanism which does not readily lend itself, in Philip Kurland's words, to painting "with a broad brush and in a single color."

To be more specific regarding the work of the Burger Court in the realm of civil rights and liberties, how does it compare with its predecessor tribunal? It may come as a surprise, for we are ready victims of snap judgments and predispositions, that, on balance, Warren Burger's Court has in effect been expanding rather than contracting much, although certainly not all, of the work of Earl Warren's Court! This is a fact of judicio-governmental life in almost every segment of civil rights and liberties except the previously noted retrenchment in the criminal justice sector, and some slight alteration in certain aspects of reapportionment and redistricting on the state, but not on the congressional, level.

Thus in the racial sector, although there has not been a hundred percent movement "forward," the Burger Court has embraced areas Warren's never did. Among these are the approval of forced busing in aid of racial integration, based on the utilization of racial quotas; so-styled "good faith" desegregation plans; outlawing of *de facto* as well as *de jure* segregation; and racial hiring quotas in housing construction. True, the erstwhile unanimity on the high bench in racial matters ceased to exist as of the 1971–1972 term of Court, after two decades of full bench agreement on the subject. But that is hardly astonishing, given the headlong judicial (and executive) rush toward reverse discrimination and preferential treatment. It was bound to terminate, given the implications of that trend—witness the remarkable dissenting opinion by Mr. Justice Douglas in the University of Washington Law School Admission Case of *De Funis* v. *Odegaard*.

In the always *au courant* issue of separation of church and state, while the Chief Justice has been undergoing a rather curious constitutional turnabout, his Court, here led by Mr. Justice Powell, the remarkable heir-apparent of justices Frankfurter and the second Harlan, has, at least so far, not given an inch on the basic "no-saying" strictures of its predecessor Court. In fact, as several cases between 1971 and 1975 demonstrate, the Court is being very strict indeed, with only Burger in some, Rehnquist in many, and White in almost all instances, opting for commingling escapades.

In the vast realm of the First Amendment other than religion, the Burger Court has, by and large, either maintained the Warren Court's momentum or accelerated it. Free speech, both in its symbolic and advocative tenets, is getting even freer; association and assembly are getting even more freely assembled and associational, with an occasional Justice Black-like *caveat* toward proscribable conduct, especially in the realm of picketing and other mass demonstrations. The two possible exceptions—and I put it in that manner because one has to await further developments—are the realms of obscenity and the currently embattled freedom of the press. But notwithstanding the cumbersome *Miller* and *Paris Adult Theatre* 1973 decisions, on the matter of obscenity I am far from convinced that, in the final analysis, the Court will not, despite its curious stance in the 1976 Virginia sexual privacy case, ultimately adopt Mr. Justice Brennan's minority position that "at least in the absence of distribution to juveniles or obtrusive exposure to unconsenting adults, the First and Fourteenth amendments prohibit the state and federal governments from attempting wholly to suppress sexually oriented materials on the basis of their allegedly 'obscene' contents." As for the press sector, depending upon how one views the Burger Court's posture, it is either harder or easier for a grievant to sue successfully in a libel case—one's judgment on the presence or absence of "liberalism" hence depending upon whose ox is gored. Also far from settled here are two other subfields: a newsgatherer's right to refuse to identify his or her sources of procured data, the most recent decision by the Court rejecting the privilege by a 5–4 vote; and the currently "hot" issue of how to draw the line between freedom of the press and a fair trial—an issue that probably defies clear-cut line-drawing.

There has been retrenchment in the criminal justice area—especially in that of searches and seizures, confessions, and self-incrimination. Moreover, it is entirely possible that the *exclusionary rule* will find itself modified by Congress in the foreseeable future. And yet there have been "advances" here as well, such as the 1972 capital punishment decision and the extension of the right of assigned counsel to *all* imprisonable misdemeanors.

Finally, what has been the Burger Court's stance in the contemporarily prevalent facets of "incorporation," "due process," and, especially, "equal protection"? In the ever fascinating realm of the "incorporation" of the Bill of Rights—that is, its applicability to the states—nothing has, in fact, occurred since the double jeopardy guarantees of Amendment Five were absorbed in late 1969. Although one might argue that interpretative extensions of provisions of the Bill of Rights already incorporated have taken place at the state levels regarding juries and counsel, the five provisions that were "out" when in 1967 I wrote the pertinent sections of the first edition of my *Freedom and the Court: Civil Rights and Liberties in the United States* are still unincorporated. They are: Amendment II (bearing of arms), Amendment III (quartering of troops), Amendment V (indictment by grand jury), Amendment VII (jury trial in civil cases), and Amendment VIII (excessive bail and fines). In the "due process of law" quicksand sector, the Burger Court has been indeed enterprisingly expansionist, rather more so than the Warren Court. Whatever its rationale and/or justification, it has plowed deep new, not untreacherous, furrows in such due process fields as school discipline, capital punishment, involuntary commitment of the harmless mentally ill, and divorce proceedings—all of which are hardly beyond serious reservation and challenge.

More than in any other libertarian sector it has been in that of egalitarianism, under the often controversially perceived mandate of the "equal protection of the laws" clause of the Fourteenth Amendment, that has seen the Burger Court's most ambitious, and most contentious, pioneering. It represents pioneering that has undoubtedly gone far beyond that of the Warren Court, preeminently in its articulation *cum* creation of the strict scrutiny or, more accurately, the "suspect" category conceptualization. Under it, legislatures must do far more than merely demonstrate, upon challenge in the courts, that they had a "rational" or "reasonable" basis for a law's enactment, which had long been viewed as the traditional, normal "equal protection" test for its birth; they must now instead meet the burden of demonstrating that they had a "compelling" reason for adopting it—an infinitely more difficult test to meet. But judicially "suspect" now, and thus subject to the latter's high-level "strict scrutiny" test rather than to the former traditional test, are "race," "alienage" and "national origin," "illegitimacy," and perhaps (although still far from clearly) "sex." Unquestionably an advanced manifestation of "judicial activism" or "judicial legislating," the "suspect" "strict judicial scrutiny" concept is indeed a controversial judicial posture, one that is both disturbing and fascinating. In addition, or peripheral thereto, are such highly contentious "new" equal protection Burger Court decisions as the 1973 *Abortion Cases* and a veritable host of landmark holdings in the social welfare-poverty sector.

As the Burger Court moves toward the end of its 1975–1976 term, the old but never-out-of fashion line-drawing issue of "judicial self-restraint" versus "judicial activism" gives promise of newly developing controversy, particularly in civil rights and liberties. It represents controversy, both troubling and exciting, nurtured by the now clearly emergent central issue of how to resolve conflicting constitutional rights, privileges, and demands between liberty and equality, free expression and societal protection, privacy and national security, fundamental due process fairness and law and order—in sum, between individual and societal prerogatives. And it may well be that the days immediately ahead will see the most troubling, yet most basic, clashes to come in collisions between liberty and equality, both specifically guaranteed by the Constitution against non-due process infringement by the letter as well as the spirit of the Fifth and Fourteenth amendments.

It matters, of course, *who* is on the Court at a particular time—an issue poignantly contemporary with the exit of the Warren Court and the entrance of the Burger Court. Men and women as justices and judges, are, in their professional commitments, justices and judges; but they are also men and women, not "disembodied spirits." As human beings, as Mr. Justice Frankfurter recognized, "they respond to human situations." They do not deliberate in a vacuum. They neither are, nor can they be, "amorphous dummies, unspotted by human emotions," or "monks or scientists." But as Mr. Chief Justice Warren tried to explain in a *Fortune* article on one occasion, they are "participants in the living stream of our national life, steering the law between the dangers of rigidity on the one hand and formlessness on the other." If this be "legislating" rather than "judging"—well, like other elements in the process of governing, the interpretation of the law, too, may at times be necessarily based at least in part on what Francis Biddle, following his master Holmes, so well viewed as the "can't helps."

Still, there are the obvious limitations on the judicial process alluded to earlier, and whereas, as Mr. Justice Holmes was frank to admit, "without hesitation," that judges "do and must legislate," he admonished us all that they can, of course, do so "only interstitially; they are confined from molar to molecular motions." While, in the magnificent language of the Court's finest literary stylist, Benjamin Cardozo, "the great tides and currents which engulf the rest of men, do not turn aside in their course, and pass the judges idly by," it is also a fact of judicial life that a member of the bench

is not to innovate at pleasure. He is not a knight errant, roaming at will in pursuit of his own ideal of beauty or of goodness. He is to draw his inspiration from consecrated principles. He is not to yield to spasmodic sentiment, to vague and unregulated benevolence. He is to exercise a discretion informed by tradition, methodized by analogy, disciplined by system, and subordinated to "the primordial necessity of order in the social life."

The two hallowed, and all-too-often oversimplified, concepts of judicial "self-restraint" and judicial "activism" vis-à-vis actions by the executive and legislative branches—concepts that are directly related to judicial judging and judicial legislating, respectively—are not incompatible. No matter how an observer may label a jurist, the jurist is never the "compleat deferrer" or the "compleat innovator," although, to a considerable degree, a good overall case could be made for associating such well-known members of the Court as Justice Frankfurter and the second Harlan with the first and Justices Murphy and Douglas with the second jurisprudential concept. However that may be— and it behooves us to be aware of facile labeling, for the Supreme Court of the United States and its personnel are so delightfully complex, individualistic, and unpredictable—the judiciary may well have the last say at a particular moment in history in a case at bar. But potentially it has the last say *only for a time,* unless it can convince the other participants in the governmental process, as well as the people, that its short-run judgment and leadership are entitled to long-run adoption. For the Court may be reversed in a host of ways. If not without toil and trouble, the other forces of the body politic may override even the highest judicial pronunciamentos. Witness Congress's speedy countermanding of the Supreme Court's 1970 decision in the eighteen-year-old state voting rights case. Well aware of this fact of governmental life, the Court understands that it can make its decisions stick only by winning a persuasive victory in the *short run,* by making its case clear at the point of initial impact; for *in the long run,* nonaccepted Court rulings will simply not survive. Hence the judiciary's educational process is an essential one, and, by and large, the Court has done an excellent job in its role as arbitrator *cum* educator, as a teacher in what E.V. Rostow termed "a vital [eternal] national seminar."

Although the Court must indeed "respect the social forces that determine elections and other major political settlements," it has not, and it should not, shy away from acting as the instrument of national moral values that have not been able to find other governmental expression, provided always, however, that constitutional bases for such action exist. Thus in tackling such major areas of public law as desegregation, reapportionment, and criminal justice—those three great preoccupations of the Warren Court from 1953 to 1969—the Court lived up to its role as the natural forum in our society for the individual and for the small group. Even at the risk of pleading *mea culpa* to a double standard, it thus has proved itself as the greatest institutional safeguard we possess. It is to the Court, the judicio-legal process it represents, that the would-be violent, the would-be lawbreaker, the constitutionally despairing, even the impatient, ultimately addresses himself, for it represents the essence and the ultimate of the enunciator and arbiter of liberty, under law, in our democratic polity. The road is a long and sometimes a serpentine one, but in the final analysis there is not only the hope and the promise but the real chance for justice under law, even for such occupants of the nether stratum of society as the famous or infamous Messrs. Palko, Mallory, Gideon, Escobedo, and Miranda of contemporary criminal justice fame. In Mr. Justice Frankfurter's often quoted words, "it is a fair summary of history to say that safeguards of liberty have frequently been forged in controversies involving not very nice people."

The Court's essential function, as Mr. Chief Justice Earl Warren consistently viewed it, is "to act as the final arbiter of minority rights"; and minority rights, often admittedly coupled with minority demands, is what so much of the constitutional crisis of our day is essentially about. Yet it should be candidly recognized that at times both the demands and their response have begun to go well beyond the pale of justification. Thus it is quite understandable that many a seasoned observer of the judicial role has been disturbed by the Burger Court's now well-advanced development of so-called suspect categories of legislation and ordinances under contemporary egalitarian interpretations of the Constitution's Amendment Fourteen, a not inconsiderable number of which are administering a rather disturbing beating not only to that amendment's libertarian guarantees, but also to the First Amendment, which contains explicit, fundamental, indeed sacred safeguards against governmental intrusion. Should, as Mr. Justice Stewart asked in dissent in the *Pittsburgh Press Case* recently, the First Amendment really "be subordinated to other socially desirable interests"? The Court must resolutely shun the temptation to become a prescriptive policy maker. It should always be alive to the frequently quoted 1964 admonition by Mr. Justice John Marshall Harlan: "The Constitution is not a panacea for every blot upon the public welfare; nor should this Court, ordained as a judicial body, be thought of as a general haven for reform movements." Although law does, of course, play a role in social reform, our courts should not be viewed as baskets of social problems.

Still it is to the judiciary, with the Supreme Court at its apex, that we should confidently set our constitutional face. Notwithstanding the 1969 unpleasantness involving one of the Justices—the first such case, let the record show, in its entire history of almost two centuries—and notwithstanding the storms that have swirled about it and buffeted it, and will indubitably continue to do so, the Supreme Court has been our national conscience and, at least on balance, our institutional common sense. It must continue to be that, for no one else appears to be able or willing. Fulfilling well—if hardly without controversy—its fascinating and delicate role of heeding the "felt necessities of the times," in Mr. Justice Holmes delightful phrase, it holds aloft the proud banner of constitutional fundamentals. In that role it will, for it must, live in our history!

Freedom and the Native-Born Stranger

Patricia Roberts Harris

For the last several years sociological chic has led to a characterization of black residents of New York and other urban centers as the latest wave of immigrants. Problems of residential segregation and educational disadvantage encountered by black persons in the United States have been analogized to those suffered by the immigrant Irish of the nineteenth century and to the more recent problems of groups such as the Italians and the Chinese. The premise, both expressed and implied, is that the problems encountered by black persons will be as historically transient as were those of immigrants from continents other than Africa. In short, black persons are urged to understand that they are not uniquely disadvantaged, but are only the latest group of strangers to confront and ultimately to overcome the hostility of those already established in this nation of immigrants.

The error and the central unfairness of this theory is clear: the first black appeared on this continent before the pilgrims landed at Plymouth Rock. The year of the immigration of blacks to this country is 1619, not 1919, or 1959, or 1969. But even if one does not accord any particular significance to the seventeenth-century arrival of blacks on this continent, it cannot be denied that blacks arrived at constitutional citizenship more than one century ago with the adoption of the Thirteenth, Fourteenth, and Fifteenth amendments to the Constitution of the United States. Thus the cavalier assumption that blacks should not feel a particular disadvantage because of problems they encounter in this country ignores the reality of the history of black persons in the United States.

Blacks who arrived with the original English settlers and who accompanied the Spanish and French explorers have been treated as if they were not present during the development of this country, and as if they made no contribution to its history. The black as a historical person, rather than as the embodiment of the institution of slavery or of the "race problem," still does not exist as part of American life. The consequence of the immigrant analogy is that the black person is assumed to have had no existence before the recognition of that existence by the white residents of this country, many of whom have but recently arrived and almost all of whom had forebears who arrived significantly later than the forebears of the blacks who are now called the new immigrants. In short, the black American whose ancestors came to these shores in large part no later than the early nineteenth century is today still a stranger in his native land.

This is not to say that developments of the 1960s, when important steps completed some of the work left undone by the Thirteenth, Fourteenth, and Fifteenth amendments to the Constitution, did not significantly alter both the theory and the reality of the environment in which black persons operate in the United States. It is clear that the 1960s represented as much of a watershed in the history of black citizens of the United States as did the Civil War. The continued refusal of many white citizens to accept the centrality of the black presence in the United States, and their refusal to acknowledge the consequences of the presence of blacks for the development of this country's political, social, and cultural institutions, leads to a distortion of perception of who we are as a people and how we came to be as we are. We have not yet acknowledged that from the beginning of our history to the present moment, we are as we are because some of us are black or have ancestors whom we acknowledge were black.

Indeed, among the mysteries of this nation's history is the racial origin of some of its citizens. Of the Founding Fathers, at least one, Alexander Hamilton, is believed to have had black ancestors (for those paranoid blacks among us, his fate was prophetic), but, in addition, there are believed to be in the United States possibly thousands of persons who live as white and think of themselves as white, who indeed have black ancestors. All of us who are black also know of people who are aware of their black ancestors and who for economic and social reasons deny that ancestry. It has been estimated that as a consequence of this passing from black to white as many as twenty thousand persons a year change from black to white on the census data. Whether this will continue with instantaneous universal computer data, or whether any would find it necessary in a society that made racial origins a matter of only happy interest, remains to be seen.

One exception to the avoidance of understanding of the role race has played in the essential development of the United States, if there is an exception, is the Southerner. Southern whites have understood the symbiosis of the racial identity of blacks and whites, and have sought to prevent the ultimate acceptance, the ultimate integration, that they knew would result from the elimination of the barriers to black-white association. The Southerner recognized that even rigidly imposed barriers to equal relationships could not prevent the miscegenation that was both openly and secretly feared by those who had never heard of imprinting, but who recognized with something akin to instinct that men cared for as infants by black women would not confine their oedipal longings to their natural mothers, and that even girl children bathed, dressed, combed, and fed by black hands could never really fear that color difference unless there were the inculcation of a socially induced fear.

Northerners who have had neither the social inclination (upper-class northern whites preferred white servants, for example) nor, for those not wealthy, the luxury of much intimacy with blacks have little awareness of black presence. It was therefore possible for Northern whites, while dancing the "black bottom," or fox-trotting to "Alexander's Ragtime Band," to assume that blacks were an annoying but not central part of their life experience in this country. Thus both Northern and Southern whites have behaved as though their obsession with the consequences of the coexistence of blacks and whites in the United States has not distorted the democratic experience and induced many of the problems faced by this country today.

A major compromise of the Constitutional Convention was the recognition that blacks who did not vote and who, as a result of their status as chattel, could not qualify as voters (as the *Dred Scott* decision was to confirm) were still human beings and therefore could be counted in determining the population of a state for purposes of national representation. This compromise with a slaveholding South led to a disproportionate influence of a minority of white agrarian Southerners over Congress, the presidency, and federal institutions. This influence existed before and continued after the Civil War. Long after the establishment of universal manhood suffrage and, indeed, of legal universal suffrage, the power of the Southern minority and their Northern allies over federal policies and institutions resulted in unmet needs and a cynicism toward government among a majority of the country's population.

Those who claim that the Old South neglected its black citizens are too generous, because neglect in its legal and ordinary intendment carries with it the sense of failure to give attention to a matter where attention would be given by a reasonable and prudent person. The condition of blacks in the South until the 1960s was a condition deliberately induced and consciously maintained, whether that condition was slavery or the successor to slavery—social and political subjugation. Although the Civil War amendments conferred *de jure* citizenship upon former slaves and their descendants, Southern interests continued until a decade ago to avoid any reversal of the initial constitutional decision to count disenfranchised blacks as voters to offset the greater number of Northern farm and urban labor voters. The major change wrought in the South by the Civil War amendments was the enlistment of white Southern urban and rural labor in the task of preventing the exercise of the black franchise. The cost of this effort is still being paid by the blacks themselves, and by the Northern urban areas to which the South, in the last few decades, has exported the victims of years of deliberate black oppression.

This peculiar status of black persons perpetuated the neglect of the white farm and urban working classes. The inability of such groups to protect themselves in a more concentrated and rapidly developing industrial society became greater after the Civil War ostensibly removed the threat to free labor which resulted from its coexistence with slave labor. Although the claim can be sustained that the continuing mistreatment of the white working class was as deliberate as the mistreatment of blacks, the white working class did, from time to time, use the vote to remedy its problems. Western territories and Northern industrializing states not only enacted protective legislation for workers in general, but also, in some instances, pioneered and extended the vote and other privileges to women. Despite the efforts of several of the states, decades ago, to improve the lot of their citizens by various kinds of protective legislation, the Supreme Court consistently reversed efforts by representative legislative bodies to protect citizen interest in decent wages, hours, and even uncontaminated food.

Not only did malapportionment result in unrepresentative Congresses and electoral colleges whose products were unsympathetic to the interest of nonbusiness, small farming, and labor interests, but it also encouraged inaction in most Southern legislatures on issues of social concern to the working and farming classes. The city of Boston might have been spared its racial travail of the mid-1970s had a more representative post-Civil War Congress carried out the mandates of the Civil War amendments. The power of a newly returned Southern elite, coupled with the venal complicity of a new aggressive Northern industrial and financial leadership, stopped such efforts and prevented the necessary action until the 1960s.

Prior to the New Deal, general social legislation was so limited as to be practically nonexistent. Only in part did this failure to deal with conditions of personal security and basic decency result from the primitive interpretation of such basic constitutional doctrines as interstate commerce power, due process, and federal law supremacy. Congress revealed its anti-humanist attitudes when it failed to exercise its powers in behalf of social progress but exercised its willingness to use the commerce clause to control business corporations—a goal that some parts of the still agrarian South were prepared to endorse along with the North. Antitrust legislation had no direct effect in improving the lot of individual human beings, but it did deal directly with power, a concern never absent from the minds of Southerners and their allies. Even the limited reformist consensus which existed after 1933 faced opposition in a Supreme Court selected by unrepresentative institutions.

What the history of social legislation might have been with the exercise of political power by large numbers of people who could not vote is only vaguely suggested by the change in the character of the Congress and its legislation since the apportionment case of *Baker* v. *Carr* (1962). The slowness of the New Deal to remedy depression conditions resulted in large part from the unrepresentative quality of the

Congress and the Supreme Court. Whatever the still unanalyzed impact of the control exercised over federal institutions and Southern state legislatures by Southern whites dedicated to the maintenance of legal disabilities affecting black persons, private responses to race in the United States have materially altered the development of American society.

The movement of Southern blacks, displaced from Southern agriculture and incurably crippled by deliberate exclusion from the benefits of American society, into cities apparently less hostile to black needs than Southern rural areas, led to a correlative white flight from those cities. That white flight was in many instances an escape from interracial association. Certainly, the white physician who sold his expensive house in Washington, D.C., when the Howard University professor of surgery moved in next door was acting on racist impulses of the most deranged kind. But for many whites the movement from the city was painful and expensive, frequently resulting not only from a racially induced panic but also from an inability to deal with strikingly different life styles or increases in both crimes of violence and the destruction of property.

But equally important in explaining the white flight from the cities was the fear that white children would be subjected to an unwanted black acculturation. Closely related to this fear was the conviction that any acceptance of blacks as peers in the schools would diminish the value of the educational experience for the white child for achieving upward social and economic mobility or for maintaining existing social and economic class status. For the entire society, North and South, black persons represented the lowest rung of the social ladder. Any identification and association with such persons seemed a threat to the class status of white citizens at any social level. Especially was this true for the lower-class whites who possessed a lesser marginal advantage in social and economic advancement. Although upper-class Southern whites and blacks frequently suggested that ordinary blacks were generally better than "white trash," the most disadvantaged white persons, North and South, received comfort from the thought that they were ultimately better than the most successful blacks. For all these reasons, including racial prejudice, whites fled from the cities in droves, and left the infrastructure of cities that supported the suburbs to which they fled with fewer taxable resources and the economically unpromising dependency of blacks who had been disabled by the years of racial subjugation in other places.

Undoubtedly the most dramatic impact of the black presence in the United States has been on the nation's culture. Its greatest manifestation can be found in the white efforts to appreciate the humanity of blacks. Here they soon discover that, whatever the number of people who have deliberately passed from black to white, all are part black. Everyone who has hummed and danced to swing or jazz, or who has enjoyed rock music, is part black. Save for Western and Country music, the most potent cultural exports of the United States to the world—jazz, blues, and the spirituals—are the contributions of the black experience. True, the African roots of jazz, blues, and the spirituals are clear to anyone who has listened to an African drum or watched a group of African dancers. Still these musical forms are unique expressions of the black religious experience in the United States. Even a glimpse of the white evangelical Southern church makes one wonder about the degree to which even that highly segregated institution has been affected by the black experience.

Certainly the presence on the American scene of a black population has materially altered the British-European base of this nation's culture. That such presence has made American culture richer and more vibrant than the culture it modified seems clear enough. But equally true is the fact that the reaction of the white majority to the presence of black persons has in many ways distorted the country's development, stunted its social growth, and given rise to the unresolved communal sense of guilt which Gunnar Myrdal described so well a third of a century ago. Much has occurred to alter conditions affecting the black population of the United States since the publication of *American Dilemma*. In addition to the school desegregation cases, the Supreme Court aided the black cause with the courageous reapportionment decisions which ended the rotten borough system that had for so long reinforced the consequences of the exclusion of blacks from the electoral process. The Voting Rights Act of 1965 terminated the blatant and deliberate refusal of the white majority to permit black persons to exercise political choices. The changes of the 1950s and 1960s, judicial and legislative, altered the appearance of the Congress and of many state legislatures; in ways not yet fully realized those changes have modified the nature of legislative concerns and enactments. The American people are beginning to see the results of an open electoral process.

To paraphrase an alleged quotation of Winston Churchill: "So much have we done; so much remains yet to be done." It is to the question of what yet remains to be done that Americans must address themselves if the specter of race is not to continue to prevent the development of the nation and its people. The two-way transmission of culture that has been part of the formation of this country will not cease. Blacks, Mexicans, and Amerindians will continue to enrich the culture of the United States, as will also the Chinese, Japanese, Vietnamese, and other newly admitted Asians. What must be avoided is the continued rejection of the principles of equality of opportunity and fairness for black Americans.

During the past two decades the United States has altered fundamentally the imposition by law of inferior status upon the black minority of this country. But in so doing, it has made no similar effort to provide for black citizens the same benefits of citizenship available to whites. Many have believed that it was enough, after three and a half centuries of legally imposed black exclusion from the benefits and effective power relationships of United States society, to remove the legal disabilities to the attainment of equality. But others have long understood that elimination of officially imposed racial disability was merely the *sina qua non* for *beginning* the task of securing for black persons equality of opportunity in this society. It did not *complete* the task.

Unfortunately the elimination of legally imposed racial discrimination did not eliminate individual and collective prejudice and hostility directed at persons of black ancestry; it did not end the exclusion of black persons from societal benefits that stemmed from individual and collective prejudice. The assumptions regarding the superior rights and competence of white persons, and the correlative assumptions of inferior rights and competence of blacks so long confirmed and reinforced by law, remained. The debate that raged twenty years ago regarding the power of law to change the hearts and minds of prejudiced men and women still continues to be heard. Whether law can achieve an attitudinal purpose remains unclear. Even if there were no First Amendment proscriptions, laws cannot be expected to change beliefs.

Still law is not ineffectual. The purpose of law is to change behavior, and in no area of public policy is the goal of behavioral change more important than in the area governing black status. In some measure the laws requiring whites to change their behavior in dealing with black persons has changed attitudes. Poll after poll in the last decade has revealed striking change in the attitudes of whites toward the acceptability of black equality. Such new attitudes seem to be related directly to changes in behavior mandated by law. The enormous shift in the attitude of whites toward integration of the schools, integration of housing, and integration of the employment line, as revealed in opinion polls, is striking evidence of the role of legal remedy in changing individual attitudes. Even today's anti-busing spokesmen disclaim any hostility to racial integration, and instead shout their attachment to neighborhood schools.

This is not to suggest that there are no strongly held segregationist feelings on the part of some whites, but the inability to enforce these attitudes has led to acceptance of new status for blacks, no matter how reluctant the acceptance. The result has been increased opportunity for black people to move into formerly segregated situations, and, in so doing, to influence directly the attitudes of white persons. Today, more whites, when generalizing about blacks, must moderate their judgments by references to co-workers, next-door neighbors, and their children's black teachers.

Unfortunately many whites acknowledge what appears to be a reverse phenomenon—the development of racial prejudices from the experience of living in a newly integrated setting. The stories of well-motivated whites who, when confronted with underclass cultures of violence, with formerly prohibited language patterns, and with criminal behavior, develop virulent anti-minority attitudes are well known to all of us. It is also true that as whites have had such anti-minority attitudes confirmed by experiences, they have also developed an ability to discern differences among members of the minority group—a positive identification ability absent in most whites at times of gross racial separation.

But whether or not the culture-clash stereotype reinforcement occurs in some situations, few today adhere to a notion that groups must earn their way to equality of opportunity. Indeed, it may be that patterns of cultural conformity and compatibility cannot and should not be expected until there exists a realistic opportunity for individual members of outsider groups to adapt to the objective conditions that produce cultural identity. Actually it should come as a surprise that so many black persons conform to white middle-class ideals of social and economic behavior despite the societally imposed exclusion of blacks from the mainstream of the middle-class behavior consensus. While avoiding the new fad of preserving cultural diversity without regard to the social and personal utility of such diversity, it is possible that people who have common experiences and common expectations will develop attitudes toward themselves and their environment that are more alike than different. The issue before the American body politic is that of providing such common experiences and expectations. In a society still largely segregated by race there must be the adoption and enforcement of policies insuring that race will not be the predeterminant of economic level and social status and behavior.

Past debate about affirmative action and remedies to be applied to black persons to help them overcome the low status which results from past racial discrimination is directly related to a judgment about the validity of pursuing the goal of common experiences and expectations for black and white Americans. There are many who question whether this society has an affirmative duty to change the conditions that have subjected black persons to disabilities not suffered by whites. Others believe that the Civil Rights Act of 1964, giving blacks—long discriminated against in seeking or retaining employment—remedies akin to those which have been present in established law, has ended the debate. They are wrong.

Common law has long imposed a duty upon persons to adhere to a standard of conduct required by law, and has imposed a money damage burden upon persons who fail to adhere to the standard. Despite the historic use of the remedy of money damages for wrongdoing, there are many today who have suggested that it is unfair to require the payment of damages for racial discrimination on the same basis that one pays damages for negligence. Most white persons find it difficult or impossible to accept remedies for black persons that include more than the grant of money. To require the placing of a black person in a job from which he was formerly excluded and which is now occupied or sought by a white is often regarded as unfair to the white person. Such action has been termed "reverse discrimination." If the employment opportunity sought by a black and a competing white is conditioned by the administering of an examination showing purported levels of proficiency, some assert that the person whose measured proficiency is greater merits the position, even though both applicants show the proficiency necessary to perform the task which the employment requires. If educational attainment is a measure of ability to perform, it is assumed that the individual with the highest educational attainment merits employment.

This approach to the competition of white and black persons for the same employment (and the same theories would apply to application for admissions to colleges, professional schools, and to college and university faculties) insists that admission to a previously denied status be determined without regard to past exclusion from the desired status. This approach establishes fairness by requiring that the decision regarding the admission of blacks to the demanded status will be made solely upon allegedly objective competitive merit. For blacks long denied the desired status because of past refusals to recognize black merit, such assertions of meritocratic procedures seemed enough to assure racial progress. Experience has shown otherwise.

First of all, employers frequently avoid the objective meritocratic selection process in situations which involve interests other than that of directly remedying past black exclusion. But even where there has been a significant effort to utilize strict meritocratic competition in the conferring of status in this society, it is clear that employers circumvent such competition when a superior interest is asserted. For example, in one city recently some citizens urged that the appointee to the vacant position of chief of police be a black man. A senior officer at the time was a black man with a master's degree. Promoted to senior status at a later date was a white police officer whose formal education terminated at the end of high school. The white officer became chief of police amid few assertions that it was unfair and improper to appoint the white man with limited education as the superior of the competent, better educated black officer. It is not difficult to imagine the cries of "reverse discrimination" had a black high school graduate been appointed to supervise a white man with an advanced degree. It appears that the contentment of the police force, both white and black, became an important factor in the appointment of the less educated person. In defining the happiness of subordinates there was present no element related to the objective ability to command, since the black officer throughout his career had been able to command and to achieve the goals of a police officer. The circumstance that led to the appointment of the less well-educated officer was a subjective judgment by the appointing authority that respect for the wishes of subordinate officers was as important as were the objective conditions of education and prior experience.

This reluctance of whites to accord remedial benefits to black persons in circumstances in which white citizens seek the same position indicates that the policy of achieving *de facto* equality for black people has a very low priority in the hierarchy of American social values. It also says that when the choice must be made between the disappointment of black persons, who have historically been excluded from any but the lowest status in the society, and the disappointment of whites, society will prefer the white claimant.

Perhaps the efforts of society to provide remedies for past inequities which it wishes to correct is best illustrated by the procedures it provided for those taken out of the competitive process by the demand for military service in World War II. To restore veterans to the positions that they might have occupied had they not been removed from the competitive process by the demands of war, the law imposed upon employers a requirement that veterans be rehired. In government employment the law instituted an explicit numerically stated preference for veterans. It is instructive to note that only after the unpopular war in Vietnam—which did not accord total approval to the participating soldier—was there a concerted attack on the concept of veterans' preference. Still despite questions from serious observers about the validity of benefits for veterans, there is as yet no revealed intent to remove the numerical veterans preference from the determination of competitive status in employment by the federal government. Society undoubtedly approves of the goal of placing the veteran in a position equal or superior to that of persons who did not serve in a war.

Thus the continued opposition to preferences for blacks which might accord them the status they have so long been denied proves that this goal has, in fact, a very low status among many white Americans. To terminate the distortions of policy that have resulted from its failure to come to grips with the racial issue, the country must demonstrate that the remedying of conditions which sustained past discrimination has the highest priority. To do so it must deflate the notion of the "innocent white" who is allegedly harmed by efforts to improve the condition of black persons.

There are many circumstances in which society does not consider it unfair to require a person, who himself has done no wrong, to subordinate his wishes to the legal rights of others. For example, if the seller of a house rented that house after the sale without the consent of the buyer, a court could order the renter to leave the premises. Certainly the renter was an innocent party if he had no knowledge of the prior sale. But would anyone suggest that the renter's rights were superior to those of an unconsenting owner? This situation is not significantly different from that in which the Supreme Court recently not only required the payment of damages to one denied employment, but also required the employer to place the discriminated-against person in the position he would have achieved had another not been employed in his stead. Thus the right of blacks includes not only the right to employment, if under a court order, but also the right to all of the privileges of that employment in full possession, just as the owner of the house is entitled to ownership in full possession.

When whites and blacks compete for the same job in an area from which blacks have previously been excluded, both are entitled to consideration. But the same social policy that provides a preference to the formerly excluded veteran should provide a preference to the formerly excluded black that would permit the remedying of a general condition. Certainly, the 4-F whose chances of securing employment are reduced because of the veterans' preference is no less innocent than the white who would be denied employment because of a policy to remedy a tradition of black exclusion. In both instances—that of the formal veterans' preference and the less formal preferences for formerly excluded blacks in employment—society has a general policy. It must, however, find the mechanics by which the policy is to be effectuated.

At the base of the veterans' preference mechanism there is a device that establishes a minimum qualifying point at which the veterans' preference attaches. In practice, the same baseline qualification requirement is made of blacks seeking employment or admission to a particular status. Despite assertions to the contrary, there is no evidence that black persons who do not meet the baseline competence requirements for actual or potential performance have, in fact, been selected for any benefit which has been denied a white who meets the baseline qualifications. If fairness requires a mechanical formula for the application of the remedial process with respect to black status, there is no reason why a numerical preference should not be assigned to all black persons, women, and minorities who in the past have suffered exclusion from desired and desirable status in society.

Such a preference would apply only to that section of society in which past discrimination has not been corrected, and where black or other minority presence is below the proportion that could be reasonably expected in the judgment of the pool of formerly excluded applicants. Such a preference would not exist for blacks in basketball or football or for women in household employment. It would exist in college and university admissions; in skilled, white-collar professional, and other employment from which blacks or others are either absent or present in very small numbers. Such a formula would establish the baseline of competence and thereafter a numerical value would be assigned to the status that in the past would have resulted in the exclusion of the individual from participation in the desired benefit of employment or education. It would be assumed that anyone who meets the baseline qualification could perform adequately in the desired task. There is considerable evidence to demonstrate that against a baseline measure of seventy percent performance the objective difference between seventy and eighty percent performance is not significant. When confronted with the difference between the seventy percent baseline competence and a ninety percent competence, a "past discrimination preference" would not change the relative competitive position of top performers and lower level performers. Such a preference system would assume only that when a white and black were equal or only marginally different, the black applicant would be employed because of a past discrimination preference bonus. Thus a person without this preference who scored at ninety would seldom lose employment to a person significantly below in baseline competence.

Probably few blacks have any particular affection for the establishment of artificial baselines of competence, because in so many cases the decision to employ a particular person is made not on objective grounds but on very subjective measures of competence. Blacks in general would permit such subjective judgments if they included an affirmative judgment that, in instances of prior exclusion of blacks, any black who could do a job which was open would be employed, regardless of the availability of a competent white, until such time as the blacks were present in the employing situation in relative proportion to their availability in the general society.

Residual questions about the priority, if any, to be given to placing black persons in positions substantially equal to those they would have occupied except for past discrimination requires mechanical formulas to persuade the white majority that remedial action is not unfair to white persons. It cannot be denied that fairness, like beauty, may well be in the eye of the beholder. There has been some acceptance of the fairness of court-imposed remedies based upon clear proof of past discrimination. But unless every black person is to be remitted to the courts for correction of all past injustices, there must be voluntary affirmative action by whites to eliminate the consequences of the three hundred years of underclass status for blacks.

Black persons will not cease to be strangers in their native land if every black claim to justice and remedial action is countered by the claim of whites that they need not share the three hundred-year burden of the terrible imposition of segregation and second-class status upon blacks. If white demands for business as usual and protection from disappointment remain superior to the claim of blacks to justice and equality, the black American will continue to be a native-born stranger to whom the full promise of freedom is truly to be denied. Black persons will cease to be native-born strangers only when whites agree that it is both fair and just for whites, individually and as groups, to share equally with black people the travail of ending the democratic distortion created by racial discrimination.

Tradition—Or Starting from Scratch

Harold Rosenberg

Artists are lovers of freedom, of course. But in art there is an ambition that goes against freedom—the ideal of the masterpiece. Masterpieces exist or are recognized only within traditions. And a tradition is a binding force, not a force for liberation, the impulse of which tends to be identified with something called "self-expression."

The question is: does new art need to be a continuation of the art that came before, because if it must it cannot be free. It is generally agreed that art is based on art—had there been no poems or paintings in the past, it is highly unlikely that someone today would invent these genres. But how much pressure does the presence of old art exert on the art of the living?

Many of you no doubt recall T.S. Eliot's celebrated essay of half a century ago, "Tradition and the Individual Talent." It asserted that the obligation of the poet was not to apply his talent to works bringing forth something personal and unprecedented; on the contrary, the poet ought to amalgamate his feelings with the ongoing life of poetry as an objective reality, in order to contribute a fitting extension to the heritage of the past. The repression of the artist's natural inclinations—that is, of his freedom to respond to individual impulses—was seen not as an unfortunate effect of a tyranny external to art, but as a fundamental necessity of art itself. Eliot spoke of finding an objective correlative, by which the poet's feelings were transformed into the stuff of art. The artist was given the choice between accommodating himself to preestablished forms, ideas, rules, and aims—and wasting himself in futile flights of eccentricity. Eliot chose William Blake as an example of genius wasted through lack of connection with a valid tradition.

Traditional arts, such as poetry, painting, architecture, and drama, are, of course, much older than individual freedom as an ideal or as social fact. Most of the world's masterworks, from Egyptian friezes to Romanesque mosaics or Russian gold crafts, have been achieved under conditions that placed severe restrictions on their makers' range of choices. In medieval Europe the signature on a painting or sculpture was often that of the patron who commissioned the work and perhaps conceived its appearance and subject and directed its execution.

The high level attained by the arts under traditional controls has supplied a powerful argument to the effect that an inherited body of beliefs and practices is an indispensable condition for excellence in the arts. On the other hand, the social situation of the artist—that he may have been a serf or a slave—has been seen as irrelevant to the quality of his product.

In sum, the arts seem to have been able to do very well without freedom, at least in the past, but not without the support and promptings of a tradition. Paintings were based on paintings, poems on poems, not on nature studies, dreams, or personal histories.

In America founding art upon a tradition has been a decisive issue since the early years of the Republic. For an American to paint masterpieces required that he make himself adept in a style from which masterpieces had emanated. This meant, of course, reverting to the European past—to the Italian, Flemish, Dutch Renaissance. To draw a horse, the American art student had to learn how horses were formally constructed in classical Greek and Roman statuary and in Renaissance painting.

What about actual horses on the farm or the streets of Philadelphia? After sufficient training in copying exalted models, the artist could sketch the horse from life without destroying its resemblance to the heroic beasts of antique art. The same for the human figure: the artist, conditioned by classical casts and by copying paintings in museums, could find heroes and gods in the crowds pouring out of his neighborhood movie theater.

From the eighteenth through the twentieth century American artists have subjugated themselves in rotation to the traditions of British portraiture, Düsseldorf genre painting, Barbizon landscapes, Italian sculpture, French and Dutch naturalism, Paris Impressionism, and other modernist schools. At the end of World War II, American Abstract Expressionism and Action Painting at last broke the hold of European traditions. In the sixties traditionalism was extended in the form of color painting and various Minimalist and abstract tendencies. Monet, Cézanne, Matisse were interpreted in such a manner as to make them forerunners and standard setters of present-day American painting. One recalls the New York School exhibition of the late sixties at the Metropolitan Museum which proposed the thesis that all the modernist art movements of Europe had reached their apogee in the paintings and sculptures featured in New York. The ideal of individual freedom and self-development once again was conceived to be irrelevant to the formal evolution of art in America.

It needs to be recognized that the great bulk of creation in contemporary society is brought into being under various degrees of outside direction authorized by one tradition or another. The products of the so-called mass media, from television plays and advertising commercials to fabric designs, follow prescriptions laid down by the past. In each genre certain formulas have been tested and proved effective in attracting and influencing audiences, and artists employed by the media are bidden to conform their creations to these recipes. In authoritarian societies direction of the arts is political; in the democracies the media strive to produce the maximum profit. In regard to artistic freedom the difference between politically motivated art and economically motivated control is negligible. Indeed "leftist" critics are prone to maintain that it is socially more progressive to manipulate people for political ends than to exploit their tastes in order to make money.

The basic distinction in regard to freedom between the arts in authoritarian countries and those in the democracies lies not in the character or objectives of their media, but in the fact that in free countries it is possible for artists to work outside the media and their aims and rules, and thus to create what they, the artists, not the media managers, choose, whereas in the Soviet Union and other culturally dictated nations all artifacts are produced under media conditions and are calculated to stimulate preconceived reflexes in mass audiences.

In the free countries (but not in modern dictatorships) there arises a conflict between "elite" and "mass" culture. "Elite" corresponds to freely created, "mass" to controlled—or, if one prefers, "mass" corresponds to socially designed and socially effective communication. Those who demand that art be useful, whether they represent media, patriotic groups, or militant minorities, are opposed to elite art. And it is true that, statistically, "elite" art is of minor status, and has little effect on public opinion or the course of social change. In our time, the arts that keep free of the media system lack both extensive popular interest and strong immediate influence; they are free because society as a whole ignores them. Perhaps this is because of their disconnection from tradition, or because the traditions that once sustained them have ceased to exist or to be honored. Poetry, painting, "serious" novels, plays, films and dance called "experimental" (that is, they lack a realistic expectation of financial success) are swamped in the public mind by their media equivalents, and are thus absolved from giving an account of themselves. They are free in being disengaged. They exist, to use a familiar phrase, "for their own sake." To totalitarians and social progressives, such arts represent individualist self-indulgence, related to million-dollar yachts and fifty-dollar-a-bottle wines.

Social and cultural tradition has come to be represented by the media. It is they who identify themselves with the Fourth of July, the Statue of Liberty, the Bicentennial. As in Eliot's conception of poetry, each new movie and TV show is joined by formal links and intellectual assumptions to the entire body of motion pictures and television performances that have preceded it. It was no doubt Marshall McLuhan's recognition of the overpowering intrusion into each creation of the medium as a whole that inspired his slogan: "The medium is the message." Movies and TV dramas are also joined to the past of literature and the theater, and are now considered in our universities in the light of these traditions under the general classification of "narrative." A striking example of how motion pictures relate themselves to cultural traditions and become their embodiments in the experience of today is Stanley Kubrick's *Barry Lyndon.* The movie recapitulates Thackeray's early novel in terms of paintings, costumes, military science, gesture, music, and interior decoration of the period in a single cultural package available to everyone, a vivid "Five-Foot Shelf" that dispenses with the need to read books or visit museums. It is difficult to recall any literary work of today that mirrors the past with more blank fidelity than this creation of Hollywood. In the great art of this century—*Ulysses, Joseph and His Brothers*—there is an irresistible impulse to parody the past and distort it by introducing modern equivalents. *Barry Lyndon* is old wine in new technological bottles, a fabrication that "quotes" the facts of an earlier period as they exist in recorded form.

In keeping with their traditionalism, the media limit themselves to what society is prepared to know and experience. The aim of the media is to convey, not experience, but what is expedient to stress as experience. Media creations permit themselves to be reshaped by the pressures of social groups so long as these are sufficiently large and well-organized to allow them to claim to be representative bodies. Plots and images are changed to correspond to, or compromise with, articulated demands based on ideological religions and ethnic considerations. Clearance officers in the networks and production offices consider the age, sex, mores, and prejudices of their intended audiences. Media expertise in attracting and holding segments of the public, the repetitive formats in which the media incorporate premeasured quantities of time (on the air) and space (in print), are founded on analysis of results attained in the past. Novelty in the media, fresh apperceptions, extend only to details. The media world is a world of received ideas and accepted fictions. Perhaps in their sum platitudes and fabrications do constitute reality of some kind.

Practiced under socially derived restraints, the media, like traditional art, are a culturally stabilizing factor, a shock-absorbing mechanism that shields the public from the impact of the information which the media convey. Images of massacre, disaster, menace are brought into the living room without ruffling the mood set by entertainment and advertisements conceived in the same formats. The media induce mental uniformity that contributes to a sense of security, an effect also induced by art in the past. But the media cannot be considered as an agency of free expression.

The communication of experience in its actual weight and density is left for the elite arts. Were it not for them, America would be immersed in an invented world, not too unlike in its arbitrariness that of traditionalist and authoritarian nations. To the nonmedia artist, motivating an

audience through appealing to a shared tradition is secondary to the
realities of *his* experience. Since every individual's experience contains
elements which are unique, such an artist can be said to start from
scratch. He is aware of tradition, but has chosen to set tradition aside
in the interest of truth. Viewed in comparison with the media, a work
that touches on reality belongs to the avant-garde, and every avant-
garde work is a rebellion. Mallarmé described the modern poet as a
"civilized primitive" (*civilizé édénique*), and primitivism, in the sense of
perceiving things without their garb of prescribed forms, is a recurrent
motif in modern art. Of course, no artist ever achieves a completely
clear slate. But the goal of eliminating clichés of thought and response
is continuously reiterated as a leitmotif of modern art. "I want to paint
like the first man," is often heard among artists—whereas tradition
requires exactly the opposite: to learn all that has been accomplished,
to choose the best, and to paint like the *last* man, the heir of the ages.

In America, to paint like the first man is a desire not restricted to contemporaries. The phrase "first man" has about it the tone of Walt
Whitman's "red Adam," the aboriginal human being, the Noble Savage.
Since the beginning of the Republic there has been a current in American art in addition to that founded on the desire to acquire the skills
and standards of the Old World, a current that would dispense with
those skills and standards and replace them with modes of experience
appropriate to experience in America.

In sum, American art has been divided between copying and adapting
European models, on the one hand, and sporadic efforts to break away
from these models and derive sustenance from the New, on the other.
It is in these efforts that freedom has found its voice in painting and
sculpture. The word "art" or "form" has been considered by these artists
to be synonymous with refinement and decorative disguise, in short, with
falsification. Reality and Truth were preferred to Beauty. George Catlin,
painter of Indians, was convinced that the American prairies provided
the best school for the American artist. Even such an accomplished
American academician as Thomas Anshutz, successor to Thomas Eakins
at the Pennsylvania Academy of the Fine Arts, valued "fact" above style
and believed that fact was to be achieved by intense looking at objects,
not by imitating European masterpieces. It is not uncommon for American artists, no matter how highly trained, to attribute to themselves the
simplicity and unknowingness of folk artists, to think of themselves as

common people and strive to behave like mechanics or regular guys. The leading sculptor David Smith called his studio the Terminal Iron Works as if it were a blacksmith shop; he drove a truck on his travels and affirmed that American art must be crude and unrefined. For him the American artist was naturally allied with Walt Whitman's "roughs and beards and space and ruggedness and nonchalance that the soul loves." Jackson Pollock's celebrated statement, "when I am in my canvas I don't know what I'm doing," may be interpreted as an effort toward a consciously acquired naivete. American romanticism is less likely to take the form of complex fantasies than to consist of one-person realism. For Gertrude Stein, truth in art consisted in getting away from "things as everybody sees them."

The primitivism, real and assumed, of American artists has several drawbacks which must be weighed against its stimulation of energy and originality. As a mode of resistance to traditional attitudes, primitivism tends also to resist ideas, to promote anti-intellectualism and a mystique of aesthetic infallibility. The idea that Americans can produce art without assistance from the European past has fostered a kind of chauvinistic self-sufficiency, especially noticeable in the past fifteen years. Claims have been made that American art has absorbed the essence of the Continental avante-garde movements since Impressionism and has gone beyond them. Such an attitude may seem to free Americans to follow their own course. Actually, it is a form of coercion in contemporary form. It demands that art must begin with the here-and-now of American art and pursue the objectives implied by this art. No room is left for the individual artist's own vision of art and life. For the old subservience to European traditions, it substitutes subservience to an American tradition, moreover one whose existence is dubious. Young artists are told that they need not look past their American predecessors—Pollock, Gorky, Newman, Smith, Hofmann, de Kooning—to the Europeans by whom these artists were inspired and whose work needs to be grasped in order to understand the Americans and their originality. The effect of this aesthetic know-nothingism has been a growing shallowness, eccentricity, exhaustion. The absence of a tradition cannot itself be established as a tradition. No longer dependent on the European past, American art must avoid enslaving itself to a past of its own.

It was Whitman who most emphatically stated the proposition that starting from scratch in the New World did not entail rejecting the accomplishments of earlier generations. "America," he wrote in the ringing opening sentence of the 1855 Preface to *Leaves of Grass*, "does not repel the past or what it has produced under its forms or amid other politics or the idea of castes or the old religions." But though the past was not to be rejected or "repelled," it could no longer serve as a guide. Whitman was aware that as an American he had no continuing tradition able to sustain his poetry, that, as he put it, "I have all to make." One might say that for Whitman, as for Poe, the past consisted of a cultural rubble, among which magnificent treasures might be found.

> Not you alone proud truths of the World
> Nor you alone ye facts of modern science
> But myths and fables of old, Asia's, Africa's fables. . . .

Starting from scratch in the perspective set by Whitman means beginning from writings, paintings, oral histories, as one finds them and where one finds them. Tradition is replaced by a new universal eclecticism. Recall how the art of the past hundred years has drawn on the forms of antiquity, of Chinese art, of Japanese, pre-Columbian American, African. This borrowing from everywhere will continue.

An artist finds works of art in accordance with what he is. The same is true of the public. An immigrant to the United States in the 1890s does not encounter the Statue of Liberty in the same way that a New England art critic encounters it, that is, as a cultural artifact, an example of mediocre French academic art set in New York Harbor for political reasons. The immigrant encounters the statue as a torch of liberation, and as a noble promise resounding across the seas. In his culture, the Statue of Liberty is both an image and an emblem by which his life has been transformed. It is thus a creation on a par with the greatest creations of man, a popular masterpiece rather than an art-historical one. "All the past we leave behind," sang Whitman in "Pioneers! O Pioneers!" contradicting what he said in his preface. "We debouch upon a newer, mightier world."

The individual without a tradition, or, as is common among Americans, with more than one tradition—traditions which are today multiplied by examples and reproductions of works belonging to all times and places—relates himself to the past by means of a one-person

culture which he pieces together from the odds and ends which he ac-
cumulates as he lives and animates by his own undefined personality.
To affirm the essence of his individual mixture of absorbed influences
and primitive apperceptions is to realize freedom. The model for such
an affirmation lies in the arts that have escaped conscription for economic
or political ends. Whatever art may have been in the past, whatever
functions it may have fulfilled for society and individuals in former
ages, in our time art's deepest reason for being is as a vehicle for self-
liberation. "The main thing is freedom," wrote Paul Klee, "a freedom
which insists on its right to be just as inventive as nature in her grandeur
is inventive." Freedom limited only by the nature of things is incompatible
with tradition. Or it is compatible with the modernist tradition of shak-
ing off inherited restraints.

The negations required by freedom are by no means easily attained—not
in politics, not in art either. The old ideas hang on, the old moods, the
old solutions. To liberate the eye, the hand, the mind from their habitual
reflexes requires subtle techniques and heroic persistence. The advanced
art of the past hundred years constitutes an encyclopedia of methods
developed in order to attain self-liberation. One could write a history
of art since Impressionism in terms of devices, theoretical and practical,
employed by artists in circumventing the controls of external form and
interior inhibition. Painting outdoors in the effort to render direct
sensation of scene and atmosphere; application of color according to
system rather than observation; derangement of the senses through displacement of metaphors; dislocation, distortion, and dismemberment of
familiar shapes in order to evoke new feelings rather than satisfaction
in things recognized; rearrangement of forms in arbitrary divisions of
pictorial space, as in Cubism—all these are incidents in the liberation of
art from traditional certainties and from the effects of rigidity of habit
and belief on the human psyche.
    The modernist tradition is the tradition of individualism, in the good
sense as well as the bad. To be an artist, one is forced to choose—that
is, to perform a free act. Freedom for art's sake accompanies art for
freedom's sake. And the morality of freedom requires that the artist
keep on choosing. To stop choosing is to cease being an artist and to
become an imitator of one's own past. If one stopped being an artist one

could relax and repeat oneself, like everyone else. But art is a profession that carries a pledge, the pledge of being free and activating freedoms.

For fifty years, de Kooning, for example, has demonstrated a continuous devotion to the principle of self-liberation as the moral imperative of painting in our time. The drawings and paintings of his latest phase are animated by a spontaneity that surpasses all his previous improvisations and refutes the belief that age must result in rigidity. A comparable growth in freedom was visible in the compositions which Hans Hofmann produced well into his eighties. Picasso once said, "When I was a child I drew like Michelangelo; it took me years to learn to draw like a child."

Spontaneity, freshness can apparently be acquired through training. The transition from the rigors of Renaissance tradition to an art that starts from scratch is epitomized in Picasso's witticism. The ideal and the necessity of the human being today is the capacity to make discoveries within constantly changing phenomena both outside the observer and within, to contrive forms in the midst of confusion, to probe the world and his own consciousness for the raw materials of knowing. Our experience is, as Yeats expressed it, that of

> images that yet
> Fresh images beget,
> That dolphin-torn, that gong-tormented sea.

Within this sea change, there is no other place to start but from scratch, the unique reality that falls to each of us.

Freedom, the United States, and the World Environment

Norman A. Graebner

With its independence two hundred years ago the United States accepted both the risks and the opportunities of a separate national existence. From the beginning geography and ideology combined to determine the Republic's basic objectives in its relations with the outside world. First, the nation's physical security from direct attack required military forces and a government with sufficient taxing powers to maintain them. That security, second, required an international environment which would minimize dangers of foreign attack. The latter objective created two specific American interests: military and political primacy in the Western Hemisphere and a functioning balance of power in both Europe and Asia. Third, the United States entered the world of nations seeking to extend, through example and action, its notions of free government to other regions of the globe. More than any people of the modern world Americans turned their concern for freedom into a national ideology; more than others they identified the nation's security and well-being with the expansion of that ideology.

This sense of mission sprang from two essential factors in the country's early experience: the providential advantages offered by the New World and the political ideology of the American Revolution. Even before his ship touched the New England coast in 1630, John Winthrop admonished his fellow Puritans: "Wee shall be as a city upon a Hill, the eies of all people are uppon us; soe that if wee shall deal falsely with our god in this worke wee have undertaken and soe cause him to withdraw his present help from us, wee shall be made a story and a by-word through the world." What followed—the profitable exploitation of a rich continent—merely confirmed that sense of destiny. It required no more than the amalgamation of opportunity and liberty to convince the leaders of 1776 that their Revolution must serve as a model for the world. Benjamin Franklin spoke for that generation when he wrote in 1782: "Establishing the liberties of America will not only make the people happy, but will have some effect in diminishing the misery of those, who in other parts of the world groan under despotism, by rendering it more circumspect, and inducing it to govern with a lighter hand." The American Revolution, as an assertion of the inalienable rights of man, had put the liberal ideas of the eighteenth-century Enlightenment into practice.

During his first administration George Washington recognized the dangers of placing American foreign policy on the altar of idealism. No less than Franklin and others, he acknowledged that the preservation of liberty depended "on the experiment entrusted to the hands of the American people." Still he refused to commit American power to the support of France's revolutionary cause. Washington warned his countrymen, in matters of foreign policy, to consult no more than the permanent interests of their country. He declared that "it is a maxim, founded on the universal experience of mankind, that no nation is to be trusted further than it is bound by its interest; and no prudent statesman or politician will venture to depart from it." Again in his Farewell Address Washington warned the Republic: "The nation which indulges toward another an habitual hatred or an habitual fondness is in some degree a slave. It is a slave to its animosity or to its affection, either of which is sufficient to lead it astray from its duty and its interest."

Washington's Farewell Address, despite its intrinsic brilliance, did not terminate the debate on the nature of a proper American approach to foreign policy. The sense of mission was too deeply entrenched. At first this commitment to the expansion of freedom aggravated the nation's insecurity, for its early leaders assumed that Europe's reactionary powers would seek to destroy the country's democratic institutions and thereby terminate its mission to the world. The Monroe Doctrine expressed that fear of European monarchy as a burgeoning threat to the Western Hemisphere. Indeed, for President James Monroe the Holy Alliance imperiled the whole democratic experiment in America. With the passing of that European danger the champions of the American experience breathed more freely. To Andrew Jackson the United States was again the confident beacon of liberty. In his farewell exhortation he admonished the American people: "Providence has showered on this favored land blessings without number, and has chosen you as the guardians of freedom, to preserve it for the benefit of the human race."

Amid the collapse of Europe's liberal movements at mid-century, Lewis Cass of Michigan looked forward to a better day. "I trust the time will come," he told a New York audience, "when not a hostile drum shall roll, and not a hostile cannon be fired, throughout the world, if we say, 'Your cause is not a just or right one.' " Abraham Lincoln responded to the threat of disunion by reasserting America's cosmic role at Gettysburg in November 1863. It was for the living, he said, to dedicate themselves to the great task remaining so that "government of the people, by the people, and for the people shall not perish from the earth." This sense of mission drove President William McKinley toward the annexation of the Philippines in 1898. During his October speaking tour of the Midwest he admonished his listeners in Columbus, Ohio: "We know what our country is now in its territory, but we do not know what it may be in the near future. But whatever it is, whatever obligation shall justly come from this humanity, we must take up and perform, and as free, strong, brave people, accept the trust which civilization puts upon us."

Such references to mission were not the actual determinants of national policy. Throughout the nineteenth century the country was preoccupied with a succession of finite goals which appeared to serve the national interest. Such idealists as Thomas Jefferson, James Madison, Henry Clay, and Lincoln were less concerned with the American involvement in revolutions abroad than in the creation of a society in America that was worthy of emulation. For them the United States was no more than an example-setter for the world. Without exception those who prior to McKinley demanded American involvements abroad in behalf of liberty and humanity were not in positions of power or responsibility. Never did they succeed in framing policies that might secure their interests in liberty. In fact, they never tried. McKinley, in defending the Spanish-American War and the acquisition of the Philippines in humanitarian terms, was the first president to affix American foreign policy to sentiment rather than clearly defined national interests. Thus the liberal revolutions of the nineteenth century responded more to the universal trend toward representative government than to the propensity of some Americans to identify the nation's interest with the cause of revolution. But with no support from American external policy the symbolic shot heard at Lexington traveled around the world. It was heard in France before the end of the eighteenth century, in Latin America and Greece shortly thereafter. In 1848 it resounded all over Europe. France heard it again in 1871, just as Italy had responded to it with the Risorgimento a few years earlier. Then the sound traveled eastward, touching off the Russian revolution in 1905, the Persian revolution in 1906, the Turkish revolution in 1908, and the Chinese revolution three years later. Already it had awakened the native leaders within the great colonial empires and laid the foundations for the twentieth-century independence movements in India and elsewhere. Jefferson once commented with considerable truth that "the disease of liberty is catching." To the delight of Americans all of the pre-1914 revolutions represented successful or at least halting steps toward liberal democracy. The nineteenth century not only exerted few external demands on the United States but also reassured its citizens that their revolutionary tradition and governmental principles had indeed established the course of history.

With good reason twentieth-century Americans have identified the American mission with Woodrow Wilson's perceptions of a new order in international affairs. In many respects Wilson's idealism was a continuation of the older dream. At the core of his thought was the conviction that the nation's political, social, and moral uniqueness had assigned it a transcendent mission to serve humanity. America had been born, he said, that men might be free. But in contemplating the damage which autocratic governments had allegedly done to civilization, Wilson gave new meaning to the American mission. Earlier expressions of idealism had focused only on the good that freedom might bring to others. Under Wilson that idealism would serve as the foundation of a new world order based on the triumph of the American democratic mission. By guaranteeing the peace this new order would serve the interests of the United States in perpetuating the status quo among nations.

Wilson's vision emerged with increasing force as the war progressed. If war comprised irrational resorts to violence, perpetrated by selfish, undemocratic governments, then perennial peace required no more than a universal triumph of democracy. "Only free peoples," he said, "can hold their purposes and their honor steady to a common end and prefer the interests of mankind to any interests of their own." Wilson's fear of Germany merely reaffirmed his determination to broaden democracy's base, for German absolutism now appeared to be the enemy of freedom everywhere. Colonel Edward House, Wilson's trusted adviser, reported on his conversation with the German kaiser in 1916: "If victory is theirs the war lords will reign supreme and democratic governments will be imperiled throughout the world." In his war message of April 2, 1917, Wilson repeated unequivocally the goals of his earlier speeches. "Our object now, as then," he declared, "is to vindicate the principles of peace and justice in the life of the world as against selfish and autocratic power and to set up amongst the really free and self-governed peoples of the world such a concert of purpose and of action as will henceforth insure the observance of those principles. . . . The world must be made safe for democracy. . . . Its peace must be placed upon the foundations of political liberty."

During 1919 the country deserted Wilson's leadership, but not his mission to make the world safe for democracy. That goal required not a universal democratic order but an international environment in which free societies could survive and flourish. Even this more limited purpose did not rule out the expectation that countries would increasingly adopt democracy and become more peaceful in their actions. Still, if those nations were to survive and prosper, they would require the conditions of peace and stability in which democracy could flourish. Thus the rise of any aggressive, totalitarian state would reinvigorate the quest for a more universal freedom as the ultimate defense against threats to democracy everywhere. The more acute the perception of danger, the more insistent would become the demand for policies that would eliminate totalitarianism and its real or alleged threats to freedom.

Tragically from that very war which seemed to presage the triumph of democracy and peace emerged two totally unprecedented forms of absolutism—Nazism in Germany and communism in Russia. By the thirties Hitler and Stalin had transformed both countries into potential military giants. Neither country, moreover, shared with the democracies any allegiance to the Versailles order. Still Hitler's aggressions of 1938 and 1939 produced a scant reaction in Washington, for an isolationist America, faced with a challenge of such predictable and frightening cost, preferred to assume the absence of a direct physical threat to the United States while it permitted the Nazi juggernaut to destroy a succession of European democracies.

Yet the burgeoning Nazi threat to the Versailles order by early 1940 committed President Franklin D. Roosevelt not merely to Hitler's destruction but to the creation of a new world order of freedom. When Roosevelt that year dispatched Sumner Welles to Europe and Myron Taylor to the Vatican, he instructed both to insist that any acceptable peace must include the restoration of all freedoms which the Axis powers had destroyed. Thereafter Roosevelt stressed the need for a world consecrated to human liberty. As he declared, "We and our associates . . . are determined to establish a new age of freedom on this earth." Roosevelt, in defending Lend Lease early in 1941, defined the struggle against Hitler as "Democracy's fight against world conquest." With the passage of Lend Lease, Roosevelt addressed the press, "We know that although Prussian autocracy was bad enough in the first war, Nazism is far worse in this." The issue facing the world was clear. "Today," he reminded the nation on May 27, 1941, "the whole world is divided between human slavery and human freedom."

As Nazism, Fascism, and communism increasingly dominated Eurasia, liberal democracy took refuge in the United States. The very magnitude of the danger encouraged Americans to reject, with Roosevelt, the need for coming to terms with it. At the same time some reasserted the American idea of a free world of free people as the only guaranty of a better future. In late 1940 a group of American and European intellectuals, which included Lewis Mumford, Thomas Mann, Van Wyck Brooks, and Reinhold Niebuhr, issued their statement, "The City of Man." America had become the repository of Western civilization. "Here and here alone," ran the statement, "the continuity of ancient and modern wisdom lies in a Constitution. . . . Here . . . the treasure of English culture is guarded, as Hellenism is preserved in Rome."

In February 1941 Henry R. Luce published his famous essay "The American Century" in *Life* magazine. For him the United States was no longer the mere sanctuary of civilization's ideals. "It now becomes our time," he admonished, "to be the powerhouse from which the ideals spread throughout the world and do their mysterious work of lifting the life of mankind from the level of the beasts to what the Psalmist called a little lower than the angels." Shortly before Pearl Harbor American and European intellectual and political leaders formed the Free World Association. In October 1941 Archibald MacLeish published a poem in the first issue of its journal, *The Free World:*

> Be proud America to bear
> The endless labor of the free—
> To strike for freedom everywhere
> And everywhere bear liberty.

In May 1942 Henry A. Wallace restated the issue before the American people: "This is a fight between a slave world and a free world. Just as the United States in 1862 could not remain half slave and half free, so in 1942 the world must make its decision for a complete victory one way or the other."

Roosevelt responded to this revival of the American mission in January 1941 by framing the nation's purpose in terms of Four Freedoms—freedom from want, freedom from fear, freedom of speech, and freedom of religion—all of them universal. Roosevelt's dreams, like those of Wilson, included the eradication of evil, the abolition of spheres of influence, and the triumph of liberal democracy the world over. In August 1941 Roosevelt and Churchill restated the ideal of self-determination for all people freed from Axis rule in their Atlantic Charter.

Unfortunately the wartime vision of a world restored to the principles of Versailles had little relationship to reality. The United States and its allies could destroy the dictatorships of Germany, Italy, and Japan and thereby establish the possibilities for free governments in those countries. But those triumphs required the full support of another totalitarian dictator, Stalin, and a military ruler, Chiang Kai-shek. The war could never result in either a victory for freedom or the reestablishment of the Versailles order, for Stalin had made clear throughout the war his determination to have pro-Soviet regimes along Russia's western periphery, in defiance, if necessary, of the principle of self-determination. Nor could the United States, at reasonable cost, prevent the postwar collapse of China's Nationalist government and the eventual victory of Communist Mao Tse-tung.

World War II carried the United States into the world arena as the world's dominant economic and military power. The failure of the Soviet Union to accept America's vision of the postwar world, anchored to the principles of the Atlantic Charter, perpetuated the country's foreign involvements. At issue for United States policy makers in 1947 was not merely the formulation of countermeasures to offset the dominant power and possible expansionism of the U.S.S.R. toward western Europe, but also the creation of an appropriate international order to replace that destroyed by two world wars. The Truman years from 1947 to 1950 were filled with intense activity designed largely to rebuild Europe's confidence and productivity, both destroyed by the war. One aspect of this postwar endeavor was the encouragement of world commerce through the greater stabilization of currency and the expansion of trade and investment through such international agencies as the International Monetary Fund, the World Bank, and the General Agreement on Trade and Tariffs. These international instruments received reinforcement from the Truman Doctrine, the Marshall Plan, the Technical Assistance Program, and a variety of regional and bilateral economic arrangements. The nation's agricultural efforts abroad triumphed in the so-called green revolution with its sometimes amazing gains in crop production.

Similarly a number of regional and bilateral military pacts, all underwritten by the United States, attempted to sustain the international stability required for economic recovery. Despite the American responsibility for financing and managing much of this postwar reconstruction, the effort in no measure exceeded the capabilities of the United States. The limited objectives of international stabilization and economic expansion marked the perimeters of basic United States interests and thus the limits of successful national action. The Marshall Plan for Europe, the rebuilding of Japan, and the maintenance of a stabilizing military and economic structure, all reflecting the country's financial and technological predominance, remained the essence of the nation's postwar international achievement.

In large measure this body of limited purpose and action lay outside the main thrust of the postwar Soviet-American conflict. Still the burgeoning fears of Soviet power and ideology after 1946 magnified the international burden of the United States in two important respects: it universalized the American sense of obligation, thereby eliminating the possibility of any diplomatic settlement, and extended the size of the American military structure beyond that required for maintaining the stability that mattered. For the gradual globalization of the Communist danger again gave the United States the apparent choice between a universal victory for peace and freedom and the total disintegration of liberal democracy as a world force.

Almost from the outset the perceptions of Soviet expansionism (not directly reflected in Soviet behavior) assumed forms which scarcely permitted any reaction at the policy level at all. Attorney General Tom C. Clark expressed his definition of the Communist danger in a 1946 speech to the Chicago Bar Association. "We know," he said, "that there is a national and international conspiracy to divide our people, to discredit our institutions, and to bring about disrespect for your government. . . . We know full well what communism and fascism practice— sometimes one taking the cloak of the other." In September of that year commentator H.V. Kaltenborn termed the Soviet Union "a ruthless, totalitarian power which is seeking domination in both Europe and Asia." J. Howard McGrath, in a speech entitled "Save Human Freedom," told the Senate in February 1947: "Today it is Trieste, Korea, and Manchuria, tomorrow it is the British Empire, the next day it is South America. And then—who is so blind as to fail to see the next step." President Lewis H. Brown of Johns-Manville Corporation argued in 1947 that Russia "is the dread of every family in Western Europe every night when they go to bed."

With time the threat became more ideological and universal, especially after the Communist triumph on the Chinese mainland in 1949. Former Ambassador to Russia Walter Bedell Smith warned the nation in June of that year: "It is extremely important for the democracies, and especially the United States, never to lose sight of the fundamental fact that we are engaged in a constant, continuing, gruelling struggle for freedom and the American way of life that may extend over a period of many years." On April 7, 1950, the secretaries of state and defense submitted their report on United States Objectives and Programs for National Security, known by its serial number, NSC-68. Again the document defined the stern choices created by Soviet ambition: "These risks crowd in on us, in a shrinking world of polarized power, so as to give us no choice, ultimately, between meeting them effectively or being overcome by them." With that context, the report asserted, "a defeat of free institutions anywhere is a defeat everywhere." For the United States, locked in a global struggle, the alternatives were victory for freedom or defeat before an insatiable totalitarianism.

Perhaps such vast challenges to the nation's will, which came with the political, moral, and technological revolutions of the forties, might have dictated caution in assaying external objectives. Actually the new dangers merely intensified the nation's dialogue concerning the country's proper objectives abroad. No longer, moreover, did the dialogue appear academic. It was now related, it seemed, to hard choices and real events. Again national goals defined in terms of world mission and the deep-seated expectations of unity and harmony as the genuine norms in international affairs aroused the expectations of Americans in the face of obdurate realities. Never before did the American sense of mission appear so limitless.

The reason for this unprecedented response was clear enough. The enemy—communism—was perceived as universal, and because communism loomed as a special antagonist and danger to values which lay deep in the American heritage, the war on it partook of two objectives. The first was security against the enormous physical power of the U.S.S.R.; the second was the freedom of those subject to the Communist system under the dual assumption that the captive peoples added immeasurably to Soviet strength and that no one living under Communist rule could be anything but oppressed. The first objective dictated and sustained the fundamental American policy of containment; the second encouraged the policy of liberation—of bringing freedom to the hundreds of millions who lived under Communist rule. Liberation, if successful, would serve both the security and the humanitarian interests of the United States.

Military containment demonstrated quickly that it would not bring freedom to the Iron Curtain countries. Still the limits of national action did not set limits to American purpose. Somehow the greater the Soviet danger, the greater its vulnerability to American ideology. Indeed, NSC-68 assumed that the United States could arrange the disintegration of Soviet authority without war. It contemplated no less than Soviet acceptance of "an international environment in which free institutions can flourish, and in which the Russian peoples will have a new chance to work out their own destiny. If we can make the Russian people our allies in this enterprise [it added] we will obviously have made our task easier and victory more certain." To achieve this goal the United States had no alternative but "to demonstrate the superiority of freedom . . . and to attempt to change the world situation by means short of war in such a way as to frustrate the Kremlin design and hasten the decay of the Soviet system." For NSC-68 the means lay in military strength, readily mobilizable, which would render containment an effective policy "of calculated and gradual coercion." Such containment, by avoiding any direct challenge to Soviet prestige, would sustain "the possibility for the U.S.S.R. to retreat before pressure with a minimum loss of face."

Such illusions of victory without war characterized the outlook of the Truman administration, and especially that of Secretary of State Dean Acheson. Acheson regarded conferences as occasions for registering the decline of Soviet power and ambition as the United States moved toward the creation of a world which conformed to its ideological preferences. John Foster Dulles, who became secretary of state in January 1953, shared those suppositions, but with less patience. He represented the burgeoning conviction that the United States could, without war, speed up the process of Soviet disintegration. He possessed a deep sense of the importance of moral force in international affairs and supreme confidence in the ultimate triumph of principle. In his article "A Policy of Boldness," published in Life (19 May 1952), he created the concept that the nation had available moral resources that could topple the Soviet imperial structure and ultimately establish the universal dominion of freedom. The time had come, he wrote, to develop a *dynamic* foreign policy that conformed to *moral* principles. American policy, he charged, must move beyond "containment," it must anticipate the "liberation" of those who lived under compulsion behind the Iron Curtain. This new concept of liberation demanded, as its initial step, that the United States shun any settlement which would recognize Soviet control over alien people.

Unfortunately the Dulles attachment to the goal of liberation, like all broad objectives based on principle, either meant nothing or it meant war. Time would demonstrate that liberation meant nothing and that the Eisenhower administration, like that of Truman, would emphasize preparedness and containment.

The demonstrable limitations which the near absence of American power and interests in Eastern Europe placed on American policy in no way terminated either the nation's ideological crusade against the Communist enemy or the presumption of ultimate victory. Confronted with the ideological choice between total victory and total ruin, some Americans continued to verbalize the goal of universal freedom. Walt W. Rostow, in *The United States in the World Arena* (1960), explained why the grave danger posed by Communist power required the triumph of freedom. Any Eurasian empire hostile to the United States endangered democracy everywhere. "It is, therefore, . . . the American interest," he said, "that the societies of Eurasia develop along lines broadly consistent with the nation's own ideology; for under modern conditions it is difficult to envisage the survival of a democratic American society as an island in a totalitarian sea." The 1960 Report of the President's Commission on National Goals observed, "We must never lose sight of our ultimate goal: to extend the opportunities of free choice and self-determination throughout the world."

Thereafter official American purpose was no less determined and universal. President John F. Kennedy phrased the nation's goal in his State of the Union message of January 1962: "Our basic goal remains the same: a peaceful world community of free and independent states, free to choose their own future and their own system so long as it does not threaten the freedom of others." Similarly Secretary of State Dean Rusk made clear that the administration's goal was not merely freedom for the American people, or freedom of one nation or one people from another, "but a worldwide victory for freedom." Perhaps no one expressed this determination more forcefully than did Richard M. Nixon in June 1963: "To the Communists who say that their goal is a Communist America, we must answer our goal is nothing less than a free Russia, a free China, a free Eastern Europe, and a free Cuba. Only such a great goal, deeply believed in, constantly repeated, selflessly worked for, is worthy of the efforts of a great people in this gigantic struggle. Only such a goal will blunt the Communist ideological offensive and regain the initiative for the cause of freedom." Again it was the concept of massive danger that demanded a global victory for freedom.

Clearly the persistent failure of the nation to dismantle the Soviet empire did not reduce the ends of policy; but it sent some men in a frantic search for other, more effective, means than containment to close the gap between the goal of total victory and the experience of limited power. In general those who continued the search found the means that assured a victory for freedom in some form of psychological warfare. Upholding such methods, Congressman O.K. Armstrong of Missouri declared: "Let us realize this great and fundamental truth: That the struggle against communism is the struggle for minds and hearts of mankind. It cannot be won by bombs and guns alone. The strongest weapon that we hold in our hands is truth itself." Such a policy would succeed, in the words of Senator Thomas J. Dodd of Connecticut, because "it is in harmony with the moral principles on which our faith and civilization are based."

Still another approach to the problem of total victory appeared in William S. Schlamm's book, *Germany and the East-West Crisis: The Decisive Challenge to American Policy* (1959). Rather than bargain with the Soviets over the future of Germany, he wrote, the West must grasp the offensive. In partnership with a heavily armed West German Republic, the United States, using threats of violence, must force the Russians out of East Germany. This would succeed, he predicted, because the Soviets would avoid war. The West, having rolled the Soviets out of one strategic position, would gain the momentum and soon drive the Russians behind their prewar boundaries. Senator Barry Goldwater of Arizona, in his *Conscience of a Conservative* (1960), advocated the same formula for victory. Should the Russians resist militarily, it would mean simply that they had changed their strategy and would have attacked the West anyway. Such risks the West must assume, for the mere desire to avoid conflict would assure the eventual triumph of communism.

For Secretary Dulles it was the superiority of freedom over despotism that assured the ultimate triumph of the West. To him the democracies, given time, could win the Cold War totally at no great cost to themselves, for the Soviet weakness lay essentially in the human spirit. By combining its military, economic, and moral assets, the West could exploit that weakness. The secretary voiced that conviction in September 1958, when he said: "If there is any one thing in the world that is inevitable, it is that human beings want for themselves a degree of personal freedom and liberty which is denied by communism. So I believe that it is inevitable, sooner or later, that desire for personal freedom will manifest itself. Therefore we do not accept the type of Communist rule that now prevails as a permanent situation anywhere in the world." What created the fallacy in the concept of total threat and total response was clear. Its adherents, from their conviction that the West could not resist Soviet ideology or subversion, demanded the eventual destruction of the Communist system. But they always discovered the promise of ultimate victory without war in the pervading weakness of that system itself.

Upon examination it appears clear that the Wilsonian concept of mission and the postwar goal of liberation were directed at a common purpose. Whatever the universals proclaimed by national leaders and writers, the actual policies of the United States in the twentieth century sought to maintain as much as possible the *status quo* that existed at the turn of the century when the United States enjoyed almost absolute security at little cost to itself. It is well to recall that Wilson at Versailles applied the doctrine of self-determination only to the defeated powers, not the victors, of the Great War. The British, French, Belgian, Dutch, and American empires emerged from the war untouched. It was the supreme historical accident that Germany, Austria-Hungary, Turkey, and, in a sense, Russia were defeated simultaneously, which permitted the triumph of self-determination in much of Eastern Europe.

Similarly few Americans in the era of the Cold War sought to apply the doctrines of self-determination, with their emphasis on freedom and justice, at the weaknesses in human society which existed everywhere, but rather at specific repressions which existed behind the Iron and Bamboo curtains. Again the national sense of obligation, when applied to external affairs, was directed less at the creation of universal freedom than at the undoing of those powers which again threatened the balance of world politics as it existed at the turn of the century and continued, at least superficially, until the mid-thirties. In general the effort failed. The Wilsonian appeal to peaceful change could not prevent the destruction of Versailles order; the postwar appeal to the Atlantic Charter could not restore it.

Thus the United States after mid-century did not reveal any genuine concern for freedom or self-determination in the vast regions which comprised Europe's former colonial empires. In some measure the reversal in the American role, at least at the level of politics, from the arch-revolutionary to the arch-conservative power of the twentieth century began with the Russian Revolution of 1917. Still it was not until mid-century that the United States transferred completely its historic revolutionary leadership to Russia. Arnold Toynbee, in his *America and the World Revolution* (1962), attributed the change in part to the rise of the United States from a relatively poor country in the eighteenth century to the world's richest in the twentieth. But the American distaste for the revolutionary movements of the postwar era resulted in part from ideological factors as well. Too often the postwar revolutions were turbulent, anti-Western, and radical; thus, even when provoking some reluctant American approval, they scarcely served any United States economic, military, or ideological interest.

Americans understood clearly enough that only nations of affluence can afford to own and operate a democratic system. Preaching democracy to nations which have no means to attain abundance has meaning only to the extent that the United States can export abundance to them. Certainly the United States made a prodigious effort to achieve that goal. It spent tens of billions in Asia and Latin America especially to stimulate production, to improve sanitation and housing, to control infectious diseases. If the results have been limited, the challenge was simply too overwhelming, the impediments too pervading. At the same time this nation *imported* much of its prosperity in the form of cheap energy and raw materials. Thus a more politicized and competing underdeveloped world could well reduce the American standard of living. The consumer economy of the United States required an empire in the form of economically controlled regions of oil, coffee, nickel, and other basic products. It is not strange that Asian and African leaders reacted bitterly, if somewhat unjustly, to the realization that the poverty of their countries contributed to Western wealth and prosperity.

Washington's fundamental decision, in the wake of the Korean War, to hold the line against Communist expansion everywhere merely accentuated the country's basically counterrevolutionary behavior. The United States soon found itself confronted with the ambiguities of supporting "free world" allies which were often repressive, narrowly based, and dictatorial. These ambiguities scarcely troubled most Americans, for the absence of freedom in most countries allied to the United States seemed of less consequence than their independence from Communist encroachment. In its concern for global defense against world communism (assumed to be monolithic in purpose and organization), the United States, with few exceptions, exerted no pressure toward freedom and humaneness among its Asian and Latin American allies. The Nixon administration, finding some dictatorships more amenable to private negotiations and agreements than democracies, managed to strain United States relations with almost all democratic governments while it cultivated a myriad of dictatorial regimes, large and small. Ultimately the quality of regimes supported by the United States, including those of Cambodia and South Vietnam, became immaterial. On July 25, 1974, Secretary of State Henry Kissinger testified before the Senate Appropriations Committee, "Where we believe the national interest is at stake we proceed even when we do not approve" of a country's policies. Human rights, it seemed, did not necessarily serve America's essential needs.

Some revolutionaries have understandably regarded the United States as the enemy of freedom. Dissidents in such countries as South Korea found their restrictive governments so reliant on the United States that they associated the achievement of their human rights with the removal of American aid. Even when Asian countries gained democracy, as did Thailand in 1973, it was without United States help. Nor did democratic governments in Asia or Africa receive any special commendation from the United States. Toynbee, who as late as mid-century hoped that the United States might hold sway throughout the world, attacked this nation a decade later because it had seemingly deserted its revolutionary mission. "America is today," he charged with some exaggeration, "the leader of a world-wide anti-revolutionary movement in defense of vested interests. She now stands for what Rome stood for. Rome consistently supported the rich against the poor in all foreign communities that fell under her sway; and, since the poor, so far, have always and everywhere been far more numerous than the rich, Rome's policy made for inequality, for injustice, and for the least happiness of the greatest number. America's decision to adopt Rome's role has been deliberate."

By the seventies the United States had given up its freedom crusade against the Communist bloc as well. Earlier there was little disposition within the country to deal with the U.S.S.R. realistically as a powerful and permanent element on the world scene. The recognition of the necessity for change came at last with the Nixon-Kissinger policies and the Moscow summit of 1972. What seemed to Washington more important than freedom was the avoidance of war between the United States and the Soviet Union. As Kissinger explained in his *Pacem in Terris* address of October 8, 1973: "For a generation our preoccupation was to prevent the Cold War from degenerating into a hot war. Today, when the danger of global conflict has diminished, we face the more profound problem of defining what we mean by peace and determining the ultimate purpose of improved international relations." Détente required some bolstering of undemocratic regimes and some blunting of American conviction, including the acceptance of the Soviet hegemony in Eastern Europe, but it appears to have abated the Soviet-American conflict, diminished the danger of nuclear war, and opened the possibilities of increased trade with the Soviet bloc.

If Americans agreed that the bedrock purpose of United States foreign policy was still the preservation of the nation's independence and freedom, they also agreed that any achieveable international order would of necessity include nations of differing and competing ideologies. Earlier the United States had ceased to care about democracy and freedom in the new nations; with the fall of South Vietnam in 1975 it discarded its former determination to prevent any further Communist expansion. This decline in American globalism acknowledged the exorbitant costs of global policies and the growing conviction that the American mission of liberation would not and need not succeed. Americans had come to realize that the pursuit of ideological goals on the international scene was an endless chase after elusive gains, leading to waste and convictions of powerlessness. Neither liberty nor democracy was prospering, even where they existed. The Third World, rejecting democracy and totalitarianism alike, supported a variety of centralized socialist regimes that responded to immediate necessities.

In this apparent failure of the American mission there is nothing strange. Whatever its power or self-assigned obligation, no nation has ever succeeded in serving much more than its own interests. Such limitations do not deny that the United States can and should sustain its devotion to the ideals of honesty and humanity in its relations with others. But principles, when permitted to create objectives which transcend the country's historic and clearly perceived interests, will eliminate the possibilities of a functioning foreign policy in like measure. Policy goals unsupported by generally recognizable interests will not receive much credence elsewhere. Thus Washington's Farewell Address remains the only effective guide to national action. The power of the United States to create a utopia on either side of the Iron and Bamboo curtains was always limited, and this fact alone eliminated the nation's general obligation to humanity. Nor did the failure of the United States to create an environment of universal freedom necessarily prevent the emergence of a stable world. For no nation, whatever its strength or ideology, would willingly permit another to invade its borders or challenge its integrity. There are many political arrangements in the world which defy the principle of self-determination. No American takes any pleasure in their existence. Still, the overriding American obligation must be to international stability, for only in that context can the interests of both the United States and the vast bulk of the world's population be protected. To the extent that the nation's considerable physical and economic power has contributed to that stability, the original, limited postwar policies of the United States have served the country well.

Freedom,
the Economy,
and the Environment

Freedom:

Past Meanings and Present Prospects

Paul K. Conkin

Our dearest words are also the most elusive and ambiguous. The word "freedom" has stood for many and varied hopes and dreams; it has evoked a spectrum of images. This essay will restrict the word to its political implications, not to one meaning but to many.

In some sense, the American people rightly associate freedom with their national origins. It is at the heart of most Bicentennial meditations. By their declared intent, the Founding Fathers fought a war to gain or to preserve political freedom. They established new governments to protect or guarantee such freedom. Their writings embrace three related but analytically distinguishable meanings or implications for political freedom. They feared arbitrary governments, and thus they wanted constitutional restraint and due process. They feared repressive governments, and thus they wanted a wide leeway for individual self-expression. And above all they feared partial governments, and thus they wanted secure personal independence and broad economic opportunities.

Although governments are necessary to protect freedom, they often pose the greatest threat to it. Governments can be arbitrary in the enactment and enforcement of laws or administrative rules. Thus one meaning for political freedom is an assurance of fair treatment or due process in all individual dealings with government, and particularly in the crucial area of criminal prosecution. Newly independent Americans sought such fairness through a new and highly original use of constitutional process. They took quite literally the old doctrine of popular sovereignty. The people of a community, they insisted, by right have and retain all ultimate power. The people rightly determine the form of, and delegate all powers to, their government. They did this in America by convening conventions to draft constitutions, by insisting upon popular ratification, by reserving the right to amend, and by according a special controlling status in their courts to constitutional law. Not only did they try to limit government by specific delegation, but also they incorporated into their new constitutions many revered safeguards already present in the English common law. Americans know and revere these procedures: early and open indictment of the accused, no ex post facto laws, no forced self-incrimination, no double jeopardy, the confrontation of witnesses, no unreasonable searches and seizures, no excessive fines and bail, no cruel and unusual punishments, the right of counsel, and the right to a trial by an impartial jury.

A second meaning of political freedom—a large leeway for individual self-expression—is today most familiar because most emphasized. Here the concern is too much government, or socially unjustified governmental intrusion into areas of private conscience and expression. Expression freedoms include religious toleration, free speech and press, rights of assembly and petition, a wide selection in the use of productive and consumer property, and, as a catchall, a wide choice in personal life style.

Such expressive freedoms are consistent with, but not necessary to, fairness and due process. One may enjoy a scrupulous and equal enforcement of laws under a government, yet live under laws that severely restrict one's opportunity for self-expression. The early Puritans, for example, honored due process, yet they tried to maintain an ordered and homogeneous society, with a common religious faith, clearly regulated economic roles, a required respect for properly constituted political leadership, and a highly disciplined and responsible life style. They wanted no freedom for diverse religious sects, for fractious political parties, or for socially destructive uses of property. They wanted no license for anyone to say or print whatever he wanted to inflict on an impressionable public. The Puritan views were not that different, or that much more repressive, than the views that still prevail in extremely parochial and homogeneous villages. And even in the country's pluralistic society, where widely different tastes and preferences are the norm, a vast majority of Americans still agree on some canons of expressive responsibility. The courts still prosecute for slander and libel and uphold some remaining rules against obscenity; laws provide indirect subsidies and advantages for certain religious organizations, penalize or strictly regulate some types of economic activity, and, perhaps more than ever before, try to discourage personally harmful modes of consumption.

The third meaning of freedom—personal liberty or independence—was most fundamental in the eighteenth century. Its meaning is much more difficult to grasp today, because of major shifts in social realities. This concept of freedom gained much of its meaning from widely held American images of European government and society as aristocratic and class ridden. There, government favoritism to a few created varying degrees of servility for the many. Most often, the working people of Europe were exploited peasants or wage-dependent employees, subject to the patronage of their superiors. A government was tyrannical to the extent that its policies abetted such servility and limited economic opportunity. A person, to be free, had to escape any unequal dependence on others and had to enjoy on an equal basis every benefit and protection of government.

This concern for personal independence provided the central themes of the Declaration of Independence. It found expression in the two unalienable rights of liberty and property, and embodied the meaning of the phrase "all men are created equal." Children are born unequal in so many respects—in genetic endowment and subsequent abilities, in their chance for loving parental care, in their enjoyment of material comfort or a superior education. These disabilities are largely beyond political remedy. But how much more oppressive if these join with inherited legal disabilities, such as an unequal claim upon a father's inheritance, a permanent exclusion from political participation, a lesser claim upon government services, no assured access to the resources of nature, no opportunity to own and manage tools of production, no protected and prior claim to the products of one's own honest labor. These types of inequality result not from nature or from accident but from human choice. They are political, and thus subject to political amelioration.

Americans easily misunderstand to what extent those of the revolutionary era sought to gain or to preserve this form of freedom and equality, and how quickly they tried to abolish the final vestiges of a hated European class system. For at least two generations, American politicians, as well as such perceptive visitors as Alexis de Tocqueville, continually argued that laws against titles of nobility, and the repeal of entail and primogeniture laws, however symbolic or even because of their symbolism, still clearly marked the most important internal changes made in America during the revolutionary period—changes second in their significance only to the successful overthrow of British authority. Americans boasted of a new political order that made possible a nation of property-owning freemen. Here there would be no special privilege, no large monopolistic estates based on laws of descent, and, slavery excepted, no large class of people excluded from ownership of the means of production. There would be no trading companies, basking in special government charters or franchises. At least all white males, despite a wide range of ability and varied levels of attained wealth, would be of one social class—the proprietary. Each man would eventually be able to own his own farm, shop, or ship. He would thus be free and independent, in control of his own life, under no lord or boss. And, indeed, an overwhelming majority of white men (about 90 percent) remained self-employed as late as 1800. Today, less than 10 percent of the workforce is self-employed.

This suggests the magnitude of change over two hundred years. Eighteenth-century definitions of freedom remain as an intellectual heritage. But in our changed society, this legacy may no longer function as a live, moral heritage, for many citizens may no longer value one or another of these formerly cherished freedoms. And even if they do, they need to ask what each means in this age, and what institutions are now necessary to protect or realize them. As a preface to such complex issues, this essay surveys the shifts over two hundred years in the context and operative meaning of political freedom in America. This task is easiest for due process and expressive freedoms. At least in a formal sense, Americans now enjoy fairer governmental procedures, and more toleration for diverse life styles, than ever before. From the Puritan concern for social solidarity and enforced, narrowly defined behavioral norms, they have come close to a completely open society, at least insofar as they use the law to control private belief and expression.

Contrary to many well-entrenched myths, the revolutionary generation was almost as close to Puritan ideas of responsible expression as to contemporary ideas of tolerance. Verbally, it was at one with the present in affirming freedom of religion, speech, press, assembly, and petition. But few people in the eighteenth century meant as much as we do by such freedoms. Almost everyone then expected a much higher and more uniform standard. None of the first thirteen states ever contemplated overt persecution for religious belief; all accepted religious toleration. Yet practically every early state constitution contained religious disabilities—for atheists, Unitarians, Catholics, or Jews. Three New England states continued tax support for a favored church. Any conception of complete separation of church and state remained far in the future, although the very diversity at the local level made it inappropriate for a federal government to show any religious favoritism.

Likewise, no American state dared impose prior restraints on speech, press, or assembly. Not one ever contemplated state censorship. Yet, even as in Britain, state courts continued to enforce stringent standards of responsibility, as reflected in continued prosecution for seditious libel and slander well into the nineteenth century. Only in 1790 did the new Pennsylvania constitution first make truth an allowable defense in libel action, although a maverick jury had accepted this principle as far back as the Zenger case of 1733. The states continued to enact rigid laws against blasphemy, profanity, and obscenity, a few of which may still be enforceable. To our forefathers, individual conduct seemed wrought with grave social implications not only when it directly, physically curtailed the rights of other people (a necessary limit on individual expression even today), but also when it violated communal sensibilities, a position reflected in a whole range of laws minutely regulating sexual conduct.

But even by 1787 one lesson was already clear. The degree of desirable and even possible legislative control over individual expression varied at each level of government. In a small, homogeneous, exclusive community, such as a Puritan town, narrow but consensual norms might be necessary for any clear sense of communal purpose and unity. Either by clear and explicit laws, or by arbitrary public opinion, such communities usually limited basic dissent or deviance. But even New England Puritans realized that they were a hated religious minority in the British empire, and thus they fought for a broader imperial tolerance of local differences. A cosmopolitan or federal government, fulfilling only these governmental needs common to several quite diverse communities, could not act like a local government. If it imposed a single standard of acceptable belief or permitted behavior, it became, by necessity, a tyrannical government for most member communities. Diversity required toleration, forbearance, or coexistence.

Here was the source of the early American idea of a federation of liberty, yet a federation almost inevitably made up of varied and sometimes intolerant local communities. Minorities excluded from local communities had one consolation—they could usually find their own fulfilling niche somewhere in the vast expanse of America, confident that they would not be forced into an unwanted conformity by the imperial center. But at whatever level a government encompassed diverse beliefs or life styles, it was almost compelled to become tolerant of differences. A few early colonies, most notably Rhode Island, New York, and above all Pennsylvania, set a precedent for later federal practice. These colonies embraced diversity from the very beginning. For example, Pennsylvania had a wide toleration for religious differences, and early made provision for such tender matters of conscience as pacifism and nonoath taking. By the Constitutional Convention of 1787, only delegates reflecting the most archaic parochialism believed the federal government should intrude itself in such areas as religion, press, speech, or assembly, either to set federal standards or to force an unwanted tolerance upon state governments. No uniform rules could be fair. Let the states decide these issues. The Constitutional Convention not only refused to delegate any power in such sensitive areas, but also the new Congress and then three-fourths of the states quickly ratified the First Amendment, which explicitly set limits on federal action.

But change came with time. The conflict over slavery revealed a growing sense, at least in the North, of one national community, united in all its organic parts and collectively responsible to the same high moral standard. Slavery was a standing affront to most national ideals. Besides, on slavery the federal government went well beyond metropolitan restraint; its policies at several points protected slavery. Being complicit in slavery, national policies reinforced a sense of communal guilt and provoked communal efforts to right a horrible wrong. At the end of the costly attempt to right this wrong came the Fourteenth Amendment, which created a national as well as state citizenship. By twentieth-century interpretations of its due process clause, it extended

First Amendment protection to people against state and local governments.

This profound constitutional shift has changed the whole role of the federal government. It has become the guarantor of both procedural and expressive freedoms, a court of last resort for suffering minorities at the local level. At the same time, extended interpretations of federal authority under the interstate commerce and general welfare clauses, and a veritable explosion in the range and magnitude of federal tax grants and services, eventually made almost any local issue also a federal concern. In the twentieth century the United States finally became one nation in legal rights and standards. This has meant a wholesale extension of federal standards of tolerance into local communities, to the immense relief of suffering minorities, but not without determined resistance from local majorities, as illustrated by such a sensitive issue as prayers in the public school.

This nationalization of expressive freedom and due process has dramatically changed American society. Until a decade or so ago, local and state governments seemed responsible for the most grievous repression of minorities and effective denials of due process. Relief lay in the federal courts, or in federal police power. Any fair appraisal of twentieth-century history cannot deny that, by and large, the federal government has more often taken the lead in protecting and extending expressive and procedural rights than have local governments. But we have all but reached the end of that story. It is difficult to imagine any major new federal initiatives against what seems, from the perspective of cosmopolitan opinion, the remaining bastions of local bias, intolerance, and prejudice. Such local opinion must now win its way by informal modes of influence, not through the legal system.

First Amendment freedoms and procedural rights seem sufficient to guarantee national standards of openness and tolerance. Yet the immediate future will be a period of fuller enforcement of existing federal laws, continued local assimilation of such laws, and major court decisions, possibly accompanied by minor strategic retreats from complete and uniform openness. We see at least a minor retreat in the present posture of the Supreme Court. For example, the federal courts have relaxed a few of the most stringent protections for newly arrested criminals, deferred somewhat to local standards on obscenity, and moved back from an earlier rigidity on church-state issues. This has accompanied a seeming change in cultural fashions. Ethnicity, sectarianism, and localism are back in vogue; problems of self-identity, of the realization of community solidarity, and a zeal for personal privacy now seem as important concerns as individual self-expression. A regained appreciation of standards and a new concern for order and discipline (reminiscent of the fifties) have accompanied a decline in the number of frontal assaults on the few remaining local or national barriers to uninhibited self-expression. In part, this is because there are so few limits to oppose, so few forms of expression that remain shocking or seem subversive.

If the American public desires due process and complete expressive freedom, then should it not be completely happy with our national achievement? Not necessarily. Three growing concerns have dampened much of the exhilaration. First, despite federal guarantees of due process and elaborate rules to safeguard the innocent, the nation has not achieved equal justice for all. Second, many citizens understand once again that the same powerful federal government, which could be such an effective tool for eliminating local repression, may itself become the most important repressor. Finally, the conditions of modern mass society have helped nullify the significance of certain expressive freedoms. We can say or publish what we want, but who is listening? The village soapbox and the small-town newspaper no longer shape even local opinion. Large news services and the national television networks have a near monopoly over public opinion. Any access to these media is limited to the few with great wealth or great ability. From a national perspective, local voices of dissent are of no great consequence; most quickly exhaust themselves in sheer futility.

It is extremely difficult to assess the present status of the third and, in the past, most fundamental meaning of freedom—personal independence. Tremendous changes in American society have transformed almost all the conditions of this largely economic form of freedom. Only one shift is clear and unclouded by ambiguities—a much greater share of Americans can now claim the right to be "equally free and independent," to use the phrase from our earliest declarations of right. In 1776 only adult white males who owned property qualified as free persons. Women, children, servants, slaves, Indians, nonpropertied wage workers, and criminals were ineligible. Americans believed generally that children were naturally dependent, and thus rightfully subject to parents. Males perceived women as naturally dependent, rightfully subject to parents or to husbands. Likewise, men without productive property could hardly be independent, masters of their own lives. Many, but not all, Americans believed blacks and Native Americans naturally dependent, either because of racial inferiority or because of cultural backwardness. Today, in the wake of over a century of struggle, women, blacks, and Native Americans have largely established their legal equality with white males. Soon after the War for Independence, the states began to drop all but minor property requirements for the franchise, which gradually became the clearest token of full citizenship. Finally, although American society still deprives convicted criminals of freedom and independence, it has gradually decriminalized several types of behavior. This has not been very significant numerically but all-important to beneficiaries from nineteenth-century debtors to contemporary homosexuals.

These legal shifts, coupled with an apparent decline in most forms of social deference, suggest that the United States has finally come close to attaining one of its great national goals—a society without formal class divisions, without any legally anchored forms of dependence or servility. Today all are liberated save children, and do not be surprised when they mount crusades to further lower the voting age, the drinking age, or the age of legal competence. But, again, self-congratulations may not be in order. One can argue either that this advance of liberty has been a hollow achievement, based on false values, or that behind the legal but increasingly empty forms of freedom most people are in actual fact dependent and servile.

In 1776, as today, the opponents of a society in which every adult is equally free and independent defended an older, more traditional form of society. To them, a structured and accepted class system, as well as subtle, personalized forms of dependence, seemed neither unnatural nor arbitrary. Given varied abilities and talents, only an organic, interdependent society could lead to the fullest measure of human happiness and fulfillment. An atomized society, made up of lonely, purportedly free individuals, could lead only to extreme personal alienation and social fragmentation. For example, such advocates of a hierarchical and communal society might argue today that a newly won but largely abstract equality for women will surely undermine the last truly supportive and organic community left in a troubled America—the nuclear family. This view reflects the preference of, at best, a tiny minority in America. But the reverse judgment—that despite all their hopes and illusions, Americans live in a society laced with special privilege and comprised largely of dependent and servile workers—seems to be winning increasing support in this Bicentennial year. It is, for example, the major theme of the People's Revolutionary Bicentennial Commission. Admittedly, almost all Americans have presumptive control over their own lives. They enjoy such valued tokens of citizenship as a franchise, and have an equal claim to governmental protection and services. Yet in a very complex, largely collective economy, they may suffer the types of interdependence that lead not to cooperative equality but to all manner of demeaning dependency. Nine of ten Americans do not own and manage productive property. Most must work in hierarchically managed corporations or government agencies. To have any bargaining power over the conditions and returns of their work, they must become members of hierarchically organized professional societies or labor unions. All Americans live under an increasingly paternal government which, often without intent, supports growing forms of dependence rather than individual or communal independence. Today, it is almost impossible to avoid unequal and intimidating relationships affected with at least some of the nuances and tensions that typified past ties between masters and servants.

Few people today enjoy what seemed, in 1776, the minimal condition of freedom—a realistic opportunity to control productive property and to dispose of their own labor. A modern disciple of Jefferson would lament the return to a type of serfdom, to a system of overlords and dutiful servants. The corporation or the government agency is the modern manor; the small managerial class, the modern nobility. The proprietary ideal now haunts only our nostalgic memories; it lingers in the atavistic rhetoric of politicians still extolling the few remaining family farms or independent businessmen, or in corporation executives who still extol an almost nonexistent free enterprise. Today, in a nonpropertied society, Americans seek fulfillment not primarily in ownership and management but in consumption. The nation's citizens once dreamed of a society that could dispense with other than temporary wage employment, with all its dependent and servile implications. Today, we set full employment as a national goal. To note the present, highly collectivized economy is to implicate the whole vast story of industrial change in America, change that came with overwhelming rapidity only in the twentieth century.

Two broad, complex policies were most basic in the gradual narrowing of proprietary opportunity. The first involved land, defined in its broadest economic sense. Governments—colonial, state, and federal—rapidly and generously transferred common natural resources to private individuals and corporations. The purpose seemed laudable—needed public revenues, rapid economic development, and, irony of ironies, increased proprietary opportunity. But except for some short-lived efforts by early Puritans, the adopted policies usually involved no conditions of access—no requirement of need, no rules for responsible use, no limits on amount owned, no public retention of the social increment. Such policies would lead to later scarcity and exclusion. They insured that later generations would pay dearly not for the improvements made by earlier owners but for primary access to their share of a common natural inheritance.

The second basic policy involved capital. The limited liability corporation is perhaps the greatest single example of special class privilege in our history. The corporate form allowed individuals, already blessed with competitive advantages because of their savings or credit ratings, to pool their wealth or credit in large aggregates, with limited liability and a type of legal immortality. They thus enjoyed all the competitive advantages of expensive and sophisticated technology, detailed labor specialization, new degrees of market control, and large economies of scale. Such exceptional, politically secured corporate advantages severely restricted entrepreneurial opportunities for individual or cooperative enterprise. More and more people of necessity gave up a proprietary role in exchange for a type of wage employment that allowed neither ownership nor management. But collective enterprise did require a form of cooperation and mutuality so lacking in a proprietary society. In a modern corporation thousands of people blend their contributions in order to attain a few goals. The corporation thus provided the form, and the agency, for a new type of communal life, although it was a hierarchical rather than an equalitarian form of communalism. And, it now seems certain, only this or some alternative form of economic association could have assured our present level of prosperity, or possibly even the survival of the country's present large population.

The change from a propertied society, and thus one that maximized individual independence, to a corporate economy, with complex relationships and many levels of dependence, came so gradually that public understanding always lagged behind realities. The proprietary ideal, the celebration of property and individual enterprise, the dream of equal economic opportunity, still shapes political rhetoric. In the perspective of these older conceptions of liberty, the large corporation was an alien institution in America, and indeed so recognized by an unending series of critics. Yet by the 1920s a majority of Americans seemed willing to accept, if not yet applaud, corporate enterprise. By the thirties, two equally alien but necessary correlates of pooled capital—large labor unions and a regulatory and welfare state—also gained begrudging public acceptance.

Any fair appraisal of the contemporary economy, and its relationship to personal freedom and equality, must embrace a staggering complexity. No easy generalizations fit. Above all, one must not confront the present with glowing, nostalgia-colored stereotypes of a proprietary past. No doubt the individual proprietor was more independent than a factory employee or even a corporate executive, but at what cost in economic insecurity and hardship? Besides, proprietary status still remains an option for some people. From early land policies to a present solicitude for family farmers and small businessmen, the federal government has always balanced off some of its favors to corporate producers. And even within the emerging corporate system, very capable people had, if anything, enhanced opportunities for high achievement along with a managerial role. Even today, the very large and impersonal corporation is not the rule; large firms still employ less than half of the workforce. At least well into the twentieth century most native-born Americans had, or had good prospects for, proprietary roles. The most dramatic changes came after 1920, with a veritable revolution in agricultural productivity and the constant shrinking of the number of self-employed farmers. Only now are family farms, and the remaining bastions of individual enterprise in retailing or services, finally succumbing either to corporate integration or to semicorporate management in contract farming or franchised dealerships.

More important, older images of master-servant relationships fit only the most lowly and unprotected types of employment. Few workers feel servile. Even with the earliest development of factory production in the nineteenth century, unpropertied workers already enjoyed the vote and would soon gain free public education, or what even then seemed either full or partial compensations for a loss of access to property and management. Even as a majority of Americans moved into the employee class in the early twentieth century, conditions of employment steadily improved. Increased productivity and secure profits permitted corporate benevolence. Consumption soared. Both unions and federal policies forced new wage and work standards upon employers. Today, salaried and highly skilled workers rarely feel the heavy hand of a boss or display any cringing deference. Finally, federal and state governments take one-third of the final product, and, in recirculating it, variously redistribute it. The redistributed gains go as often to the top as to the bottom, but the principle is clear: today governments are the final arbiters of real income, and to this extent Americans have a politicized economy. But it is clear that political intervention has so far worked to alleviate the worst abuses of economic subordination, to create benevolent masters, not to assure any but a minority of Americans a masterless and truly independent status.

Beyond the present status of political freedom are profound moral and philosophical issues. These will provide the themes for a final section of this essay.

Early American writers seemed to assume that all normal people, or at least all normal adult white males, both desired and deserved all three forms of political freedom. They also assumed the ultimate primacy of the individual, however much he found fulfillment in social relationships. This did not mean, even in a more parochial eighteenth century, that such freedoms had the exact same practical implication in every cultural context, or that it was ever easy to move from broad moral principles to appropriate legislation. But the Founding Fathers did assume enough common human needs, and enough common problems in organizing a political society, to justify an objective and universally valid moral defense of political freedom.

Except for the more extreme degrees of expressive freedom, such a defense lay, ready made and fully developed, in the main body of Western moral philosophy, and particularly in matured seventeenth- and eighteenth-century concepts of natural law and right. According to this tradition, any arbitrary, repressive, or enslaving government was tyrannical and wrong. It violated an objective standard of right, and by so doing released its citizens from any obligation. Political freedom seemed an essential attribute of man, necessary for any human happiness and fulfillment. If right prevailed, everyone would enjoy such freedom. It was in this sense, a now almost archaic and nonlegal sense, that such freedoms constituted "rights." The primary reason for having government was to protect such rights. If any government adhered to moral principles, it had to respect and protect them.

What arguments vindicate such rights? If one reads the polemical literature that preceded the American Revolution, two interacting and traditional arguments predominate. One appealed to authority; the other to utility. Reality, or what unalterably is, seemed the ultimate basis of political freedom and for all universally valid rules of human conduct. Such rules were surely rooted in God, in His orderly creation, and above all in the more constant needs and aspirations of man. Thus such rules or standards were morally unalienable. The autonomy and worth of a person was not a gift of man or a product of political choice. It was a birthright, and in some sense sacred. Individual rights were in no sense "democratic," subject to votes or majority will. But even as they were anchored in the highest and most objective authority, and in fact precisely because of this, such rights seemed supremely utilitarian. Enlightened people had to affirm and support an environment of freedom, because only such an environment offered any long-term prospect for individual happiness. Only a legal order fully protective of human rights could pay off in the greatest realized good for the greatest number.

Behind these rational arguments lay a profound but rarely articulated insight. Given a personal desire for either of the political freedoms, consistency suggests today that we must universalize such freedom. If one perceives due process, a wide leeway for self-expression, or a high degree of realized autonomy and independence, as necessary for his own happiness, then he has a compelling, although not a logically necessary reason, to attribute the same needs to all other adults. If he does not attribute the same needs to others, he must contend that other people have inherently and not just circumstantially different needs than he does, and that they are incapable of his degree of enlightenment or moral sensitivity. If he is willing to see others, at least to this extent, as in the same moral situation as himself, then universal obligations fall easily into place.

Such universality has been present in almost all great, sweeping ethical ideals, from Jesus's Golden Rule to Immanuel Kant's categorical imperative. If citizens want their individual rights respected, they must respect the same rights in others. If they want to be safe from killers and thieves, they cannot make murder and robbery rules of conduct in their society. To enter the necessary modern·caveat—that such generalized rights will entail different conduct in culturally different societies—does not reduce the force of the argument. The level of generality easily accommodates cultural differences. Thus the image of Americans as deservingly free, their affirmation of what this entails for others in their behavior toward them, is only another way of affirming the common rights and the moral equality of all mankind. Such an affirmation seemed normal (not ever-present) in the eighteenth century. To the extent that Americans continue to affirm it, it remains their norm. But, obviously, everyone does not accept it as a norm or respond to its imperatives. Self-hatred, fear, and a desperate craving for paternal care, for the security of a master, are facts of life as well as the basis of alternative affirmations, affirmations which universalize concepts of moral inequality and dependency.

Such psychological insights give an ultimate, subjective aspect to all arguments for human freedom. At one point or another, one is pushed back to one's own beliefs and preferences as a starting point. Since some citizens perceive each of the three types of political freedom as desirable and important, they can respond to the logic of natural rights, to objective arguments in their behalf. Thus the source of America's highest moral commitments is not in God or nature, not in some view of reality, not in some object beyond man, but in man himself, in his most ambitious definitions of himself. The commitment is a product of cultural creativity. Such a challenging self-definition, once affirmed, can find support or justification in common human needs, or in an understanding of inescapable necessities present in the surrounding world. This recognition of subjective involvement, prior to objective appeals, does not detract one whit from the moral cogency of the nation's ideals, or offer any exemptive escape for those who find such ideals beguiling, a necessary component of self-identity and self-respect. But it does suggest a crucial, factual question: to what extent do Americans today understand the meaning of these political freedoms, and to what extent are they morally committed to them? Surely the future of freedom in America is fully as dependent on the answer to this question as it is on the related material and institutional structures of society.

The first form of freedom—due process or freedom from arbitrary government—is easily understood. Even the most conventional of people, for whom the slightest leeway for daring self-expression seems threatening, or even a contented slave who unhesitantly gives his life over to command of another, can still appreciate the horror of whimsical, unpredictable, and unjust government. It is hard to conceive of anyone who would want to live in a society subject to arbitrary arrest, summary executions, or completely capricious laws. Americans may not reflect intense concern over due process, but this only means that, for most, it is safely assumed.

Expressive freedoms involve endless problems of discrimination and judgment. They overlap and often conflict with each other as well as with other types of freedom or with other values. Such freedoms always require the acceptance of a continuum, which slopes from a repressive or totalitarian society, which defines as socially significant and legally weighed almost every aspect of personal belief and expression, to a fully libertarian society which restricts private expression only at the point of overt, physical harm to other people. The totalitarian position is logically persuasive. It is hard to find any private conduct that does not have social implications. Anything one does may offend another person, or it may harm himself, and thus lessen the happiness of all who love him. When most people in a society share consensual values, then individual dissent seems clearly to do greater harm to the whole than any possible good it may bring to the deluded individual. Yet, as the libertarian so well understands, coercive restraints limit, and at some point destroy, any possible happiness for the individual who cannot, in good conscience, embrace communal values. How then does society draw the line between the group and the individual? Generally, even in America, where individuals have had to learn tolerance for great differences, those of more conventional (i.e., average) beliefs and life styles rarely appreciate the value of expressive freedom to other people, and often resent the freedom allowed to those they perceive as deviants or irresponsible dissidents. Thus today, as in the past, the most active support for specific expressive freedoms comes from eccentrics, from minorities, from those with an immediate stake in a given freedom (newsmen and freedom of the press), or from a few intellectuals who embrace broad and abstract principles.

Personal independence is the most complex form of freedom. As no other form, it touches on the sense of identity and self-respect. Yet, one is compelled to ask: is it likely that medieval serfs always burned with resentment of their lord and bitterness over their lowly station? More probably, they gloried in his success and basked in the diffused light of his greatness. A person may assimilate himself to larger wholes—nation or state or local village, to family or sect or party or profession, even to a private corporation—and accept a humble and dutiful and subservient role without protest or any sense of frustration, at least so long as he is kindly treated and his primary needs find fulfillment—food, home, appreciation, companionship, games, a hope of immortality. In such a perspective, the definition of a good society entails not autonomy in all areas, not liberty in the vital economic sphere, but a secure social role, adequate material returns, and some socially approved badges of respectability. This is perhaps where most Americans are today. If so, society might be most fairly judged not in how well it has supported personal independence or liberty in the economic sphere but in how effectively it has made a humane and fulfilling adjustment to its absence, to a new form of structured communalism, to new and dependent work experiences, to massed urban life, to paternal employers and paternal governments.

This may seem a very pessimistic conclusion in the wake of so many recent liberation movements. But personal liberty, to the extent that it depends upon economic independence, does seem out of date, a fond souvenir of past ages. It is an artifact of a completed, simple, expansive stage of American or even Western history. For a time, at least on the expanding frontiers of European exploration and expansion, a proprietary society seemed possible. The very possibility helped underwrite new concepts of liberty and property as advocated by European philosophers such as John Locke. But by our perspective, the expansive attitudes now seem part of an exceptional historical interlude, of one brief age when a part of mankind could escape an economy of relative scarcity and avoid any form of communal economic organization. Perhaps this stage ended in America before it had to, and in part because American proprietors placed their greatest emphasis not upon the primary moral meaning of property—the universal right of all people to have access to nature—but upon a secondary and morally distorting meaning—the right to retain what one had acquired, however large and however much it foreshortened opportunity for others.

For those who value the fullest dimension of political freedom, the most pressing challenge of the present and the future is in the area of political economy—to find some political means of restoring proprietary independence, of lessening the subordinated, dependent, or even servile characteristics of work in large collective organizations. Still any wholesale return to small productive units, to individual ownership, to freedom of enterprise seems out of the question because of their staggering economic costs. Nothing is more radical and more utopian than a proposal that the country return to a propertied society. Less radical proposals may turn out to be merely cosmetic. It is doubtful that increased stock ownership by workers, or even compulsory worker representation on corporate boards, will significantly change the status of employees. Americans have bought their present affluence, their national preeminence, at a great price. Never have they been more aware of this, although they may easily discount some of the present human costs. Despite all the labor reforms, despite all the welfare, their affluence still rests on a wage system, on very demanding work disciplines, and on an acceptance of an ordered and hierarchical command system. And the ever-growing number of people who do not have competitive skills, who cannot find employment, are even worse off. Fully dependent on the direct patronage of government, they have no reason for pride or self-respect.

Thus at the end, a question. Have all the economic returns been worth the cost? Americans must necessarily refer to their own values and preferences, as well as their own economic experiences and achievements, in answering this question. It seems clear that a vast majority of them still accept the bargain as the best one among realistic alternatives, and thus that they are still willing to pay the personal costs inherent in such a political economy. In this sense, in a vastly different environment, the American people have turned away from one of the aspirations of the Founding Fathers, from one of their most valued conceptions of freedom. Instead of permanently eschewing the hierarchical models of Europe, they have embraced them in their dominant economic institutions.

Freedom
and the Economy

Thomas C. Cochran

In defining freedom as "a state of exemption from the power or control of another," Webster's Dictionary implies the basic dilemma from which we never escape. One man's freedom from control is often based on restricting another person from exercising power. From the restraints imposed on members of primitive hunting bands not to steal from each other, each step toward a more complex society has carried some new forms of restraint. Yet the restraint against stealing imposed on the strong or cunning opened a new dimension of freedom to the other hunters, who did not need to protect their catch by continual vigilance and physical strength.

In fact, in civilized society freedom exists only because of restraint. Without law, order, and the security of property, economic freedom would be largely useless. The good society therefore results from a satisfactory balancing of freedom and restraint, and the proper recognition of their reciprocal relationship. In this balance "satisfactory" is the important word. Economic freedom is a subjective feeling, based on comparisons of what is with notions of what should be. An American might feel economically constrained in Sweden, whereas the native takes pride in his freedom.

As in all nations, American ideas regarding what should constitute economic freedom are parts of a fabric woven from the national experience. If one starts by analyzing the current patterns in the fabric, each set of threads lead back to some formative experience in the past. But in few cases does a national tradition ever preserve past patterns intact. Often the enduring elements in any custom or tradition could not even have been foreseen at an earlier time. Thus while Americans have an important heritage of particular economic freedoms stemming from the Colonial period, these liberties were set in an accepted pattern of regulation that would be thought oppressive today.

The paternalistic or mercantilistic state was regarded as normal in the colonies, as it was in Britain. Workers expected to have their wages regulated by justices; farmers accepted provincially set prices for wheat, tobacco, and other staples; uncomplaining artisans applied to municipal authorities for licenses to pursue their craft; and for over a century merchants were reconciled to the imperial acts of trade. The important new and enduring freedoms were of two types. First, while artisans or shopkeepers needed to acquire licenses, these were granted automatically, whereas in England and on the Continent urban manufacturing and services were controlled by old and exclusive guilds which generally accepted members on a hereditary basis. American journeymen workers had their wages regulated, but they moved freely from city to city as they heard of better opportunities—perhaps outside the imperial laws. The system thus provided an unprecedented freedom to work at any occupation.

Second, the common law doctrines concerning land titles were modified in the direction of freedom of exchange. In a society that was more than ninety percent agricultural, acquisition or sale of land was the most important type of transaction involving capital. English and, even more, European law had evolved to protect the orderly inheritance of property by the eldest heir and to make it difficult and expensive for landless men to acquire real property. By entail or deeds of settlement land could be preserved in a single family for generations. In America land was seen as a capital asset which could be sold when it seemed advantageous and new land could be bought from the great unused acreage further west. Consequently, the courts tended to use only those doctrines of the common law that facilitated transfers of title for full ownership, or, in legal talk, in fee simple.

The modification of the law in the direction of greater freedom of action in regard to land titles, however, was only the most important aspect of a general modification in the direction of simplicity. Neither judges nor advocates in the seventeenth century were specially trained in the law. The more literate read copies of the English jurists Coke or Dalton, who themselves provided a simplified version of the forbidding complexity of English law, and the colonial judges then applied only those principles that seemed best suited to the local situation. A Marylander who didn't like the very personalized judgments of its high court wrote:

> Twice a year they gravely meet
> Some to drink and some to eat,
> A swinging share of county treat.

The courts provided neither a learned nor a democratic process, but one biased in favor of freedom of action for the property holder; to influential contemporaries that seemed the essential economic freedom.

Shaping the character of the law and relying on it, in turn, has been the continual movement of people and families. Perhaps the greatest differential between European and American society over the past three centuries has been the exercise of the economic freedom to move elsewhere. Migration became a type of value in itself. Before the Civil War, except for the rich, only slaves and ne'er-do-wells stayed long in the same place. If one did not achieve moderate economic success within a few years, the solution was to move—a maxim as true in the colonies as in the modern corporation; and even if one did get ahead, the best response often seemed to be another move.

Thus the restrictive parts of the Colonial heritage, such as local regulations and arbitrary governmental power, were largely lost in the creation of new governments during the Revolution and its aftermath. This left the free sale of physical property and easy movement to new jobs and localities as the two most important colonial elements contributing to the emerging national tradition of economic freedom.

To understand the unusual acceptance, from 1790 to about 1837, of the idea that the state, national or local, was a power to be used to develop the region or the nation economically, one must take into account the international situation of the young republic. Looking back we see a people full of self-confidence, living without fear of foreign pressure or conquest—a luxury seldom enjoyed by those of any nation in history. Consequently people saw no need for a strong government and a military bureaucracy. Unlike the strong and prestigious governments of Europe, the weak American governments in state and nation were not feared by the very broad middle class. Businessmen could readily see immediate advantages from subsidies, loans, or charters that more than counteracted any fear of ultimate coercion or higher taxes.

The spirit of cooperative state and private development was manifest in the speeches and writing of the leading business thinkers of the time, such as Alexander Hamilton, Tench Coxe, or the Careys. Although Scotch professor Adam Smith had spread the doctrine of the self-regulating economy through free competition, and the French physiocratic philosophers had coined the phrase *laissez-faire,* these eighteenth-century Americans were not followers of either view. Rather they represented an American school of economic nationalism that advocated using all possible means to speed development. Hamilton was particularly favorable to state subsidies, the Careys to protective tariffs, and all advocated mixed state and private corporations.

Although state-chartered corporations and state-owned public works might create monopolies, initially they seemed to curtail no one's freedom and promised more economic benefits for all. In this situation one can understand the wealthy and able Gouverneur Morris telling the New York State Legislature that private enterprise was not competent to build the Erie Canal and that the state should act promptly.

Back of Morris's insistence on haste was a powerful motivating force at this stage of eastern development: intense state rivalry. Massachusetts, New York, Pennsylvania, and Maryland, possessing the major seaports, were all afraid that if they did not speedily penetrate the back country their neighbors would contrive to channelize all the trade through their ports. In a sense these were four city states. Boston, New York, Philadelphia, and Baltimore carried on warfare for control of the vast western back country, but the weapons were not swords or bullets, but dollars, picks, and shovels. The economic warfare, however, produced very close ties between businessmen and their governments; temporarily, at least, economic progress seemed far more important than abstract doctrines of *laissez-faire.* The real divisions in interest during this period were between those farmers and landowners who would not benefit from a particular work, and therefore opposed state or federal action, and those who saw the promise of gain. This division largely inhibited action by the federal government, because geography dictated that some states would inevitably benefit far more than others from internal improvements.

This period of superficial contradiction between immediate practice and long-run attitudes emphasizes the fact that in the United States "economic freedom" never developed into a philosophical theory or doctrine. It has always been what at any given time and place served the business interests, and normally the nation, best. Hence Professor John Roach has called the result "entrepreneurial freedom" rather than freedom based on a specific philosophy. There is no reason why business spokesmen should quarrel with such a definition.

This honeymoon of government and business terminated abruptly with the panic of 1837, but arguments against it had begun some years before. Up to the War of 1812 businessmen had been active in politics in the East and practically dominant across the mountains to the west. In the easygoing world of the merchant, lawyer, and real estate dealer men could spare the time to promote a proper commercial influence in government. But as business grew in complexity everywhere, and new technology and types of enterprise demanded increasing entrepreneurial attention, business began to leave politics to professional career politicians, or to those with direct interests in government action. This withdrawal was gradual, occurring first in the older industrializing areas and not until after the Civil War in some agricultural states.

This professionalization of politics produced the spoils system of rewarding party workers with all available offices, strong party organizations that could look after their loyal supporters, a lack of a permanent civil service based on ability and security, and a consequent need for support from outside sources for politicians temporarily out of office. Many of the latter became lawyers with offices at capitals or county seats and, when not on the public payroll, were particularly anxious to represent business interests. This led to permanent lobbies for corporations such as those in finance, real estate, or transportation that had continuous state or federal relations. But the personal withdrawal of the businessman from politics meant that he was forced to deal with men he could not altogether trust. The professional politician had to weigh votes and balance opposing interests; he could not always do what business wanted. Furthermore, as successful businessmen came to make far higher incomes than most politicians could hope for from all sources, the latter came to be regarded as second-level operators not up to the ability of entrepreneurs.

This gradual rift between business and politics was rapidly widened by the results of the panic of 1837. States defaulted on bond issues and left public works uncompleted. State-supported banks were allowed to fail, and government temporarily ceased to be of much use to business. When recovery came in the mid-forties, some private groups were strong enough to buy up and complete the previously state-financed works. In other words, by 1850, except for railroad construction, tariffs, and a few ship subsidies, business no longer needed government help, and the doctrine that "economic freedom" meant no interference by government began its long ascendancy.

American historians have generally seen the last half of the nineteenth century as a period of dominant, excessively free, self-seeking, and irresponsible businessmen, the strongest of whom, Commodore Vanderbilt, was as early as 1851 compared to the "robber barons" of the medieval Rhine valley. Such men often appeared to control politics, because in this period of continuing industrialization most American legislation was necessarily enacted to meet the needs of new enterprises. If we grant the hypothesis that prior to 1933 no law was ever enacted by Congress, or even by the state legislatures, without the support of some business interest, it does not imply unusual protection of economic freedom. Better legal conditions for one group of businessmen might have meant more restraint for another. The average shippers, including farmers, wanted equality in railroad rates, or freedom from the exactions of monopolistic railroads or corporate groups. But such laws after 1870 spelled loss of freedom to railroads and their biggest customers.

Business actually restricted its own freedom by creating a mosaic of regulatory laws, state and federal, each of which was desired by some special interest. And as the society grew and became more industrialized the patterns of the mosaic became ever more complex, until only a specialized lawyer could read the meaning of the design. There were, of course, many regulatory laws passed under the rubrics of police power or public health, such as those regulating housing or hours of work, that only a few businessmen wanted and the great majority opposed. State legislation during the late nineteenth century, however, has generally been regarded as constructive. Laws seeking to assure more honest weights and measure, reliable quality or healthier cities, benefited all legitimate business even though they restricted economic freedom.

When state or federal laws appeared seriously to injure a particular business activity, injured businessmen resorted to the courts which generally took a restrictive view of the powers of the state. Up to the momentous reversals of the spring of 1937, the courts from the lowest to the highest generally held to strict construction the limits of the police or public welfare power, or other powers claimed by governments. In fact, cases can be found, such as some involving contested decisions of the Interstate Commerce Commission, where most railroadmen sided with the judgment of the Commission rather than with the doctrines of the Supreme Court. Here the latter insisted on a freedom of action that the roads no longer thought practical.

By the 1890s American state and local governments had become unusually, in some cases incredibly, corrupt. In all cases they did so in the service of some politico-economic interests, but often at the expense of too many other business groups and with the loss of all appearance of honesty and integrity. As Lincoln Steffens said of the boss of Rhode Island, he "received in the sheriff's office the lines of visitors who had business with the State, openly. And openly he did that business. He ran the Legislature across the hall. He said so; everybody knew it; and he ran it for businessmen." But only for businessmen prepared to pay for the favors received. By 1900 not only were chambers of commerce and other commercial associations favoring reforms, but also the businessman's estimate of politicians was at a low point, and the responsible citizen's distrust of government, in general, was probably at its highest.

The resulting reform movements, initiated by commercial organizations and business leaders, as well as by those in education, journalism and religion, were illustrations of the dilemma that what was increased freedom for one interest was more restriction for another. Perhaps the concept of restriction of "economic freedom" is wrongly applied to these political reforms. The reformers wanted a more profitable market for local business activity through lower taxes, better services, and economic growth, not necessarily a freer one. This rather frequent contradiction runs through the ideas and actions of the Progressive Movement and

Wilson's summation of "The New Freedom." More impartial and efficient politics and extensions of the police power were accepted by most businessmen because they seemed essential for more orderly and reliable markets. Some limitations that appeared between the end of the century and World War I, however, seemed more questionable, and often deeply divided the business community.

Government restrictions on goods offered for sale were an example. The classic market was described by economists as a meeting of free buyers and sellers, each with all the knowledge necessary to bargain for a fair price. It is doubtful that any such market could exist in reality. Perhaps at a time when the scope of most transactions was local and the commodities thoroughly known, the condition may have been sufficiently approximated, although there was always the possibility that with truly full knowledge either buyer or seller might seek another market. But as the American market became nation-wide and processed goods ever more complex, the resemblance of the real to the theoretical market became more and more remote. Yet there was until about 1925 no new theory to modify the classic conceptions. In these confused markets the general doctrine was *caveat emptor.* The buyer at each of the stages from businessman acquiring raw materials to consumer-purchaser was expected to bear the risks of imperfect information, although often the cost of proper knowledge was prohibitive. When bad purchasing imposed only economic loss, middle-class Americans of the nineteenth century were inclined to accept the risk. The successful seller of wooden nutmegs was a smart fellow, not a criminal. Similarly, despite spectacular scandals, the security markets remained self-regulated. But when lack of information led to sickness or death, educated citizens became alarmed.

Hence one of the first direct negations of *caveat emptor,* of the buyers' economic freedom to be wrong, came with the congressional food and drug acts of 1906 and 1907. These were designed to protect buyers, who could not conceivably do it for themselves, from dangerous preservatives, narcotics, or bacteria arising from careless preparation. Interestingly enough, the larger producers were in favor of most sections of these laws. They had newer, more efficient processes that made preservatives less important to them than to their small competitors. Fred Pabst, one of the three big brewers selling in the national market, went to Washington to urge passage of the pure food law of 1906. In fact, one may generalize, as Gabriel Kolko has, that some big business preferred limited regulation to unrestricted competition.

In resisting state or federal regulation and in bargaining with labor, the common law doctrine of the freedom of men to enter into private agreements—as well as constitutional guarantees of the sanctity of such contracts—has been an important weapon for business. The sanctity of contracts clause of the federal Constitution was strengthened by the assertion in the Fourteenth Amendment that no state shall deprive a person of property without due process of law. A verbal agreement by a worker to give so many hours of labor at a certain price had from time immemorial been legally regarded as a labor contract by which he sold his services. The contract could be terminated at any time by either party, but the fact that the worker was on the job signified mutual acceptance of the agreement. The assumed legal right of each worker to negotiate his own contract stood in the way of both union agreements and state regulatory laws regarding hours and other conditions of work.

Unions may be seen as mutual brokerage associations in which the members pay a fee to a middleman to have him negotiate a written contract of sufficient advantage to repay the cost in dues. Until 1842 the state courts held that such joint bargaining was a common law conspiracy in restraint of trade. Thereafter the courts regarded unions as legal organizations, but often restricted their activities. During the nineteenth century all but a handful of professional economists believed that wages reflected productivity in a competitive market and could not be raised arbitrarily without disastrous consequences to the firms involved. Before 1935 many businessmen continued to hope that in the United States trade unions would encompass only a few skilled crafts; to a large degree employers succeeded in curtailing union expansion. From the view of freedom post-New Deal labor relations became a three-sided struggle involving freedom for employers, organized workers, and individual workers in which a gain for one compelled the others to lose some prerogative.

An even more confusing contest from the standpoint of economic freedom has been the never-ending competition for profits and markets between small and large businesses. Size offered advantages to firms that could purchase, transport, and sell in large quantities. The advantages in marketing under brand names, backed by national advertising, were great enough. A semi-monopoly of some part of processing or selling, at least in theory, would secure large profits. Since, basically, the advantage of semi-monopoly would accrue from a selling price above a truly competitive level, the courts regarded effective restraint of competition as a violation of freedom of the market. From the early nineteenth century state courts had viewed agreements between competitors to fix prices or limit quantities as common law conspiracies in restraint of trade. Since neither British nor European courts took such a view, such rulings seemed to reflect a stronger attachment to freedom of activity in American culture. In reality, the uniquely strong emphasis on free competition resulted perhaps from freedom of movement and abundant opportunity rather than from any formalized beliefs.

When in 1879 the new trust organization brought competitors together through a common group of trustees, the states responded with antitrust laws. In 1889 New Jersey circumvented these prohibitions through a general holding company act that made trusts unnecessary. Merely by filling out the proper forms and paying the attendant fees, a corporation could be chartered that might hold and vote the stock of other companies. Yet all but a few of nearly two million American businessmen and twice that number of farmers wanted to restrict the economic freedom of trusts or monopolies in the interest of what they conceived to be the freedom of the small enterpriser. When six million voters, many with good political connections, want a law and only a few thousand, no matter how powerful financially, oppose it, it is probable that sooner or later the restrictive act would be passed. In this case action came very quickly. To marshal additional votes for the McKinley tariff in 1890, pro-tariff forces gave small business and farm representatives the Sherman Antitrust Act. The law prohibited "every contract, combination in the form of trust or otherwise, or conspiracy, in restraint of trade or commerce among the several states."

Interpretation of the law required a generation. For the first fifteen years it appeared that a monopoly of manufacture was not necessarily one of trade. In 1911 the Supreme Court decided to use its judgment as to what practices and what share of interstate markets constituted evidence of probable restraint, and in later decisions it stretched the limit of the share beyond fifty percent. Meanwhile, to tighten restrictions the small business majority in Congress passed the Clayton Act of 1914 which specifically defined certain actions that would constitute restraint regardless of the size of the companies involved. The prohibitions included agreements to sell fixed proportions of products to other firms, called tying agreements; certain types of interlocking directorships; and the acquiring of stock in other companies to lessen competition. One exception to both antitrust laws were monopolies produced by ownership of patents.

Whether the antitrust laws restricted the freedom of large corporations to expand is a moot point. The laws may have discouraged efforts at monopoly through cutthroat competition, yet Ford reduced prices far below those of his competitors without achieving a monopoly. Some old monopolies, such as American Tobacco and Standard Oil, were broken up, but the latter, at least, was already becoming vulnerable to competition from the owners of new sources of supply. England and Germany, without antitrust laws, experienced a similar rise of large corporations, none of which achieved secure monopolies without the aid of patents. Furthermore, many of the semi-monopolistic businesses organized in the stock market boom from 1897 to 1904 were created more for selling securities than achieving efficiency from size.

Following the business revolution of the late eighteenth century, the range of choice of one desiring to enter business continually expanded. More specialized commercial activity, more intricate and varied products, more complex marketing structures, and more types of services broadened the opportunity to enter business other than agriculture at a rate faster than the growth of the population. In addition, the rapidly expanding number of positions in the larger corporations could lead to wealth more reliably than the pioneer enterprises of the nineteenth century. Among the major areas of economic activity, at least up to 1929, only agriculture and manufacturing were leveling off in number of enterprises. If, by definition, "economic freedom" included a range of occupational choice, freedom steadily increased.

There are people, particularly in the Southwest, who still argue that if government limited its actions to the prevention of crime and the civil protection of property rights every virtuous citizen would be better off. The argument cannot be answered factually because no such industrial state has ever existed. Historically, every national government has taken over about the same types of welfare functions at some point in its development, and variations seem to have been more related to geography, tradition, and international diplomatic pressures than to ideas regarding economic freedom. French farmers and small businessmen, for example, have maintained a relatively high degree of economic freedom in spite of the rather widespread system of government ownership of industry and transportation created to serve some national interest. The national security of the United States weakened the force of any argument, based on national defense, to extend federal ownership or regulation, while a high standard of living lessened the need for welfare. Consequently, the nation reached 1932 with government ownership largely limited to highways and education, regulation to transportation and public utilities, and welfare to inadequate or non-existent state systems.

Seen in this light the depression of the thirties, whose unequaled severity resulted to some extent from the lack of the cushioning effect of welfare devices, merely forced a rapid catching up with the practices of other industrial nations. The shock—and no one who lived through the period will deny the reality of the alarm felt by many businessmen— came as much from the suddenness of the change as from the content of the laws. The handful of important new commissions, for example, were difficult for the businesses they regulated. Initially able and devoted commissioners were compelled to interpret loosely drawn laws. Lawyers appearing for business clients did not know what to expect because precedents were nonexistent and the commissioners themselves lacked familiarity with the problems in their sphere of authority. Ultimately these difficulties tended to disappear: the rulings of commissions became well-known, many later members were men from the businesses they regulated, and the bodies became oriented more toward the wants of industry than toward abstract ideas of public interest.

In 1950 *Fortune* published an issue (later a book) called *U.S.A. The Permanent Revolution,* which attributed to the New Deal a large portion of those features which, the editors held, marked the superiority of the new capitalism over the old. Only a few laws, such as the National Labor Relations Act and portions of the Securities Exchange Commission and Social Security Acts, remained generally obnoxious to thoughtful businessmen. Yet the increased public security for incomes, property, and health reduced the economic freedom of businessmen substantially. A society of farmers and small businessmen represented a high degree of freedom. Mass production and urbanism seemed inevitably to involve more and more collectivity. Industrial cities could not grow without restraints demanded by business itself, and to 1976 these restraints became steadily more pervading.

Meanwhile, complex chemical processes had effects on public health and the social environment not foreseeable by the entrepreneurs who controlled the producing enterprises. In a very real sense pollution destroyed the economic freedom of those it disabled. Still any effort at relief negates the classic doctrine of personal assumption of risk by anyone choosing a particular occupation or residence. It involves government restriction of risk-taking for both employer and employee, creating a sometimes onerous interference with private rights, but one that has been committed by all democratic governments.

The growing importance of government as a customer emerged as another, more subtle restriction of economic freedom. Since 1939 educational, health, and housing facilities have represented large federal and state investments, but still smaller than government expenditure for defense. In the older, freer economy individual demands and private business decisions, through competitive methods, largely determined allocation of the national product. Currently over a fifth of total production is mandated for government use. In this sector "economic freedom" exists only to the extent that contracts must be competed for and firms, some of which would fail without the business, are not compelled to participate. Businessmen involved recognize their loss of freedom; many would prefer private contracts but are hopelessly geared to governmental demand.

Economic freedom depends on the character and policies of government, on technological change, and on the resulting evolution of the business system itself. The political structure and public policies of the United States have been strongly resistant to radical modification. Written constitutions, a supreme judiciary, and fifty state governments inhibit easy change. Europeans delight in referring to the American governmental system, regardless of the party in power, as the most conservative in the world; it is in fact the only government in a major nation that has undergone no substantial structural change since 1787. Watergate was an excellent, although accidental, example of the operation of the constitutionally designed balance of power to forestall extralegal change. In this crisis the legislature, with the vital cooperation of the judiciary, prevented an unauthorized increase in the traditional power of the presidency. Watergate made clear that the existing governmental system, for better or worse, will not be easy to alter.

For the ten- to fifteen-year future (beyond which it is surely useless for historians to speculate), it seems reasonable to assume the continuance of the economic freedom that depends on the legal guarantees and present character of state and federal governments. These two levels of authority undoubtedly constitute the most expensive political system in the non-Communist world. As the growth rate of per capita income in the United States declines in relation to that in the more compact economies, the expense may appear exorbitant. But the drastic reforms called for to eliminate unnecessary layers of government, improve honesty of operation, and, in general, readjust to less extravagant spending will be so gradual that little may happen before 1990.

Predicting changes in business that may affect economic freedom requires judgments regarding changes in technology, organization, and demand which make conclusions more uncertain than in the case of government. There is some relationship between the size of the bureaucracy in which one works and a personal sense of economic freedom; any shift toward employment in smaller organizations may produce a gain for freedom. Increasing use of chemical processes, substitutions of plastics and fibers for metals, and reliance on computers all reduce employment by automating large parts of production. Were it not for the amount of handwork on custom-made defense equipment, employment in manufacturing would be declining considerably faster than it is. In 1960 production workers in manufacturing were 7 percent of the population; in 1970 they had only fallen to 6.5. The effects of the computer and new automation were only beginning to be felt in fabrication. The chairman of the board of a large southern textile company, for example, declared in 1973 that he expected his mill employment to drop from 20,000 to about 5,000 in the next ten or fifteen years, chiefly as the result of automatic Swiss looms. In some mills half a dozen electrical engineers would constitute the work force.

The computer is affecting middle management as well. Calculations that required trained accountants, inventory experts, and others able to exercise discretion based on education and experience are being displaced by self-regulating systems. The same applies to clerical and secretarial work. Countering this pressure is the tendency for the information-digesting parts of business to grow rapidly. Americans have come to live in an information-rich world, and someone has properly to evaluate the knowledge. Therefore, it appears that blue-collar jobs in manufacturing will decline faster than white collar or managerial, but that both will continue to diminish in relation to trade and a rapidly growing range of personal, professional, or governmental services which are easy to expand and more difficult to mechanize.

This shift from employment in manufacturing will induce changes in the business structure, just as did the rapid reduction in the number of farmers between 1945 and 1970. This earlier shift was easier to accommodate, however, because the United States and Western Europe had labor shortages. The largest individual corporate employers are all in manufacturing. In the rest of business, embracing three-quarters of the working population, only Sears, Roebuck approaches the largest industrials. Banks, trading companies, insurance, and even the large retail food chains are only medium large employers. Hence the movement toward the trades and services will reflect a declining work force in giant companies. But some aspects of trade and service raise questions about freedom. Whereas ninety-five percent of American enterprises are small or medium-sized, a considerable number of them are tied in one of several ways to some of the larger corporations. Many of the more than 200,000 small manufacturers, for example, supply components to only a handful of firms and thus have their economic freedom limited by the policies of their few customers. In trade the relationship is often quite similar. Dealers in high-priced items such as automobiles or farm or construction equipment have their operations carefully scrutinized by their suppliers. They are in one sense merely selling on commission. In service, franchising is a common method of operation. Restaurants and motels are run on franchises granted by national chains that require the operator to buy food or equipment from the controlling corporation and submit to various auditing procedures.

Have these tied dealers or franchised operators lost economic freedom in the form experienced by earlier businessmen? On the negative side they do not buy in a free market; they may or may not have title to their stock of goods. They may not own the equipment they use and in many cases their methods of accounting are prescribed. On the positive side, they alone deal with their customers, they hire their own employees, and they may fail or succeed very handsomely; in a word, they are risk-taking businessmen. Since it seems likely that this will be a permanent type of arrangement in the service sector, whether economic freedom is growing or declining will depend partly upon one's view of franchising. Perhaps the ability to earn profit is the most reliable guide to what constitutes free enterprise; franchised dealers are merely submitting to the kind of regulation, by private interests, that government imposes on transportation and public utilities companies.

If one accepts this argument, the future for economic freedom appears promising. The number of separate enterprises, now totaling about ten million, will probably continue to grow faster than the population; and whereas their proprietors will no doubt have a more limited range of freedom to act in any way they choose than did the owner-manager of 1776 or 1876, the opportunities for success within the limits imposed by a complex economy on all its members should be very much greater than a century earlier. The great majority of mid-nineteenth-century businessmen failed at least once, and most had only limited success in the end. The carriage maker in a small city, for example, could design his own handmade vehicles, but he could expect only moderate returns from his small trade. In contrast, the automobile dealer with a franchise for a good sales area has no control over the design of what he sells, but if successful he will become a millionaire.

Such reasoning calls attention to the many meanings of freedom; as the white rabbit said to Alice, it is a "portmanteau word." It covers a variety of degrees that in specific cases may even be measured. Freedom also varies according to its utility. A worker in a union shop has fewer theoretical degrees of freedom than one who is completely at liberty to sell his labor to any employer at any price. But the limited freedom left to the union member may be more useful in that it produces physical betterment; subjectively, control by the union is self-government whereas control by the employer is not. The same types of distinction, with their emphasis on security, apply to the partially controlled entrepreneur.

To be meaningful, economic freedom must imply a possible sphere of operation, and must provide its possessor with the opportunity to use it. The worker is more secure today than a hundred years ago in the enjoyment of the freedom he still possesses; no less so is the franchised dealer or executive in a medium-to-large company. American society is still the most competitive in the highly industrialized world, but by imposing some restraints, the politico-economic structure has given added security to the areas of economic freedom which remain.

Freedom
and the Environment

Barry Commoner

There is a growing sense among the people of the United States that their freedom is eroding while the government's power, often without the consent of the governed, has increased. Many Americans sense that the government's power, isolated from the people's will by an elaborating bureaucracy, has grown more absolute. The nation's freedom, achieved two hundred years ago with independence and a new constitution, is now once more threatened—not by a foreign monarchy, but by the very government that the American people created, that they support with their own earnings, that they have empowered with laws enacted by their own representatives.

What is the connection between this assault on our freedom and the recent threat to the environment in which we live? In the last ten years, with startling suddenness, the nations' citizens have become aware that the air, the water, and the soil have become so fouled and degraded as to threaten the collapse of the ecological processes that support their livelihood and existence. In response, the nation has undertaken to control environmental degradation. In only a few years a series of powerful and pervasive new laws—among them the National Environmental Policy Act, the Clean Air Act, the Water Quality Improvement Act, the Occupational Safety and Health Act—has created a system of regulation and a growing bureaucratic machinery to set limits on environmental degradation and to curtail the activities that worsen it. Laws now mandate that the levels of noxious ingredients of smog may not exceed certain limits; laws give the Environmental Protection

Agency the right to enforce these limits through performance requirements for automobiles, and, if need be, by restricting the flow of
traffic. Similarly, substances that cause cancer can be forbidden to commerce, restricting the use, for example, of DDT and other insecticides.
But despite the new laws, abuses continue: new toxic chemicals appear
in the workplace and old ones continue to spread in the environment.
Further constraints seem needed to curb the hazards.

Thus a major outcome of the national effort to improve the environment has been the establishment of many new legislative constraints
and the creation of a rapidly growing superstructure of regulations,
reports, inspections, monitoring, hearings, civil and criminal proceedings, suits and countersuits, court orders, injunctions, and fines. Whatever our concerns for the environment, realism and candor require that
we recognize these outcomes of our environmental concerns for what, in
truth, they are: stringent and pervasive limitations on freedom. And
we must recognize, too, that the new bureaucracy we have created to
enforce these constraints adds new costs to a government which already
inflicts on many of its citizens a heavy burden of taxation.

We hear complaints that the growing bureaucracy enmeshes our lives
in an increasingly fine net of complex and burdensome regulations. This
swells the power of a government already so powerful as to have engaged—as we now know from the shameful revelations of Watergate
and the congressional investigations of the FBI and the CIA—in vicious
and dangerous violations of the very laws the government is obligated
to enforce. In our zeal to defend the environment we have added to the
growing burden of bureaucracy and to the power which it wields.

Why should this be true? Clearly, as a people we *must* preserve the
environment and conserve our resources, for otherwise we perish. Are
we caught in a cruel dilemma—that we can improve the environment only at the expense of political freedom? This question ranges
far beyond environmental issues. It is the same question that is being
asked about the conflict that some people see between personal freedom and the government's growing power to regulate such activities
as agricultural production, industrial practices, transportation systems,
patterns of housing and schooling, and the provision of medical care.
This is the tangled knot of issues that continues to frustrate the political
process and that, so long as it remains unsolved, discourages belief in
the value of the democracy that we created two hundred years ago.

In some measure the problem is reflected in the growth of the federal bureaucracy. During the years from 1948 to 1952 the federal budget was 15 percent of the GNP; it is now roughly 20 percent. However, at the same time the portion of the federal budget assigned to federal regulating agencies has increased by 150 percent. In short, regulating agencies have grown far more rapidly than other branches of the government.

The environmental issue, properly understood, sheds light on the reasons for the extraordinary growth of federal regulatory powers. We now know that the degradation of the environment and the wasteful depletion of oil and other nonrenewable energy resources are the inevitable consequence of the deeply faulted designs of the instruments of production. We are growing food, increasingly, with heavy applications of chemicals that overburden the natural cycles; we ship goods, increasingly, on trucks that consume four times more fuel—and produce that much more air pollution—than shipment on a railroad; we build factories that consume more and more fuel to produce the same amounts of goods; and we even convert fuel into synthetic materials that, unlike the natural materials they displace, cannot be assimilated into natural cycles.

The environment is polluted and energy is wasted because the production system—the farms, factories, and systems of transportation—have been developed with almost no regard for compatibility with the environment or for the efficient use of energy. In turn, this faulty design has been imposed on the production system by the economic system, which invests in operations that promise increased profits rather than environmental compatibility and the efficient use of resources. Yet we know that we cannot survive unless environmental quality is maintained and resources are renewed. If our system of production were governed by this social need it would be designed to harmonize with the environment rather than assault it—to renew resources rather than deplete them. But it is not, and it is this inherent fault which gives rise to environmental degradation and the wasteful use of resources. The new constraints, the laws and regulations, are intended to superimpose on these inherently faulted instruments of production added constraints and controls—physical as well as administrative—in hopes of keeping the damage within bounds. They are necessary only because the production enterprises themselves remain at fault.

Let us recall that we live on the surface of a planet. Everything we need, everything we use, comes from the thin skin of that planet—the layer of air, soil and surface waters on the earth's surface, and minerals that lie beneath it. This is the source of all of our resources—food, oxygen, and raw materials. We speak of this thin layer as the ecosystem—the network of biological interaction between living things and their environment that sustains life on the planet.

Thus we, and all other animals, breathe oxygen which is put into the air by the green plants. Geological evidence makes it clear that before green plants appeared on the earth there was no oxygen. The fact that there is oxygen in the air now is a result of ecological processes that have occurred since then. We can breathe and burn fuel—which also requires oxygen—because the ecosystem includes green plants.

Similarly, we require clean water for life as well as many industrial processes. The purity of water is determined by the ecological networks in rivers and lakes. And biological processes have created all of the oil and the coal—the fossil fuels. In sum, the ecosystem is the source of the resources that, fed into the production system, lead to the goods and services that we use.

But pollution tells us that we have so designed the production system that it damages the ecosystem on which it depends. We have designed the production system without much regard for its impact on the environment, and without much regard for its present, nearly exclusive, dependence on nonrenewable stores of fossil fuels.

As an example of how the production system operates in ways that run counter to its dependence on the ecosystem, let us look at the effect of the production system on ozone. Ozone is a form of oxygen which contains three oxygen atoms. It exists largely in a sphere around the earth—high up in the stratosphere—and provides a shield against ultraviolet light from the sun. Ozone was formed around the earth only after oxygen appeared in the atmosphere; as we have seen, the latter event was itself a consequence of the emergence, in the course of evolution, of green plants. Until then the earth was bathed with very intense ultraviolet light, a very vigorous type of energy that can do a great deal of biological damage: it will kill bacteria; it will also cause skin cancer. (Even now the incidence of skin cancer is highest in the "sun belt" of the United States—the South and Southwest.)

During early stages of the earth's development, before the appearance of green plants, oxygen, and ozone, there was such intense ultraviolet radiation on the earth's surface that no living thing could survive except under rocks or thick layers of water. Only later, when the green plants produced enough oxygen, which in turn gave rise to the ozone layer, could living things come out from under the rocks and emerge safely on land. Since then, all living things—and human society as well —have lived in an environment protected by ozone.

In recent years chemists have discovered that certain chemicals are capable of depleting ozone in the stratosphere. For example, chlorine can interact with ozone and destroy it. And chlorine is being introduced into the stratosphere because we now use very large amounts of synthetic chlorine-containing chemical compounds (usually called Freons), for example, in the compressors that drive air conditioners and refrigerators. Freon is a very stable organic chemical. Because of its stability Freon will not react chemically with cream, furniture wax, or insecticides. At the same time it is very volatile and will develop pressure in a closed container, which, when released, will expel the contents in a stream or fine spray. That is why Freon has been used as the propellant in a variety of aerosol spray cans.

But Freon quickly loses its stability when it is exposed to ultraviolet light. Being light and volatile, once released from a spray can (or a compressor) it readily rises into the stratosphere where the ultraviolet light breaks it down and causes the release of chlorine atoms, which, in turn, destroy the ozone. When researchers warned of the possible ozone destruction, a number of companies stopped using Freon in their products and returned to the use of squeeze containers and finger-operated pumps.

Thus something had happened in the production system which thoughtlessly assaulted the ecosystem and threatened to make it unable to support us. Why was this done? Why did industry make Freon-pressurized cans of furniture polish and whipped cream? Was it done to meet a social need? Did it suddenly become obvious that everybody needed pressurized whipped cream and we had to invent it? Actually this development responded to no social need. Society already had whipped cream, furniture polish, insecticides, and deodorants. There was no compelling social need for squirting these things out of a spray can. Yet they were produced.

The reason is clear. In our economic system, which is governed by the principle of private enterprise, private individuals have the right to use resources and capital, if they possess them, for the manufacture of whatever they can legally sell at a profit. Spray cans were invented, manufactured, advertised, and sold because various private entrepreneurs decided they could sell them profitably. Clearly spray cans performed well in the free marketplace. Here an exchange took place; the manufacturers sold the spray cans for profit; and customers bought them for whatever benefit seemed to arise from the convenience of dispensing wax or whipped cream by pressing a button. Both sides in the exchange benefited, but neither was aware that the benefit was accompanied by a potentially serious social cost—the loss of ozone and the possible increase of cancer and other ultraviolet-induced harm.

Why was social cost not taken into account in the exchange process? The reason is that exchanges in the marketplace of private enterprise are, indeed, *private;* they are based on the costs and benefits that accrue to the private participants in the exchange, not to society as a whole. Social costs and benefits do not enter into the exchange; they are "externalities."

The development of aerosol sprays was a mistake in the design of the production system; but because it was an externality there was no way to prevent the error, to avoid the resultant environmental harm. Because the economic mechanism that determines what we produce does not take such social consequences into account, we have to wait until the mistake is made, and then take steps to ameliorate the resultant damage —if we can.

The petrochemical industry is responsible for the appearance in the environment of hundreds of new chemicals, the biological effects of which we are just beginning to discover. Four hundred synthetic organic chemicals which never existed before are now found in the drinking water of various cities. Several of them cause cancer. One dangerous petrochemical is vinyl chloride. Chemical workers who have worked with vinyl chloride have suffered a high incidence of a type of liver cancer. Again we are confronted with a serious social cost, external to the economy of the marketplace, and not taken into account by it.

Now consider the social costs of the wasteful use of resources, such as energy. Again, the petrochemical industry is a good example, for as the industry's synthetic fibers have displaced cotton in the marketplace, the energy required to produce the same amount of cloth has increased. Production of a synthetic fiber requires at least five times more energy than cotton production (counting all the energy used, not only as tractor fuel, but to manufacture fertilizer and other agricultural chemicals). The postwar displacement of natural materials such as cotton by synthetic ones has increased the amounts of energy we use to feed and clothe ourselves. The productivity of energy—goods produced per unit of energy used—has decreased.

In addition to resources such as energy, there are two other major inputs to any production process—capital and labor. How have the postwar changes affected the productivities of capital and labor? These relationships remind us that a productive process must do more for society than to yield a given product. In addition, it must yield sufficient economic gain to support the accumulation of capital that is needed to sustain the production system itself—to replace worn-out machines, or to provide new kinds of machines. Thus one function of a production process is, so to speak, to reproduce itself—a role in which the productivity of capital (output per unit of invested capital) is important. Another important social function of the production process is to provide opportunities for meaningful employment. Labor productivity (output per unit of labor) tells us, among other things, how many jobs need to be filled to achieve a given amount of output.

Thus, in examining a postwar productive change such as the displacement of leather by plastics, we need to compare their relative productivities with respect to energy, capital, and labor. A useful basis for making such a comparison is the unit "value added"—the value (or sale price) of the product less the cost of the raw materials used in producing it. In 1971, for all manufacturing in the United States, the average value of energy productivity (value added produced per million BTU of energy used) was $14.42 per million BTU. For leather production, energy productivity was much above average (about $62 per million BTU), and for the petrochemical industry generally, which produces plastics, it is much below the average ($2–5 per million BTU). In other words, for the same amount of energy society can obtain more value from a natural product such as leather than from a comparable synthetic product of the petrochemical industry.

As to the productivity of capital, for all manufacturing an average of $1.13 of value added was produced per dollar invested in capital. For leather production the figure was $3.64, and for the petrochemical industry it was in the range of $0.34–0.80. Leather is more sparing of capital than synthetics.

Now let's look at labor. In 1971 the value added per man-hour of labor was $12.00 for all manufacturing. The leather industry is below average—$6.25. The petrochemical industry has the highest labor productivity of all industries— $28.00 per man-hour. This is an example of a very general relationship: the production of synthetics uses less labor, more capital, and more energy than the natural materials which they displace. The petrochemical industry, together with transportation, the industrial complex that depends on petroleum, represents 28 percent of the gross national product. But it employs only 2.7 percent of the labor force. It is a big, expensive, polluting, energy-using operation that does not employ many people.

We can regard unemployment as an important externality. Like environmental pollution or the waste of energy, it is an unaccounted-for by-product of the economic process. And like environmental pollution and the waste of energy, unemployment has been heavily influenced by the postwar transformation of the production system—for example, the shift from natural to synthetic materials. And just as we have been shifting from industries that use energy sparingly to industries that use energy wastefully, we are shifting from industries which use *capital* sparingly to industries which use capital wastefully. Businessmen now complain of a shortage of capital. The New York Stock Exchange reports that within the next ten years there will be a $650 billion shortage of capital. The Chase Manhattan Bank places the shortage at about $1,500 billion. A chief reason for this problem is that the postwar transformation of production technology has tended to reduce the productivity of capital—so that more and more capital is needed to produce both energy and the production machinery that energy drives.

This, then, is the reason for the mounting list of regulations, for the growing bureaucracy, for the erosions of freedom that have followed in the wake of our determination to improve the environment. There is, deeply embedded in the design of our systems of production and economics, a basic fault that is the common cause of both the degradation of the environment and the erosion of our freedom. The fault, I believe, is that we are governed in what we produce, and how we produce it, by the aim of maximizing private profit rather than social value.

We can resolve this fault by creating a production system that judges the value of its products by their use and not by their profit, and an economic system that is committed to serving social needs. Only then can we find the means to secure *both* our freedom and the quality of our life.

This, I believe, is the outcome of the close connection between freedom and the environment. It brings us face to face with the most profound question that the United States must confront in the third century of its life. Our economic system is failing us. It allows destruction of the resource base which supports it, and deprives the people it is supposed to serve of meaningful employment. How can it be transformed into a system which more effectively meets social needs, and thereby sustains the personal freedom which is the historic foundation of American democracy?

Creating
Chosen Futures:

The New Meaning of Freedom
in America's Third Century

Victor C. Ferkiss

The United States has always prided itself on being a free society. But as the nation enters the third century of existence its citizens seem less confident than in the past about their ability to remain free. The individual and American society itself seem to be buffeted about by forces beyond individual or collective control—new technologies of surveillance and manipulation; shortages of resources, energy, and space; pollution and decay in both natural and man-made environments. Can the American people survive these new assaults without resorting to authoritarian government? Is it possible for freedom to flourish in a world of rampant technology and threatening scarcity? Americans can look forward to a third century of life in freedom, but only if they understand clearly the nature and origin of the new threats to their self-realization as a people and are willing and able to act courageously and decisively in that knowledge. But, while possible, such understanding and action will not be easy, because the conception of what freedom is and what its preservation and extension in the future entail is clouded by philosophical misconceptions, by misplaced emphases, by an incomplete, one-sided approach to freedom which past history seemed to justify and confirm.

Freedom seems to be a simple idea, permitting the individual to do what he wants to do, without being compelled to do what he does not want to do. Freedom is infringed when one human being can control the life of another. Slaves are not free because they have masters. Employees are not free to the extent their actions are governed by bosses. Citizens *feel* their freedom abridged by the power and actions of government officials. The freedom for which the colonists fought in the American Revolution obviously fell within this definition. The British government forbade Americans from doing certain things and compelled them to do others—it controlled their commerce and manufactures, levied taxes without colonial consent, quartered troops in American homes without approval. The Declaration of Independence was an impressive litany of complaints against British infringement on freedom.

But national freedom from external control is hardly the sum total even of political freedom. Many nations in the Third World today speak of themselves as being free. But outside observers perceive many of their governments as squalid dictatorships, in which a narrow elite or single tyrant dominates the masses. Some of these nations themselves complain that freedom from colonial political status has resulted in what they call "neo-colonialism," in which outside forces continue to control their economic, social, and cultural life despite the fact that formal political freedom is now theirs.

Obviously, then, freedom is not a simple concept after all. The power to control one's own life can be menaced not only by the actions of individual human beings or governments but by impersonal social forces as well—economic, cultural, technological. The concept of freedom is further complicated if men and women cannot imagine or desire that which they might. How much freedom of choice exists for the ignorant, or for the mind enslaved by drugs or dogma? How free are consumers and citizens enthralled by advertising or propaganda or the host of techniques and technologies of behavioral engineering?

Given the complexity of the nature of freedom, it is understandable that there are almost as many definitions of freedom as there are commentators on the subject. But a useful synthesis is provided by the British political thinker Sir Isaiah Berlin. He argues that most concepts of freedom can be subsumed under two broad points of view. First, he notes the "negative" theory of freedom which, it is quite obvious, is the concept normally assumed by Americans who ordinarily think of freedom almost exclusively in political terms. To quote Berlin: "I am normally said to be free to the degree to which no man or body of men interferes with my activity. . . . Coercion implies the deliberate interference of human beings within the area in which I could otherwise act." Freedom by this definition means, in sum, being let alone by other discrete, identifiable human beings. But there is a second definition of freedom, of venerable ancestry, which Berlin describes, even though he seems to find it less congenial and more dangerous than the first in its implications. In this definition he regards freedom as self-realization: "Freedom is self-mastery, the elimination of obstacles to my will, whatever these obstacles may be." This is what the classical philosophers of antiquity normally meant by freedom. It is the definition implied in everyday speech when Americans talk of being free or not free from the encumbrances of poverty or obligation. Some cannot go to the movies because they are broke or cannot come to a party because of a sick child, feeling the same infringement of compulsion upon freedom as if someone physically barred the door of the theater or the party-giver's house.

This latter meaning of freedom is the one which must command any analysis of the future of freedom in America. In this definition freedom is the ability to choose among alternative futures, to create desired futures—personal and social—within the framework of the opportunities nature presents to individual citizens. "Freedom is the power to make a choice between the means offered to our activity," writes philosopher Yves Simon. This freedom may be menaced by discrete, identifiable human beings or groups, or by laws written by and enforced by impersonal and diffuse social forces, by man-made artifacts, by blindness or weakness of will. In some sense, of course, freedom is also bounded by the limitations of physical nature, our own and that of the universe as a whole. Still it is not only useless but in a sense meaningless to include these as limitations on freedom, because they constitute the very identity of that which seeks to be free. That a square cannot be a circle is not a limitation to its freedom, unless it yearns for self-annihilation.

Americans have historically thought of freedom primarily in the negative, exclusively political sense because of the nature of their country and its historical origins. Nature was an obstacle to be conquered, not a constraint. It did not present them with conditions to be lamented and endured, restricting their actions, but with opportunities to be seized, increasing their ability to grow and prosper. Some social constraints imported from Europe did restrict American behavior, especially at first, but these were quickly and easily abolished. Primogeniture took no roots in the New World, dissolving much of the foundation for restrictions based on class. Indentured servants found in the beckoning frontier a means of bettering their status, often even before their legal terms of bondage expired. (The black slave remained unfree, but his captivity did not shape the country's early national consciousness.) Established churches soon lost much of their power, in fact but especially in law. A frontier life style inevitably entailed the breakdown of many traditional social controls.

Nor did technology constrain early American activity. Early technology was weak and faltering by English or European standards. Colonists saw the machine not as frustrating their desires but as fulfilling their purposes; they were not in thrall to experts. Even the power of received ideas in science, philosophy, and the arts they could eventually set aside, as Alexis de Tocqueville noted, under the pressures of egalitarian democracy.

In the beginning, John Locke once wrote, all the world was America. He was, of course, speaking of the Indian tribes, existing in the state of nature without a common overlord, without civil government. But for the colonists as well the state of nature was almost a reality. Natural anarchists, relatively unconstrained by nature, by social institutions, or by the machine, the colonists attempted to exist in the state of nature to the greatest extent possible. The one obstacle to their freedom was government, the great remaining residual constraint on the fulfillment of their desires—a distant, hostile, or simply useless and unresponsive force. Thus the major perceived constraint on American freedom was political, embodied in the power of the British government—its laws, its taxes, its restrictions on trade and commerce—administered through its agents whether imported or locally bred. It was not strange, therefore, that for Americans freedom early came to mean—primarily and almost exclusively—freedom from government.

Eventually the colonists rebelled against these restrictions on their freedom. But after they destroyed the power of Britain over their lives they retained the fear of government. Some states briefly called their governors "presidents," so hated had the traditional term become. Others constitutionally forbade laws restricting hunting and fishing. Freedom for Americans of the eighteenth century was the absence of government. That government governs best, according to Thomas Jefferson's well-known aphorism, that governs least. Alexander Hamilton might view government as playing a positive role by encouraging capitalism through the creation of both a national debt and an industrial bourgeoisie, but few Americans consciously shared his ultimate goals. They wanted to be the creators of their own futures—and the obstacles were untamed nature and a few power-hungry fellow men. Free men would bring about the utopia of their dreams—a society of prosperous, property-owning equals (slaves and women always excepted, of course), each paradoxically capable of becoming, through his own industry, a lord and grandee in his own right.

One can argue that this view of freedom as the absence of coercion by a government of men, bounded only by a few easily understandable written laws made by delegates, was not only inevitable, given the nation's historical origins, but that it served well in taming a continent. However, the question which faces Americans today is not how they understood freedom in the past and how this understanding has conditioned the present. The question today is whether the traditional, partial understanding of freedom is adequate to enable the American people to remain free human beings—indeed perhaps to remain human beings at all—in the future.

The veneration given the traditional American liberal ideology, with its negative definition of freedom as the absence of direct interpersonal coercion, by virtually all historians and political thinkers, has not prevented some adventurous minds from asking nagging questions, especially since the final triumph of American capitalism in the early twentieth century. No one was more in the mainstream of the liberal historical tradition than the late Carl Becker. In his 1944 lectures on *Freedom and Responsibility in the American Way of Life* he argued, however, that the liberal concept of freedom was not the last word. "Freedom unrestrained by responsibility," he writes, "becomes mere license," and "one man's liberty may be another man's bondage." Speaking as a historian, he notes that "the freedoms enumerated in our constitution are mostly defined as freedom from governmental interference with the activities of the individual." For Jefferson and his contemporaries the essential freedoms were those most commonly lacking elsewhere in their era—freedom of opinion, freedom of occupation and economic enterprise, and freedom from arbitrary governmental interference—freedoms all directly denied by governments throughout the world. Rising capitalism took advantage of this negative concept of freedom. Despite the fact that *laissez-faire* economic theory was largely the rationalization of middle-class interests, few saw this, wrote Becker, because the theory "was formulated in terms of the magic word 'liberty.'"

Until recently, Becker argued, traditional American attitudes served well enough. "We were so rich," he said, "that we could afford to be careless and extravagant. We could afford to exploit our natural resources with a minimum of care for their long-term use." We could assume that individual enterprise would take care of maximizing production and optimizing distribution. "We could afford, in short," he sums up his indictment, "to let the public business ride." But that era had ended; technological society made more government regulation inevitable, compelling Americans to insist less on individual liberties and place more emphasis on their communal responsibilities.

Becker's argument indicates that common sense can pierce the intellectual dogmatism that encapsulates American ideas about freedom, but he, unfortunately, tended to obscure the central philosophical issue. He held that the problem was one of balancing liberty with responsibility to meet the demands of a new age, but he assumed that freedom must in fact be curtailed in the name of other values. This, however, was really not the issue. Meeting the problems of modern society is not a matter of grudgingly sacrificing some degree of freedom for other ends, it is a matter of recognizing that freedom takes many forms and that social action for common ends is an enlargement, not a diminution, of freedom.

At the beginning of their third century the American people are facing a basic crisis of contemporary global society, one which marks the passing from one historical era to another—from the modern industrial state to what has been variously called postindustrial, technetronic, or technological civilization. This crisis has four major aspects: the ability of humanity through its technology to radically alter man's biological and social nature; the ability of humanity through its technology to largely degrade or even destroy, through pollution and war, the physical environment which the race inhabits; the end of the possibility of uncontrolled growth in population and resource use; and the pressing political and moral need to diminish glaring inequalities in the ability of the inhabitants of an increasingly interdependent world to achieve personal survival and fulfillment.

The ramifications of this crisis are almost endless. Still the major implications of this fourfold crisis for America as a nation are clear: it must in its third century learn to master its technology, protect its physical habitat from war and pollution, conserve its resources both physical and social, and reallocate them equitably both internally and externally. Americans can no longer assume that unfettered economic growth will enable them to avoid the problems of just distribution for their society; they can no longer assume that there is enough social space between them so that they can each do their own thing without reference to the impact of their actions upon others. They are, in short, called upon to create a new society to meet the challenges of a new age.

Such a call is not, of course, foreign to American ears. This nation began as a utopian vision. Place names—New York, New London, New Haven—bespeak not simply homesickness but the desire to begin life anew. Virtually every American state has its Salem, and Salem is a contraction of Jerusalem. But early dreams of utopia were forged out of religious millennarianism and a rejection of the challenges to human freedom posed by feudalism and the new emerging dynastic monarchies of the Old World. The new utopian vision stems from an attempt of some Americans to free themselves from the toils of the bureaucratic state large-scale democracy has become, to escape from the tyranny of corporate technology, to find a new harmony with nature and themselves. Creating this new society in the country's third century will involve not a partial surrender of freedom or its qualification, but an expansion of freedom.

What then is freedom? It is the ability to create a desired future condition, or in economist Kenneth Boulding's words, "the process whereby an image of the future is consciously realized." "Freedom in general may be defined as the absence of obstacles to our desires," Bertrand Russell once argued. Our freedoms consist not merely in being able to resist the direct imposition of the purposes of others upon us but, above all, in the realization of our own aims and goals. "The essence of freedom is the practicability of purpose," the well-known philosopher Alfred North Whitehead has written. "If there is anything which men value," says another distinguished philosopher, Edgar Sheffield Brightman, "it is freedom to carry out their purposes," Man, another modern philosopher writes, "is a world building animal. Man builds and shapes his world. This activity is his freedom." Freedom seems to "lie in some *ratio* between our desires and our capacity to satisfy them; between what we can intend and what we can achieve."

Freedom thus is not negative but creative. Theologian Paul Tillich has written, "Creative freedom has three conditions: Freedom for *meaningful* activity, freedom for *autonomous* creativity, freedom for *self-fulfilling* creativity." Such freedom must be exercised in society rather than against or outside it. As the humanist and scientist J.B.S. Haldane once wrote, "The Greeks had a word for the man who used his freedom to turn his back on society. The word was . . . in English, 'idiot.' " Freedom is something free people exercise collectively, for as a noted disciple of John Dewey concluded, "a moral democracy is a society of free men freely choosing at each moment its own future."

Freely choosing its own future. . . . What are the choices before the United States today? What are the forces which menace its freedom? How can citizens act to create a better future and realize America's promise in its third century?

One source of danger to our freedom to create a desired future stems from a combination of the impersonal forces of scarcity and population growth. Some scarcities are inherent in nature: there is little rainfall in the deserts of Nevada, few beaches are to be found near the major population centers, limited amounts of oil lie beneath the surface of the soil. Scarcity does not in and of itself constitute a fundamental limit to American freedom: it provides the raw material of choice. But natural scarcity which is accentuated by the socially uncontrolled use or the monopoly of scarce resources by other human beings, or by the manipulation of prices and of access to these resources, *is* a menace to freedom. Generally, the more scarce a useful good, whether food or oil or parking space, the greater the extent to which it can be a means of control by some over the futures of others, and the greater the necessity for social control and allocation.

Population growth contributes to scarcity for all, including the new increments of population themselves. Whereas the actual generation of new human beings is a highly personal process, the impact of a growing population is felt as an impersonal pressure upon all—the crowds at such places as parks or museums become larger, traffic on the roads increases, the cost of land for housing goes up. Whatever contributes to population increase affects the future of everyone and therefore affects the freedom of everyone. Scarcity of resources is increasing in the United States and, despite claims to the contrary, cannot be totally alleviated by technological advance or the forces of the market. Despite a dramatic drop in the birthrate, the American population will be greater in the next century—certainly in its early decades at least— than it is today. A people desirous of exercising the freedom to create their own future will therefore need to gain some control over the way in which scarce resources are allocated and over the growth and distribution of population.

The second source of danger to freedom comes from corporate technology—what John Kenneth Galbraith has called the "technostructure." This includes not only private business corporations which introduce and use technology in accordance with the dictates of corporate profit but also quasi-private, quasi-governmental institutions such as the health and education industries. The litany of the various ways in which corporate technology affects the daily lives of individuals without their full consent—that is, infringes on freedom by determining their future— is almost endless. Business corporations dictate who will work, where, and how. A company moves a new plant into an area. Job opportunities may increase but streets become more crowded, prices go up, and, possibly, taxes also. A firm moves from an area and leaves workers stranded and a community in economic decay. Lending institutions decide which parts of our country will become new housing developments and which will be "redlined" and become or remain slums. Private corporations constantly menace the privacy of employees and customers.

Corporations continue to pollute air and water and to generate waste despite feeble attempts at public control. Their activities scar the landscape or wound the delicate processes of nature itself. Despite talk of market mechanisms and consumer sovereignty and some faltering attempts at regulation, the exigencies of corporate profit or sheer inertia produce certain kinds of cars, certain kinds of food, certain kinds of appliances, so that little effective choice remains in consumer hands. A health industry dedicated to its own profit and convenience mechanizes medical care and ignores preventive medicine, preferring to cure rather than prevent illness, at an ever increasing cost. The education industry routinizes and trivializes the nation's cultural heritage and skews the development of children. A whole literature—some but by no means all of it hyperbolic—details the ills of our civilization. But the most important aspect of our present situation is often overlooked. Not only are many of the offenses committed by corporate technology and its collaborators destructive of health, beauty, physical well-being or even sanity, but they are infringements of freedom. Someone else is choosing our future for us.

The third source of danger to our freedom is government itself, at all levels. This, of course, was the chief—indeed the only—source of danger to freedom postulated by classical American liberalism. It remains a real menace. Government agencies invade the citizen's privacy or interfere with his personal and political rights through arbitrary and often illegal actions, as in the case of the CIA, the FBI, the IRS, and the Narcotics Bureau, or the activities of many state and local police agencies. Government often takes money through taxation simply for purposes of its own institutional aggrandizement, creating hordes of often unnecessary civil servants. Government often uses economic and human resources for dubious military and political projects abroad or for the maintenance of an overgrown, often inefficient military and foreign policy establishment.

But perhaps the greatest menace government presents to American freedoms is not the result of what it does but of what it fails to do, not the offenses it commits but those it condones and even supports on the part of others. It menaces freedom by permitting and even underwriting the assaults on freedom by impersonal forces and corporate technology. Through subsidies and monopolistic practices masquerading as regulation it collaborates with and makes possible many private attacks on liberty. Much of the government bureaucracy exists to serve private and especially corporate interests. Increasingly historians are recognizing that many government regulatory agencies were not simply captured by the industries they were supposed to regulate but were in fact created to give political and legal sanction to the exercise of private power. Government is often simply the junior partner in a giant conspiracy to create a future for us which we do not want and have not chosen, to create our future under conditions which do not permit our participation. Government, not simply by sins of commission but by sins of omission, denies us the opportunity to collectively create and implement a vision of the future; all too often it is our government which prevents us from being free.

It is a measure of America's continuing intellectual thralldom to inadequate concepts of freedom that its citizens usually fail to see that this is so. If the traffic officer on the corner holds out his hand and forbids pedestrians to cross, they feel their freedom of movement diminished, even if they accept his directions as necessary. But if the collaboration of the highway department and the builders of a new shopping center creates a six-lane roadway which pedestrians cannot safely cross, the same citizens fail to see that their freedom has been equally curtailed. If government takes tax dollars to support a regulatory agency, Americans resent paying their taxes and complain about the high cost of government, but if that agency permits food processors to infuse their diet with carcinogens, they do not regard that as a form of tyranny.

How can individual citizens regain their freedom from the impersonal forces, corporate technology, and inadequate government which threaten most fundamental liberties, especially that of creating their own future? Both intellectual symmetry and moral duty require some attempt to sketch out the broad outline of how the American people might go about recovering and extending their capacity for social self-actualization.

The first step must be a change in basic philosophical attitudes. Americans must understand that freedom is not simply freedom from but also, more importantly, freedom to: freedom to create their own collective future as well as their own individual futures within the framework of this collective future. They must foresake the notion of America as simply a place for individual and material advancement and indulgence—the "Great Barbeque," the "big PX in the sky"—and return to the earlier utopian concept of America as an "errand into the wilderness," a "New Jerusalem." They need to recognize that their new society must be one in which they look upon nature not as an adversary but as a partner, and upon society and government not as adversaries but as settings in which they as individuals can grow and attain happiness and full stature as human beings.

In a recent book, the distinguished European political thinker and activist Ralf Dahrendorf (a sometime resident of the United States) speaks of the need for all citizens of the Western nations to think in terms of a "new liberty," and to shape a world in which not growth but improvement is the goal. A necessary part of this process, he avers, is the assertion of the primacy of politics over economics. For America in its third century these words have special meaning. It must use collective social action—ultimately political action—to create a physically sustainable society (Dahrendorf speaks of the "economy of good husbandry" in which technology is humanity's servant rather than its master). This will require technology assessment that is not simply advisory, but regulatory, which will encourage alternative liberatory technologies which conserve resources and protect amenities rather than waste resources and degrade the quality of life; alternative technologies which diminish rather than increase bureaucratization and the subordination of human beings to each other in either the private or the public sectors; technologies which will protect rather than imperil privacy and individual choice.

It will require governmental activity at all levels to protect the natural environment and to improve the man-made environment. It will require mechanisms for economic planning which not only will control inflation and minimize undesired unemployment but also will regulate land use and redistribute income and utilities throughout our society, both for the sake of justice and to provide the necessary political support for the shift from an economy based on heedless, unfettered economic growth to an economy based on improved quality of life and good husbandry.

Stated as generalities, all these goals may indeed sound utopian, but one of the most hopeful signs for America as it enters upon its third century is that throughout the land and to a lesser extent abroad as well, thinkers and tinkerers, social scientists and technologists are hard and productively at work spelling out in detail what such goals imply and require. In many cases they are making great strides toward showing others how they may be able to operationalize their dreams.

But can this nation's political institutions provide the means to reshape its economy to humane ends? That is a more difficult question. Many minor institutional changes would help—reorganization of the congressional committee system, with its present archaic overlapping boundaries, to enable Congress to focus effectively on problem areas such as energy, land, or technological development; alteration of the composition of committees so that membership and control will be less reflective of special and partial interests and more representative of the nation at large. The needs of society demand also similar reorganization of the focus and constituency relationships of executive agencies. New social institutions enabling the average citizen to take part in choosing his or her own future can be created—mechanisms for making possible "participatory futurism" or "anticipatory democracy." State-wide exercises for involving citizens in the process of future planning have already occurred in several American states. Planning, it cannot be overemphasized, need not be a top-to-bottom, arbitrary, inflexible exercise; such planning is indeed doomed to fail because it does not take into account the individual choices which are the basic elements of the social process.

But the greatest political need of our nation as it enters a century in which the American people confront the possibility of creating their own future is a restoration of political community itself. If they cannot reach consensus about where they want to go, it is obvious that no amount of tinkering with the engine of government to make it more effective will be of any use.

Some theorists would argue that consensus on political goals is impossible. Human beings—including Americans—are different and hence have different interests. They belong to different religions, races, and ethnic groups, live in different sections of the country, are rural or urban. They have different levels of income and derive it from different sources. Therefore their interests necessarily clash. The only way to attain agreement in a pluralist society, these theorists argue, is by admitting—indeed articulating and stressing—these differences in interests, and then arriving at compromises between and among them. This is the way American politics normally operates and its consequences are frequently disastrous. It is a perfect formula for inaction, drift, control of society by impersonal forces; it ignores underrepresented interests, and all too often produces consequences exactly the opposite of what people in fact want. The politics of group conflict often operates counter to the basic interests of the most powerful groups involved in the interest group struggle.

The United States today, Americans generally agree, is dominated in its day-to-day politics by one interest group—the middle class. At the same time that class is prey to an inflation which threatens it above all others. This situation, as a leading political scientist sagely notes, stems from the tendency of government to grant special privileges to v..rious segments of the middle class, which threatens the group as a whole. Raises or subsidies to some creates higher prices or higher taxes for others. Together Americans create economic distress for all.

Clearly the middle class must recognize that it has a common interest in halting inflation, an interest superior to the individual interests of particular subgroups in the policies which produce inflation. That is, the middle class must reach a consensus that inflation is destructive to the interests of all its members.

What is true of aggregates such as the middle class is true in many important instances of the nation as a whole. There are common interests shared by all which are more significant than all special interests, because Americans have common characteristics as human beings which are more significant than their special characteristics. The alternative to the politics of the pork barrel and compromise is the definition and pursuit of those interests which people have in common, the creation not of compromise but of consensus (sometimes at the cost of confrontation when individuals and groups are forced to reassess their positions and priorities under pressure), and the embodiment of that consensus in a consistent and relatively long-range program. Only true consensus can be the basis of the positive and sustained action which can take the creation of the future from the hands of impersonal forces and special interests and return it to the nation as a whole.

There are two prerequisites for a politics based on consensus rather than compromise. One is that a people possess sufficient sense of community and sufficient public spirit to create a consensus on the nature of the public interest. The concept that virtue is the foundation of republican political institutions was a commonplace in the formative years of the American republic. More recently Becker reminded us of this requirement when he asserted that the future of freedom and democracy will depend, in the last analysis, not on constitutional prescriptions but on the level of virtue among the American people. Dare we speak of virtue after Vietnam and Watergate and generations of corrosive philosophical doubt? We can and we must.

But popular virtue alone is not sufficient. A nation of over two hundred million people involved in a multitude of social and economic relationships cannot organize itself to create its own future without leadership. Individuals and groups must come forth—both inside and outside of government—to criticize the old, propose the new, and coordinate the decisions necessary to implement the popular will. The desire for alternatives and the willingness to follow new paths probably exist among Americans at large. Public opinion polls have indicated a willingness to experiment with new economic and political programs. New political leaders, breaking away from the sterile liberal-conservative dichotomies which have long paralyzed the country's everyday political thinking, are beginning to emerge at state and local levels. Will the political parties, press, and electoral system help or hinder the rise of new leadership? That is an open question. Whether or not they work toward making new leadership possible depends ultimately on whether or not the public insists that they do.

Any new movement toward the restoration of American freedom will meet with opposition. Freedom has always had its enemies—in part because individual freedoms often conflict to some degree at the level of particulars, in part because the institutionalized anti-freedom forces have their beneficiaries and hence their supporters. The freedom of action of kings was circumscribed by the growth of democratic institutions. The property rights of slaveholders—their freedom to own and buy and sell other human beings—were radically altered by emancipation. Collective bargaining and restrictions on child labor were regarded as a diminution of the freedom of employers and of actual or potential employees as well. The compulsory education of children, giving them the freedom to know, was for some an infringement on the freedom of parents and children alike.

Americans should not be surprised, therefore, that there are those who assert that the freedom to pollute, to waste resources, to carry guns, to release cancer-causing agents into food, water, and air, to sell dangerous drugs is a God-given, constitutionally protected right. They will resist the creation of a future which curtails such activities in order to give all the freedom to breathe clean air, drink or swim in clean water, have access to adequate resources and bequeath them to future generations, lower the homicide rate, escape death from cancer, free children and fellow citizens from drug addiction. Others will resist in the name of particular and partial liberties the freedom of all to create a desired future for the community through comprehensive economic and social planning, the freedom to restore urban life and use land optimally, to stabilize the economy generally so that individuals can have a secure backdrop against which to plan their own lives. Every effort of the nation's citizens to create a truly free society in the new historical era will be condemned and resented and resisted by some, and each particular of any new future society will, for moral as well as political reasons, require the attention of all, or it will not result in the creation of a free future for a free people.

Still Americans cannot shirk the awesome task before them, take refuge in a false and partial concept of freedom, or accept the counsel of despair that people are powerless to create their own future. They *can* master the technological and economic and social forces which threaten their freedom now and in the generations to come. They *can* use their intelligence and will to preserve and extend their liberty in the coming century. America was built upon hopes and dreams. Other nations can perhaps persist in the contemplation of ancient glories and the warmth of a shared kinship and fate. America cannot; without dreams resting on a shared past and a shared future it will perish. Thus the Bicentennial celebration must become not merely a nostalgic commemoration of past glories and fading hopes but a time for thought about future goals and the means of achieving them—a time for regrouping before setting out again on the long march to extend the blessings of liberty throughout the land.

Index